Occupi

Occupied Minds

A Journey through the Israeli Psyche

Arthur Neslen

LONDON • ANN ARBOR, MI

First published 2006 by Pluto Press
345 Archway Road, London N6 5AA
and 839 Greene Street, Ann Arbor, MI 48106

www.plutobooks.com

British Library Cataloguing in Publication Data
A catalogue record for this book is available from the British Library

ISBN 0 7453 2366 9 hardback
ISBN 0 7453 2365 0 paperback

Library of Congress Cataloging in Publication Data applied for

10 9 8 7 6 5 4 3 2 1

Designed and produced for Pluto Press by
Chase Publishing Services, Fortescue, Sidmouth, EX10 9QG, England
Typeset from disk by Stanford DTP Services, Northampton, England
Printed and bound in the European Union by
Gutenberg Press Ltd, Malta

For Baha

If I am not for myself, who will be for me?
If I am only for myself, what am I?

Rabbi Hillel

Contents

Acknowledgements

If every book is a collaborative process, this one was a near-commune at times, but without the support and encouragement of Natalie Groissman, Amir Hallel and Ktzia Allon, it would look very different. My family in Israel, particularly Ava Carmel and Sheila Levenkind, were also there for me when I needed them and I'll always be grateful for the warmth and friendship of Tanja G and Shahar and Adi, whose parties and Shabbat suppers picked me up when I was on my last legs.

Every project needs a patron, and without the faith shown in me by my publishers, and particularly Dave Castle, this one would never have got off the drawing board. Of my London friends, Rachel Shabi was more inspiring than she knew while Armen, Chris, Dan, Dave Watson, Jessica and Matt all helped keep me cheerful while I was on the road.

Many others gave me assistance along the way, particularly Akiva Orr, Daniella, Ido, Idith Zertal, Inigo, Itzik at the New Israel Fund, Lior, Linda Benedikt, Michal, Miri Krassin, Rafi, Roland, Seumas, Tania, Tirza, Yehudit Iloni and all the Israeli anarchists who lent me a hand or a book. I'm particularly grateful to Smadar Lavie, whose fascinating interview I was sadly unable to include. I will always owe a debt to the people who let me interview them. I hope that their humanity shines through.

If the photos in the book tell a story, it will be one that includes Max Reeves in Shoreditch and Janice Jim in Ontario who were generous in sharing their camera skills with me. While editing in Toronto, Kim, Ellie, Tim and Robert Priest were all supportive beyond the call of duty, as were all my Canadian family. More than anyone, though, my final thanks are reserved for Diana, Chaim and Esther Neslen to whom I owe everything and for whom words will never say enough.

The opinions expressed in this book are those of the interviewees, and not necessarily those of the author or publisher.

Introduction

In 1970, Golda Meir addressed the Knesset in a debate over the ethnic nature of Israel's nationality laws. 'More than anything else in the world, I value one thing,' she said, 'the existence of the Jewish people. This is more important to me than the existence of the state of Israel or of Zionism, for without the existence of the Jewish people, the others are neither necessary nor can they exist.'[1]

There was a sense then that Israel depended on Diaspora Jewry for its life blood. In the *cheder* I went to as a child, teachers who had made *aliyah* would come back enthusing about the wonderful advances Israel was making for us all. Sometimes, they would speak about Israel's creation as a kind of cosmic payback for the Holocaust or a miraculous resurrection of the Jewish people. But when talking of Judaism and Zionism, even they understood the difference between cart and horse.

By 2005, the tables had turned to the extent that Tony Bayfield, the leader of Britain's Movement for Reform Judaism, could write that, 'If the state of Israel were to cease to exist... Judaism would, I believe also cease to exist, except perhaps for a tiny remnant of Jews.'[2] For Jews like Bayfield, the unrelated phenomena of diaspora assimilation and rising Palestinian birth rates meant that Zionism was no longer protecting the religion and culture of the Diaspora. It had become the religion and culture of the Diaspora and so much for two thousand years of history.

I grew up in Britain in the 1970s and 1980s, with parents who held to the traditions of the Bund, a secular and anti-Zionist Jewish socialist party that once was the mainstream of East European Jewish life. In those days, it was still possible to find a space in the Jewish community for such a perspective. Today, Israel has come to dominate Diaspora existence and anyone defining themselves as Jewish has to do so in relation to it. I wanted to write about Israeli Jewish identity to analyse the construct that was coming to define the Diaspora. The subject fascinated me, not just because I felt that Israel's actions in the occupied territories were tearing the Diaspora apart but because I wanted

1. *Knesset Debates*, official publication, Jerusalem, vol. 13, p. 770, debate of 9 February 1970.
2. Tony Bayfield, 'We need a new kind of Zionism', *The Guardian*, 23 March 2004.

to turn the spotlight back on those who were creating the context within which I, my family, my history and culture were being understood.

Shortly after the Second Intifada began, I went to a picket of a shop that was illegally stocking goods made by settlers in the occupied territories. A passing Israeli woman harangued the demonstrators. She was angry with the other picketers, but when I told her that I was Jewish she became incandescent and shouted that she wished my forebears had been killed in the Holocaust. I'd previously only heard such comments from neo-Nazis and wanted to fathom how another Jew could say such a thing. What I found in Israel was that a self-righteous tornado had been unleashed, within which, such comments only constituted a tail-end. The storm rages across the occupied territories, deep inside the 1949 armistice line and within Israelis themselves. But its full force is felt by Palestinians.

During my first visit in March 2003, Tel Aviv was gripped by war fever. Gas masks were flying off the shelves, and a travel agent near my hotel had put mock adverts in his window advertising tickets to Baghdad on the back of a US F1–16 fighter plane for $5. 'Next year, Tehran $3! 2005, Gaza $1!' his sign read. The clamour for war was everywhere, even if the fear of suicide bombings on busses was driving well-heeled Israelis to use Arab-driven *sherut* taxis. On one *sherut* I took to Jerusalem on the eve of war, an Israeli radio station was playing songs tailored to the mood of the moment. One, a version of Chumbawamba's 'Tub Thumping' had a rewritten chorus that went something like, 'Just knock him down, shoot him in the head, there's another dead Iraqi boy.' The Israeli Jews on board laughed out loud and then sang along with the next number, a version of the Beach Boys' 'Barbara Ann' with the new chorus: 'Bomb, bomb, bomb, bomb-bomb Iraq.' I left Israel the next day.

When I was seeking accommodation in Tel Aviv before I returned in June 2004, a prospective agent sent a stormy email regarding a client's property. 'Please do not feel offended if I ask you what type of author you are,' she began. 'Both she and I are very, very loyal Israelis and we wouldn't even want to consider anyone writing anything bad about Israel or consorting with Arabs. I am sure you will understand this. In the meantime we have only your name but Arabs, especially Palestinians, take on Jewish-sounding names and try to pass themselves [off] as Jews and even as Israeli Jews, especially to get accommodation in main centres.'

The journalist Graham Usher once told me: 'Whatever you think you know about Israel, when you go there, you'll find the truth is more complicated.' Yet I always seemed to find the situation to be even more black and white, albeit with profoundly upsetting implications. Journalists can't help but anticipate the stories they will write, and on the plane to Tel Aviv, I was expecting the people I interviewed to confirm a monochromatically racist and nihilistic picture.

But Graham was right insomuch as I found a more complex and sad picture emerging.

The Zionist 'counter-identity' is something I still find ugly, but Israelis themselves are rarely monsters – and never two-dimensional. As human beings, they are frail and contradictory, however they try to mask the fact, and there are many sincere Israeli humanists, operating in a context more fraught and dangerous than that facing those who would instinctively condemn them for their nationality. I hope it will not sound manipulative to admit that I anticipated a story of how Israel betrayed the Jewish people. I also found unexpected cause for long-term optimism.

Occupation is not just a state of forced control. It is also a state of mind, a way of keeping busy and of passing the time. Individuals in societies that see themselves as permanently at war often view each other through military field glasses; as combatants, infiltrators, morale boosters and traitors. Zionism, the belief in an ethnically centred Jewish state, still commands overwhelming support among world Jewry. Israel is revered as a safe haven *in extremis*. Yet since its creation in 1948, it has existed in a state of national emergency for every year bar one, 1966. This book is an exploration of the world through the Israeli mind's eye.

Palestinians often accuse Israeli Jews of living behind mental and actual fortress walls. They may not know that the ancestors of today's Israeli Ashkenazim (ethnically European Jews) typically lived on the other side of them. In Israel, Ashkenazim today hold the most important centres of political and economic power, but for centuries their forebears led a precarious, often nomadic existence in which persecutions of the most barbarous kind were all too common. Isolated in scattered communities (often little more than ghettoes), they were frequently banned from professions, forced into rent collection by landlords and used as lightning rods during peasant uprisings.

By contrast, Mizrahi ('Eastern' or 'Oriental' Jews) were traditionally well-integrated into the Middle Eastern societies where they lived and the majority tended to see themselves as Arab Jews. In Iraq, for example, Jewish social and religious institutions flourished and Jews were entrenched at every level of the country's civil society. Jews served as government ministers, as Communist party leaders and they practically invented the country's financial and monetary system in 1932.

But political Zionism was a European invention, and its treatment of Mizrahim who migrated to Israel in desperate circumstances is still a cause of bitterness today. Upon arrival in the Promised Land, the same Baghdad Jews who had led Iraq's cultural renaissance were sprayed with DDT and sent to tin shack transit camps. The attitude of Israel's first prime minister, David Ben Gurion, towards the Mizrahim was not considered illiberal in the 1940s:

> Even the immigrant of North Africa, who looks like a savage, who has never read a book in his life, not even a religious one, and doesn't even know how to say his prayers, either wittingly or unwittingly has behind him a spiritual heritage of thousands of years.[3]

The Ashkenazi *halutzim* wanted to build a modern, secular European-style Jewish national identity in opposition to those that existed in the Mizrahi – and Ashkenazi – Diasporas. As an 'Arabised' people in a land at war with its indigenous Arab population, Mizrahim posed a particular problem for the early Zionists. But so did the attitudes of Eastern European Ashkenazi immigrants, a traditionally mercantile community, who had lacked a territorial base from which to organise self-defence, when attacked by anti-Semites. Their dominant communal strategies for dealing with conflict involved camouflage, pleas to rulers, negotiation and compromise.

Violence was seen as a dangerous tactic both for those carrying it out and for the Jewish Diaspora as a whole. During the Chmielnitzki pogroms of 1648, which claimed an estimated quarter of a million Jewish lives in Eastern Europe, there was little effective self-defence. The Jews of Tulczyn in Poland even refrained from attacking the Polish nobles who betrayed them to the Cossacks after their leaders told them: 'We are in exile among the nations. If you lay hands upon the nobles, then all kings of Christianity will hear of it and take revenge on all our brethren in the exile.'[4] Such attitudes were and are anathema to Israelis.

As socialist ideas spread through the *shtetls* of Russia and Poland, communities belatedly began to organise to protect themselves. During World War II, however, Jewish partisans were haunted by the same dilemma that faced their co-religionists almost 300 years before. Still, from Baghdad to Braslav, living 'perpetually in enemy territory', as Herzl put it, also helped bequeath diverse and vibrant cultures with their own foods, dress, humour, music, languages, schooling, behaviour and politics. The Zionist pioneers aimed to transcend them with a new identity, that of the robust 'new Jew', who was stereotypically blond-haired, blue-eyed and muscular.[5] Ironically, Ashkenazi Jews who fitted such a Teutonic bill, probably only did so owing to the prevalence of rape against Jewish women in medieval Europe and the inability of male Jews to defend 'their' women.[6]

Supplanting the weak ghetto Jew stereotype, Zionist pioneers constructed a national identity based on a connection to the land, the 'pure' Hebrew language, shared privileges over the indigenous population, a collective experience of

3. Tom Segev and Arlen Neal Weinstein, '1949', *The First Israelis* (Owl Books, 1998), p. 157.
4. Aviva Cantor, *Jewish Women, Jewish Men* (HarperCollins, 1995), pp. 81–2.
5. Michel Warschawski, *On the Border* (Pluto, 2004), p. 155, Benny Morris, *Righteous Victims* (Vintage, 2001), p. 21.
6. Cantor, *Jewish Women, Jewish Men*, p. 87.

military service and, ultimately, a blurry commitment to Judaism. The essence of their appeal to a traumatised Diaspora in the years after the Holocaust was the *sine qua non* of security. Some Israeli writers, like the activist Michel Warschawski, argue that the price was a virtual ideological pogrom against Jewish identity as it had previously been known:

> From its inception, Zionism always carried within it a rejection not only of Judaism but even of the Jew himself, or at least of a certain way of being Jewish. That Jew was crudely characterised by the ideologues of Zionism [as] primitive, reactionary, unproductive, parasitic, passive, effeminate – in a word degenerate... Being an Israeli means deliberately breaking all continuity with the history of one's grandparents, their cultures and the values they embraced, reducing the links to the past to some mythic relationship to a 2,000-year history.[7]

Certainly, Zionist grandees such as Nordau, Pinsker and Zangwill were assimilationists who saw a nation state as the precondition for acceptance by gentiles. The father of modern Zionism, Theodore Herzl, on one occasion proposed a mass conversion to Catholicism. On another he wrote:

> We might perhaps be able to dissolve ourselves without a trace in the surrounding races if we were left in peace for only two generations on end. But we shall not be left in peace... It is only pressure that forces us back into the parent stem, only the hatred encompassing us that turns us into strangers once more.[8]

To Herzl, becoming 'a nation like other nations' involved the dissolution of traditional Jewish identities in a nationalist cauldron. However, dispensing with any connection to Judaism would also have meant dispensing with any claim to statehood. Jews are a people defined by religion and Jewish identity is only *ethno*-religious insofar as it is a religion inherited matrilineally. As cases such as Father Daniel Rufeisen's[9] demonstrated to secular Zionists in the mid-1950s, religion is at the root of Jewish identity. From the word go, Israel didn't just need religious support for international legitimacy – it needed it for communal credibility and new immigrants.

In 1948, Zionism was still a heresy to the majority of the world's religious Jews because it rejected holy scriptures, which prophesied the state's founding only after the Messiah's arrival. In the end, the religious were won round by a 'status quo' agreement that institutionalised religion at the heart of the state. But

7. Warschawski, *On the Border*, p. 154 and p. 210.
8. Theodore Herzl, *The Jewish State* (Tel Aviv: Newman, 1956), p. 60.
9. Rufeisen was a Polish Jew who converted to Catholicism and subsequently tried to immigrate to Israel. A heated national debate ensued with secular Israelis arguing for him to be allowed citizenship on the basis that ethnicity should not depend on an acceptance of religion. The High Court ruled that, in accordance with religious law, Rufeisen was still a Jew (because his mother had been) but that according to secular law, his conversion disqualified him from Israeli citizenship.

tensions remained until 1967 when religious Jews embraced Zionism en masse, interpreting Israel's military success as a sign that the Messiah had returned. But the religious believed that Israel's destiny was to become 'a light unto the nations' rather than a nation like any other. They could at least point to a contiguous Israeli Jewish identity or a 'continuation of the ancient past', as Ben Gurion put it,[10] albeit it was one that had not existed for two millennia. Yet this was not an insurmountable problem for the religious, as their attachment to Israel was based on faith, rather than a desire for security.

In the European Diaspora, Hebrew was rarely spoken as a day-to-day conversational language. Even in mandate Palestine, the religious orthodoxy opposed the introduction of Hebrew as a daily language until the 1920s. According to tradition, Hebrew was a holy language that would be corrupted and deformed by mundane use. Instead, Sephardic Jews in southern Europe spoke Ladino – a mix of Latin, Arabic, Greek and Hebrew – while Mizrahi communities in the Middle East often mixed classical Hebrew with Arabic dialects. The East European diaspora spoke the fully fledged language of Yiddish, a mix of Germanic, Slavic, Aramaic, Romance languages and Hebrew. In Yiddish, a word that defined Jewish identity for millions was 'b't*o*chen', which meant 'faith'. In modern Hebrew, the word is now pronounced 'bitach*o*n' and means 'security'. Unsurprisingly, many Diaspora Jews view the transformation of the word as a deliberate attempt to debase Jewish identity itself.

The Zionist pioneers actually rejected Yiddish as a corrupt and archaic language. Yiddish posed a challenge to Zionism when Israel was founded in 1948. It was the first language of the Ashkenazi masses and heavily associated with the socialist Bund, which until the Holocaust was the most popular European Jewish political organisation. Viktor Alter, a member of the group's executive committee in Poland, explained how Bundist objectives diverged from Zionist ones:

> We Bundists cannot accept, even for a moment, the trappings of a capitalist society. [The Zionists], on the other hand, wish to remain within these trappings. Because they adapt themselves to the existing capitalist society, they cannot understand the urgency of our struggle in Poland. We wish to shatter the existing economic frameworks and show the Jewish masses how a new society can be built not by escape but by struggle. We link the essence of the Jewish masses' life to that of humankind.[11]

Armed with a universalist Jewish philosophy that saw solidarity with non-Jews as key to Jewish and human emancipation, the Bund had won fierce

10. Akiva Orr, *The UnJewish State* (Ithaca, 1982), p. 29.
11. Viktor Alter, 'I. Hart, Henryk Erlich un Viktor Alter', *Neyer Folkseytung*, 19 February 1937, p. 29.

battles with East European Zionists for the hearts and minds of the Jewish multitudes. But particularist Jewish traditions that stress Jewish separateness and uniqueness have always been equally well founded in Judaism. Israel's biblically based Law of Return, for instance, allows any person of Jewish descent anywhere in the world to claim Israeli citizenship. The corollary is that Palestinians may not.

Ethical debates about the particularist–universalist continuum still rage across the pages of the Israeli press but their fruits are affected by the climate. Tony Bayfield, for instance, inaccurately described the debate between particularists and universalists as being about 'a people in a [Jewish] land and a people in Diaspora'.[12] In fact the universalist position on Israel first articulated by the Israeli cultural Zionist Martin Buber (in opposition to David Ben Gurion) was that the new Israeli state should meet the needs of all its citizens, not just its Jewish ones:

> No contradiction could be greater... than for us to build a true communal life within our community while, at the same time, excluding the other inhabitants of the country from participation... Closed-minded attitudes inform the dominant type of nationalism, which has gained so many adherents among us – the most worthless assimilation – which teaches... that one must evaluate one's own nation on the basis of its greatest era and all other nations on the basis of their lowest points... The open minded attitude of humanitarian nationalism... demands that we judge other nations as we wish to be judged ourselves...[13]

Buber argued that Palestinians and Jews shared a 'common fate' and that mutual security could come only through equality and joint endeavour. But in 1948, Ben Gurion signed the declaration of independence, pronouncing only 'the natural right of the Jewish people to be masters of their own fate, like all other nations'. Israeli advocates of Judaic particularism frequently take God's covenant to Abraham as a starting point and proceed to a literal reading of the 'God's chosen people' story. It had formerly been popularised as a defensive riposte to European anti-Semitism and Christian supercessionism.[14]

Zionism grew out of the Haskala, a secular Jewish reformation inspired by the Enlightenment that lasted from the 1770s to the 1880s. But it was formed in the constellation of European anti-Semitism and, according to Golda Meir, needed a moderate dose of it to continue attracting new migrants.[15] Indeed, pessimists argue that without Israel's war-related gravity and the background

12. Bayfield, 'A new kind of Zionism'.
13. *The Martin Buber Reader*, ed. Asher D. Biemann (Palgrave Macmillan, 2002), 'The National Home and National Policy in Palestine (1929),' pp. 281–8.
14. Cantor, *Jewish Women, Jewish Men*, p. 41.
15. Warschawski, *On the Border*, p. 154

radiation of anti-Semitism, the centrifugal forces of Zionism might become dangerously weak. The animosities between secular Israel and religious Jewry constantly threaten to implode.

Faith and security may hold together the 80 per cent of Israel that is Jewish, but it also tears them apart. Secular Zionists who were once patrons of the Gush Emunim (Bloc of the Faithful) project to repopulate Judaea and Samaria (the West Bank and Gaza), now see holding on to all of the occupied territories as a threat to Israel's security. Religious Zionists interpret any withdrawal from the perceived borders of biblical Israel, with its implication that 1967 might not have been a herald of the Messianic age – or worse, that the secular Zionists might be obstructing its development – as a threat to their faith.

In *Ha'aretz* in June 2005, Zvi Bar'el complained that the settlers were 'trying to settle in our hearts'. The truth is that a particularist identity-type has settled in the Israeli mind. In 1891, the visionary cultural Zionist Ahad Ha'am (a pen-name meaning 'One of the People') issued the following warning:

> The secret enabling our people to survive is... that already in antiquity its prophets taught it to respect only spiritual power and never to admire physical power. Therefore, it has not succumbed, like all ancient people, to a loss of identity when faced with stronger adversaries... However, a political idea alien to the national culture can turn the people's heart away from spiritual power and produce a tendency to achieve its 'honour' by achieving physical power and political independence, thus severing the thread linking it with its past and losing the base which sustained it throughout history.[16]

Ha'am went on to argue that whether the Zionist enterprise succeeded or failed it would imperil Judaism because of the colonial and assimilationist ideas of its figureheads:

> [All our leaders] even if loyal to the state and wishing it success will necessarily seek this success in terms of the alien culture which they have absorbed. They will implant this influence through moral influence and even by force... Such a state of the Jews will be mortal poison to our people and will grind its spirit in the dust... This small state... will survive only by diplomatic intrigues and by constant servility to the powers that happen to be dominant... It will really be, much more than now, 'a small miserable people', a spiritual slave to whoever happens to be dominant looking enviously and greedily at the fists of its mighty neighbours, and all its existence as a 'state owner' will not add an honourable chapter in its history. Isn't it preferable for 'an ancient people which has been a light unto nations' to disappear from history rather than reach such a final goal?[17]

16. *Collected Works of Ahad Ha'am* [Hebrew] (Jerusalem: Dvir, 1950), p. 24, cited in Akiva Orr, *Israel Politics, Myths and Identity Crises* (Pluto, 1994), p. 163.
17. Ibid.

I hope that a small and optimistic part of the answer to Ha'am's existential question might be found in the words (and silences) of some of the people interviewed in this book. The project was conceived as a platform for an unrepresentative but enlightening cross-section of voices to tell their own stories in their own way. It was written in the months leading up to Ariel Sharon's disengagement plan.

1
Into the Kur Hitukh

In 1948, the founders of Israel began the process of state-building with what they called a *Kur Hitukh*. The term literally meant a 'melting reactor' for newly arrived Diaspora Jews, but came to denote the more US-friendly 'melting pot', a place where old Jewish identities would be dissolved and fused into a nation rising from the ashes of the Holocaust. With the birth of Israel, Adele Grubart explained, 'A new Jew was born, a Jew no longer forced to grovel as he had been for over two millennia, one who valiantly defended his homeland, his family and his people [and] though the cost was incalculable, was to walk with dignity, and build a country that would re-emerge as a light unto the nations.'[1] From the beginning, the project aimed at transcending rather than augmenting existing Jewish identities.

The qualifications for citizenship were straightforward. A person with a Jewish grandparent had only to make *aliyah* to the Holy Land to be offered generous financial, language and housing aid packages. The Law of Return, which governs the process, is enshrined as an inherent right of any Jew dating back to antiquity and is thus not governed by the state. 'Equal opportunities', in the western sense of the phrase, are arbitrarily applied to non-Jews, whatever their familial, legal or historic ties to the land. To remain a 'Jewish state', given the region's 'demographic' trends,[2] Israel needs more Jewish immigrants – or fewer non-Jewish Israelis.

Since 1948, there have been successive waves of Jewish immigration; from Europe after World War II; the Middle East in the late 1940s and early 1950s; South America in the 1950s; North America after 1967; Ethiopia since the 1980s and most significantly, the former Soviet bloc in the early 1990s.[3] All of these

1. Adele Grubart, 'David Ben Gurion in Jewish history', *Jewish Frontier*, vol. LXVI, no. 6 (638), November–December 1999.
2. Arnon Sofer, a professor at Haifa University, has estimated that by 2020, the Muslim population of the territory currently controlled by Israel will exceed the Jewish population by more than two million.
3. Jewish Virtual Library, <http://www.jewishvirtuallibrary.org/jsource/Immigration/Immigration_by_region.html>.

groups have faced absorption difficulties related to issues as various as language, climate, housing and jobs. But inter-generational problems have largely been the reserve of Mizrahi Jews, who make up around half of Israel's population and suffer structural and systemic discrimination. Unlike other immigrant groups, third-generation Mizrahim still look like locals.

Visitors to Israel often note an ersatz and improvised feel to the society or complain of an inauthentic cultural Americanism. Outside East Jerusalem, much of pre-1948 Palestine has been gentrified or concreted over. Beneath the beaches lie the cobbled stones. Naturally, the bulk of the funding and support for Israel's development has come from a United States sensitive to Israel's strategic benefits, but the two nations anyway share deep similarities. Israel also came into being by a force of will rather than organic development. It too was built on a promise to welcome immigrants in flight, and it has waged war on an armed indigenous people who were determined to defend their land from incursions by new émigrés. But America fought its war against the Indians centuries ago and was never as outnumbered or dependent on outside help as Israel.

Notwithstanding the Holocaust and other particular characteristics of Jewish history, a permanent atmosphere of 'precarity' permeates Israeli society. Like émigrés anywhere, Israel's *olim hadashim* find themselves constantly reinventing their life narratives but on shifting and crisis-ridden desert sands. Many have suffered anti-Semitism, others are refugees. Some have sought a better life, or even a sense of being Jewish. All are experiencing degrees of loss, uncertainty and disquiet in a *Kur Hitukh* unable to examine that which it melts.

EZRA LEVY

No particular place to go

Before the creation of the state of Israel, more than 80,000 Jews lived in Iraq. Hailed by some as the original Mesopotamians because of an unbroken lineage in the area stretching back to Babylonian times, they were one of the most successful Diaspora communities. Yet by the time of the second Gulf War, fewer than 100 Iraqi Jews remained. 'Ezra' Levy was the rabbi of Baghdad's last synagogue, the Mer Taweig, and one of the community's most influential figures. In 2003, he turned down an offer to sit on the American-led coalition's Iraqi Governing Council. Instead, he made *aliyah* to Israel and now lives in an old people's home in Ramat Efal.

Ezra Levy. *Photo by Arthur Neslen*

I was born in central Baghdad in November 1922, the son of a Hebrew teacher. I had four brothers and two sisters. All of them came to Israel in 1951.[4] Only one brother and two sisters are still alive.

In Iraq we spoke Arabic because we couldn't speak Hebrew. We are Jews of the world and wherever we are, we speak the language of the people we live with. If we spoke another language, trouble. If we spoke Arabic, we were the same as them.

As a young boy, I went to an Arab school and people there knew I was Jewish but I never had any problems. Arabs were always my friends. In 1941, I was working as chief engineer in the railways office on the day [that Rashid Ali began a revolt].[5]

The night before, a Muslim friend in the police had warned me to stay at home that day. But I'd gone to my office anyway until the trouble started. Then, like everyone, I hid in my house. From this place, you can't imagine how it was then. The sun does not always rise.

I was an Iraqi Jew, not a Jewish Iraqi. I lived quite separately from other Jews. I ate and slept in my family's house but that was it. I saw other Jews only in synagogue. I went every Saturday but there was never a *minion*.[6] We didn't have ten people. Sometimes we didn't have three. For the last five years I was the rabbi at the Mer Taweig synagogue, we could pray but every time without a minion, what could we do?

The Muslims were more than a family to me. I don't know why I left them to come here. It's better to have good friends than Jewish friends. I like Jews, but there is a difference between the mind of a Jew and a non-Jew. We prefer to stay amongst our own.

When Israel was created, people became concerned solely for themselves. They thought that coming to Israel would be a pleasure. But I heard the news from Israel all the time. People told me that my friends who had made *aliyah* were living in the rain, in broken tents. When my family left for Israel, the only words I said to them were 'bye bye'.

My life was with the Muslims. Sometimes I'd go to Hilla or Samarrah for three or four days, sometimes I'd ride a horse from the Palace of King Faisal. I could go anywhere because I was free. Saddam Hussein was not always friendly

4. In 1951, tens of thousands of Iraqi Jews made *aliyah* after a series of bomb attacks on Jewish targets sparked panic in the community. See interview with Yehuda Tajar, below p. 58.
5. In May 1941, hundreds of Iraqi Jews died in anti-Semitic riots led by a retired army officer, Rashid Ali, during a brief revolt in which a pro-German regime was installed in Baghdad.
6. For a religious service to be held on the Sabbath, ten men are needed to form a 'minion'.

to the Jews. At the beginning, they hung some people in Iraq.[7] We were small people. We didn't even have electric lights. But I was happy in Baghdad, until my wife died.

When she died on 1 April 1991, the day after our 30th wedding anniversary, I died with her. It was after the war and her blood sugar level had become too high. There were no doctors, no hospitals, nothing, and so she had had to have her legs cut off. I don't know what happened to the world in 1991. I only hoped that my life would soon end. It's true that the Americans offered me a job on the Iraqi governing council in 2003 but I told them I couldn't do it. My life is passing quickly to the end now.

After the war, reporters came knocking on my door. One day, a big man came from Israel with an American captain and two soldiers protecting him. I told them 'Welcome!' but they just sat in the hall. The Israeli asked me, 'Why you don't come to Israel?' I said 'Please, this is a question only for me.'

A friend in a shop in Marat said, 'Why don't you go? Your son is in Amsterdam. Why stay here? Go! *Wali*! Go!' He wanted a better life for me but now that I am here, life is very hard. Nobody comes to see me. I don't know any place to go if people won't take me. I have many friends in Israel who came in '71 and '75 but I don't know where they live. My son asked me if I would like him to buy me a car. I said no because I don't have any place to go to. Mostly, I just sit and watch television.[8]

When I arrived, many people came to speak with me, even the Israeli president, Moshe Katsav. He asked he me if I was happy being here and I replied, 'Why not?' But after that, nobody came. No telephone calls even. I feel sad now, living in this castle. The people here make like they like me. They say 'hello, *Adon* Levy!' because they saw me on the television. I don't know them. They are good people but only to say 'good morning' and 'good evening' to.

In Iraq, they would have thought I was a Muslim. My name there was Ezat. People would always shout 'Hello Ezat!' But in the hotel when I came to Israel, they were going, 'Ezra! Ezra!' I asked my sister, 'Who's Ezra?' She said, 'Brother they are calling you!' I didn't know. I still think of myself as Ezat not Ezra.

Now, my son who stayed in Iraq is the rabbi there. I don't know if he will come to Israel. In the synagogue here, they are all Ashkenazi and we are Sephardit. If I read the Hagada (prayer book) with an 'aiyin',[9] they ask 'What are you reading?' I know only my God. I must go to other people's synagogues to pray.

7. In 1969, nine Jews were hung in a central square of Baghdad after being accused of spying for America and Israel.
8. When I arrived Ezra was watching the MBC Arabic TV network.
9. The correct literary pronunciation of the Hebrew letter that approximates to the English glottal stop. It remains used in Mizrahi dialects but has been replaced in colloquial Hebrew by the Eastern European 'ch'.

How do you feel about the conflict with the Palestinians?

I don't like it. It is not for me. There are many people who this land belongs to. But what can I do? If I say something, what will happen? Nothing, because who am I? I am a Jewish man who dreamt all his life of coming to Israel, and now I am here. I am here but I am alone.

RAFAEL KATZ

A greater sense of security

Argentina is home to the biggest concentration of Jews in Latin America but it is not necessarily a place that most of them would call home.[10] Long before a bomb in a Buenos Aries cultural centre killed upwards of 85 people in 1994, Argentina's Jews identified themselves in national terms, partly because of the militaristic and uncertain climate in which they lived.[11] During the repressive and anti-Semitic military junta of the 1970s, up to 10 per cent of the 30,000 '*desaparecidos*' (disappeared ones) are thought to have been Jewish, despite Jews making up just 1 per cent of the population. There was substantial criticism of Israel's friendly relations with the Argentine regime in this period,[12] but it did not stop a steady migration. Between 1948 and 1995, more than 43,000 Argentinean Jews made *aliyah*.[13] However, the differences between their largely secular aspirations and the religious qualities of the state they were moving to were not always easy to bridge. Rafael Katz, a gay scientist, was one Buenos Airian who found sexual liberation in Tel Aviv.

10. Ya'ir Sheleg, 'Report: 25% of Argentine Jewry under poverty line', *Ha'aretz*, 29 November 2001. In the 1990s, around 25 per cent of Argentinean Jewry was thought to be living below the poverty line and 30 per cent were unemployed.
11. Raanan Rein, 'Together yet apart: Israel and Argentine Jews', keynote speech, LAJSA conference, Tel Aviv University, June 2004, <http://www.acad.swarthmore.edu/lajsa/2004%20site.html>. 'Being Zionist in Argentina... has been one of the strategies espoused by Jews in order to become Argentines. Like every other immigrant community, Jews needed to have their own Madre Patria. Just as the Italians had Italy and the Spaniards had Spain, so Jews had their own imagined Zion, or Israel. This brand of Zionism was about becoming Argentine while staying Jewish, and not moving to Palestine.'
12. Marcel Zohar, *Let my people go to hell* (Zitrin, 1991). The Israeli government, Jewish Agency and other bodies refrained from processing immigration applications from left-wing Argentinean Jews in the 1970s so as to preserve good business and political links with the junta. In this period, arms sales worth around $1 billion were concluded between the two countries.
13. Jerusalem Report, cited on Virtual Jewish Library, <http://www.jewishvirtuallibrary.org/jsource/Immigration/immigration_by_country.html>. The Argentinean Jewish population is thought to number around 200,000.

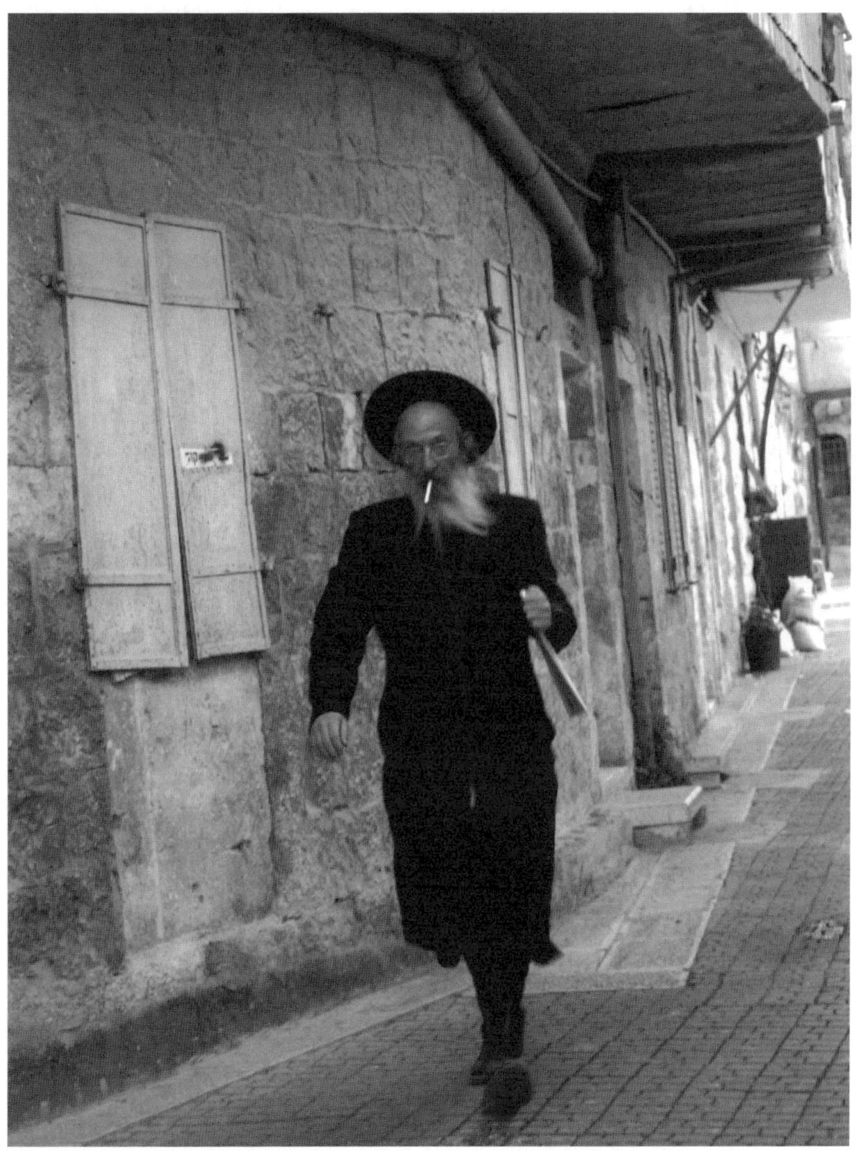

A Haredi Jew hurries through Jerusalem's ultra-orthodox Mea She'arim district. Rafael Katz did not wish to be identified. *Photo by Arthur Neslen*

As Jews, what we did in Argentina didn't amount to much. We used to go to a Jewish sports club at the weekends but that was our major contact with Jewish people. At school, in a class of maybe 30 people, there'd be around five Jews. I always knew that I was somehow different from the others. There was something about me that was not Argentinean.

I never felt anti-Semitism during my childhood. It was the 1970s and we were growing up in a bubble. We didn't know much about politics and what was going on then. Later, when you realise that all the democratic values weren't there, it's shocking because you say, 'What was I doing all that time?'

Everything was very unstable and uncertain. You couldn't make plans. I wasn't even aware that I wasn't living in a democracy. The generals were against Communism and rebellious or 'uprooting' ideas, not against the Jews. They tried to restrain society by killing people. It was terrible.

Even my family in 1973, were planning to make *aliyah* because the situation had become so difficult. But then the war broke here and they decided not to come. They still supported my decision to emigrate in 1988. As a Jew, I felt that I didn't belong in Argentina and I couldn't be out because I was living with my parents.

I really think that coming here was one of the better things I did. I only came for a year originally. I was 21 and I bought a one-way ticket to give it a try. Outside Israel, I'd always had to worry about being a Jew or doing things to feel Jewish. Here I didn't, and it made me realise how that might – or might not – be important for me.

I liked it a lot when the *Ulpan* teacher said 'Shabbat Shalom' the weekend I arrived. That was strange. We used to say that in Jewish centres in Argentina and it made me feel like I was at home in some ways. Now, though, I feel a lot of pressure from the orthodox Jews.

They think they know better what it is to be a Jew, and you are not – secular people are not. In a way it's started to make me feel a bit against Judaism. I don't want to be a Jew if it means being orthodox and narrow-minded. I don't feel it's a part of me that will be difficult to give up.

It's also what these fanatics who live in the territories and don't go to the army are doing to the country. They're so irrational and different things move them, like faith. They pay less taxes, and get money because they have like a thousand kids and who pays for all this? People like me. More than a third of my salary goes on taxes.

Yet they despise gay people. Homosexuality is against what is written. I think they feel the same way about people who eat shellfish. But gay people threaten and disturb them more because we don't build families in the usual frameworks.

Making *aliyah* helped me to come out. I was alone here, with no family around so I went about my business. I never went to Jerusalem because the tension and religion made me so moody. But Tel Aviv is a very gay-friendly city.

There was an Israeli gay centre in Tel Aviv where I started to meet people. The first was a guy from a gay beach. I remember one time he gave me a kiss in the street and I went mad because I was afraid – I wasn't completely accepting my homosexuality – but in time I got over that.

The situation for the Palestinian gay community is the worst because they could be killed if they're found out. In that way, Israel is more western than the Palestinian community. There were Israeli Arabs at the Gay Pride parade. I know someone in a relationship with a friend who was there. But I don't have any contacts with Palestinians. When I was living in university dorms, the Palestinians and *olim hadashim* would sometimes stay at the weekends because they had nowhere to go. But I wasn't close to them.

I didn't serve in the army when I became a citizen because I was already too old to be drafted. Now, I don't know if I would serve. No-one can deny how important the army is to Israel. It's a pity it should be like that. But the army also does things that I don't believe in. I wouldn't fight for these orthodox people in the territories. I will refuse.

It's different to Argentina though because here, everyone is in the army. In the beginning, it's shocking to see so many soldiers but then after a while you don't see them any more. They're like regular people. It's part of the country. In Argentina, the army is your enemy. They are the ones taking power, making all this uprootedness, and destroying democracy.

I feel a greater sense of security here. I feel safe even though I travel by bus all the time. Once, in 2002, I ran for the bus and if I hadn't caught it, I would have been on the one after, which exploded. When that happened, I had goosebumps. But now when I catch a bus, I just do it. You have to. Of course it means you end up living in a bubble.

I work as a senior scientist in a biotech company and I take four buses every day to work. But I sit in the back because statistically, they say that explosions usually happen in the front of buses. You know, I had a brother who died in an accident and there was no bus involved. Sometimes, things just happen because they happen or they have to happen. The world is very screwed up but if you want to live in Israel, you can't think about that.

I like my life here. Argentineans are not very nationalistic. They're not taught to love their country. But Israelis think they live in a great place, even though their buses might be bombed. They see it as the price of living here. I'm not for it. I would like the Israeli army to withdraw from all the territories. But that's the way it is. You have to take it as an option. That might happen.

ALEM GETACHEM AND CONOJO AMARA

Our real name should be Jews

Since 1948, more than 80,000 Ethiopian or Fallashmura Jews are thought to have travelled to Israel. Some made *aliyah* as individuals. Others were brought in mass airlifts in 1984 and 1991, following a policy shift that began with the late Israeli prime minister, Menachem Begin. To this day, some religious figures in Israel question the religious authenticity of the Fallashmura, because of differences in religious custom and the number of forced conversions in their community. But despite their intense religious commitment to Zionism, many Ethiopian Jewish groups have complained of a pervasive racism in Israeli society. By the summer of 2004, about 20,000 Ethiopian Jews were still languishing in displacement camps in Ethiopia's Gondar province. Many had been waiting years for government officials to process their applications, and end restrictive quotas. One Israeli official explained to *Ha'aretz*, 'The last thing we need is for people to start saying, they don't have any place left to bring new immigrants from, so they're bringing us blacks from Africa.'[14] In Israel, Ethiopian Jews have been disproportionately housed in remote development towns or ghettoes like the Mevasseret Zion absorption centre, outside Jerusalem. The day before this interview was conducted there, the town's mayor Carmi Gillon blamed increases in vandalism and sexual assaults – and falling property prices – on the presence of the Fallashmura. The following day, hundreds of Ethiopian Jews marched through Mevasseret Zion in protest.[15] As the result of a crisis meeting, my anticipated contact was not at the office when I arrived at the centre. Instead, Alem, a genial, loud and spirited man, instructed me to send home my translator, so that he could translate an interview with himself and Conojo Amara, for a price to be negotiated. He was cagey about which questions he would answer and his English was poor. But then, so was the neighbourhood.

14. Amiram Barkat, 'Out of Africa? Not yet', *Ha'aretz Week's End*, 23 July 2004.
15. Amiram Barkat, 'ADL joins condemnation of Gillon for slurs on Ethiopians', *Ha'aretz*, 26 August 2004.

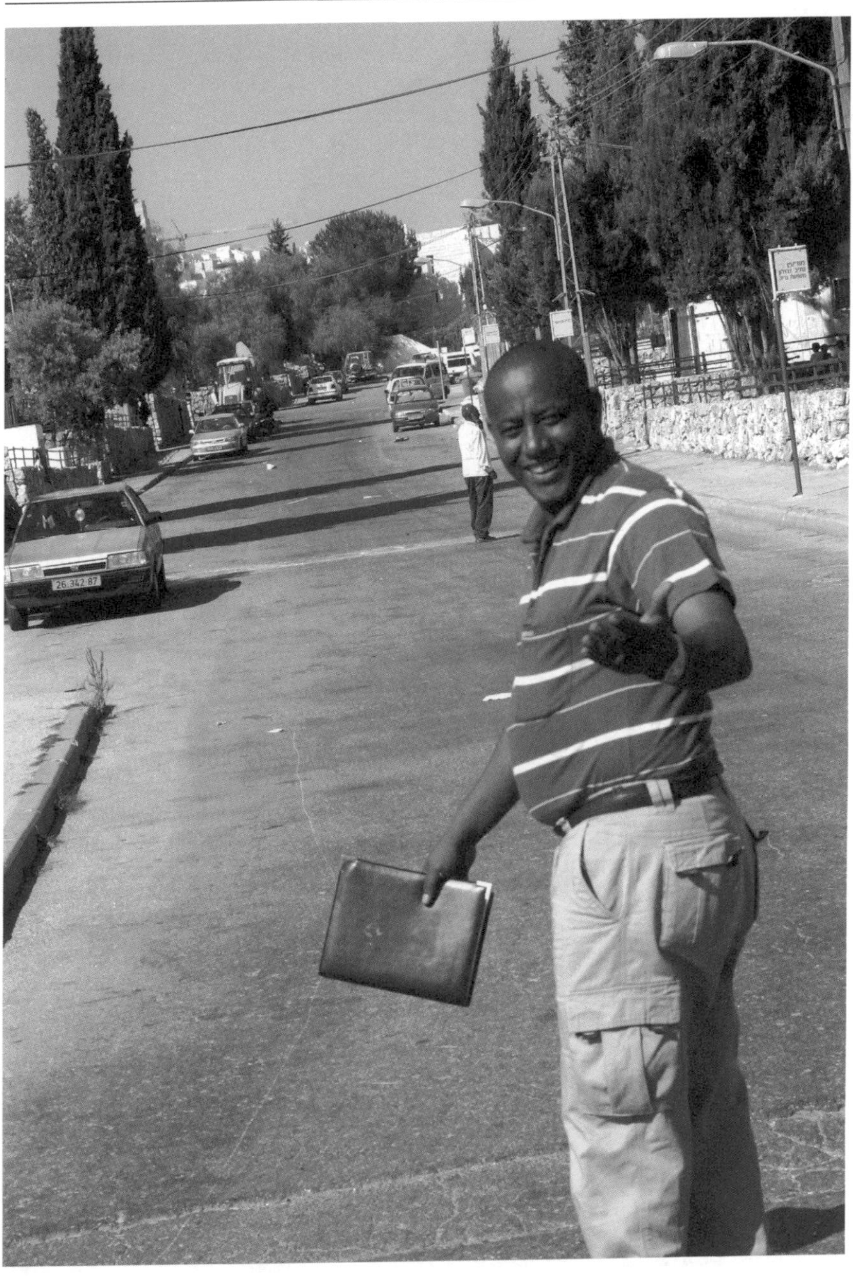

Alem Getachem in Mevasseret Zion. *Photo by Arthur Neslen*

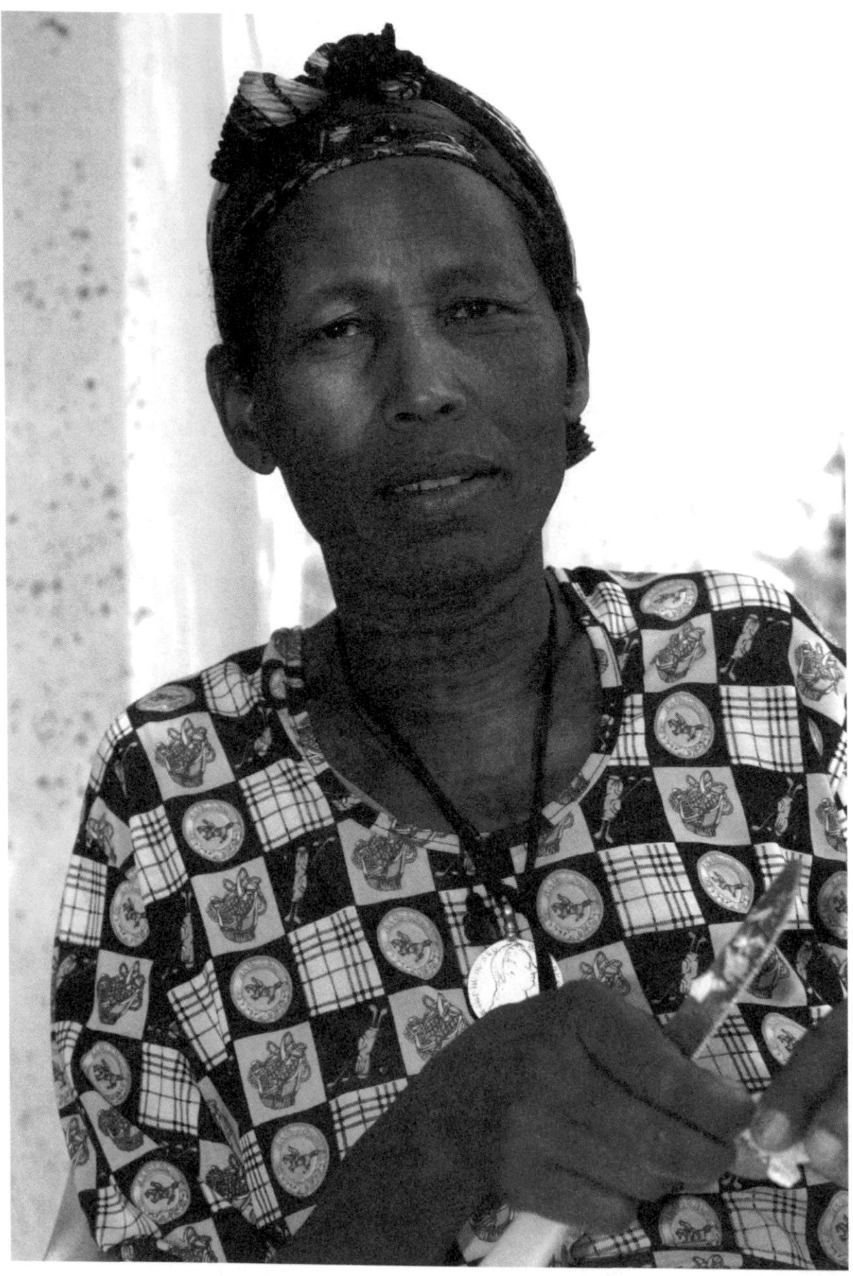

Conojo Amara in Mevasseret Zion. *Photo by Arthur Neslen*

Conojo: I'm 55 years old and I come from Balloha near Kwara. In our day-to-day lives there, we farmed, made pottery and dug for iron. I was a vegetable farmer until I migrated to Gondar[16] in 2000. Two years later, I came to Israel but I had to leave my children behind. One of them is now 31, the other is 40.

Alem: I have seven children and I also arrived here from Gondar in 2002. I'm from Dembia originally. In Ethiopia, I taught English, mathematics and history but there is no work here now. I am unemployed so the Jewish Agency gives us 2,600 shekels [approx. £325] a month.

Conojo: All I came here with was my God. I made *aliyah* because an uncle who was a rabbi came to Israel before me, but all I do now is sit here. I am simply sitting. There is no work. The Jewish Agency gives me a loan of 1,000 shekels for a month, which is not enough. I have to send half of it to my children in Ethiopia, and pay 350 shekels a month for my house. There is nothing to eat, except Injera [bread]. It is not a good life. It is no existence.

Alem: I came because my grandfather made *aliyah* 20 years ago. I was just living in Gondar, feeling lonely and so I came here with my parents. We are natively Jewish, the religion that was passed down to our fathers from their fathers. The Ethiopians call us Fallashmura[17] but our real name should be Jews. There is a religious problem for the so-called Fallashmura in Israel, because of the forced conversions to Christianity. We don't have *mikvas*[18] and also they make circumcisions here. It is a bad thing for us. It is a problem.

Conojo: I went to synagogue always in Gondar, on Succot and Pesach. The service was exactly the same as here.

Alem: We suffered from anti-Semitism in Ethiopia. The Christians would say that we had 'budda', the evil eye, and 'djaratum', the so-called tails. They thought that Jews had tails. The Holocaust also affected the Fallashmura, we felt it so

16. The Ethiopian Jewish community was historically centred on Gondar province, near the Sudanese border. During the 1984 famine, the Israeli government airlifted thousands of Ethiopian Jews from staging camps in Sudan to Israel in a mission dubbed 'Operation Moses'. More Fallashmura were airlifted from the region in 1985 and 1991, but many of the Jews of Kwara were unable to reach the camps because of the volatile situation in southern Sudan. An unknown number subsequently died in the processing camps of Gondar, as they waited for their immigration applications to be dealt with – and for immigration quotas to be liberalised.
17. 'Falashas: The Forgotten Jews', *Baltimore Jewish Times*, 9 November 1979. The 'Falashas' name given to Ethiopian Jewry by their neighbours literally means 'the alien ones' or 'invaders'. Ethiopian Jews traditionally called themselves Beta Israel and lived in the region with a relatively high degree of autonomy until the thirteenth century under the Solomonic empire, when fighting broke out with other tribes in the area.
18. A *mikva* is a ritual bath used for conversions to Judaism. Ethiopian Jews are highly religious and many have refused to use the *mikva*, seeing it as an insult. The provenance of secular and irreligious Ashkenazi Jews is often taken for granted.

much. In the famine in 1984, most of us weren't affected because we migrated to Gondar. But the people who didn't migrate died from disease because there was no aid. I feel a connection with the Jews from America.[19] They came to help us. I love them. They call us Fallashmura but they are also native Jews. They have been living there for 20 or 30 years, yes?

Conojo: There is no connection for me because we came from Kwara and only saw [American] Jewish people on the plane.

Alem: They are connected but she doesn't know how. She is coming from the countryside and they are not learned there.

Conojo: When I saw the *kippa* [Jewish head covering], I loved them. We also wear *kippas* in Ethiopia, in the synagogue. But my children are still there and it is driving me mad. They've been in Gondar for four years now and I'm going out of my mind waiting for them. Always, I think, think, think. I have no mind any more, because I am thinking only of my daughters. We ask repeatedly why they can't come. It says in the Bible that this is their land.

Alem: They've waited for six, seven, ten years.

Conojo: The immigration ministry says it is difficult to bring them here. It is bureaucracy, you know? All my relatives have come except my daughters. I am always crying. Before I weighed 60 or 70 kilos, now I am only 50 kilos. The children are going round and round in my head. Ariel Sharon promised that all the Fallashmura would be brought here but still we wait.

Alem: He didn't keep his promise. Still, they are coming little by little, a few people here and there. The French Jews are more welcome because they know the language and they are rich enough. We are poor. In Israel, some people think that because Ethiopian Jews – particularly our children – are black they know nothing. They think we are slaves. It's an apartheid system.

Conojo: Myself, I think that black is good.

Alem: I also think that black is good but they don't think that in this society. The biggest problem for me here is providing for seven children. I want to teach but it's very expensive to get the right qualification. If I had more money, I would think about serving in the army, even though I didn't serve in Ethiopia.

19. Barkat, 'Out of Africa? Not yet'. An American Jewish organisation, the North American Conference on Ethiopian Jewry, administered the compounds in Gondar and Addis Abbaba, where the remaining 20,000 Fallashmura were housed at the time of the interview. 'Sometimes it seems that the Israeli establishment – government ministries and to a lesser extent the [Jewish] agency – are as repelled by the idea of the Fallashmura being photographed [at Israeli airports] as the Jewish community in the US is charmed by the idea.' The United Jewish Communities (UJC) in the US has lobbied Congress extensively on behalf of the Fallashmura, and in 2004, it obtained a $50 million grant for the Jewish Agency to absorb 'refugees' from Ethiopia and the former Soviet Union.

I don't believe in the Palestinians' cause. They are against Judaism so I reject them. They are bad for the Jews.

Conojo: I've never even seen a Palestinian. I believe in the *kippa*, not the Muslims.

Alem: I still love Ethiopia, though. It is a good country. In Ethiopia, there is a good air, a suitable air. In Israel, there is suffocation. In Ethiopia, we were free. In Israel we are suffocated. But this is a civilised country and I am so happy to be here. I have a house with a television, a small porch, and a comfortable life. We have no work now but we believe in God and I am happy here, with my children and wife.

DAVID WEIZMAN

Happy as a Jew in France

After the outbreak of the Intifada, the international media became enthralled by the story of a new insecurity gripping French Jewry. According to one poll in 2003, more than 25 per cent of French Jews had considered emigration because of anti-Semitism.[20] Journalists noted that cemeteries had been vandalised, religious Jews attacked on the street and, in the summer of 2004, there was worldwide revulsion when a non-Jewish woman claimed to have been attacked by Arabic-looking anti-Semites on a train. The claims turned out to have been false but they provoked the Israeli Prime Minister Ariel Sharon to complain of a 'wild anti-Semitism' in French society, which made *aliyah* 'a must' for French Jewry. A diplomatic freefall between the two nations ensued. Two weeks after Sharon's comments, in a Tel Aviv café, David Weizman, a 37-year-old French PR executive, looked wistful when I told him that Paris was beautiful at this time of year. He had made *aliyah* a year before.

My name is David Weizman. I think we pronounce it 'Weitzman' in English. I was born and raised in Paris and I studied in Grenoble. In the 1930s, my family followed my grandfather to France from Poland. Seven of my father's brothers and sisters were killed when the Vichy regime began deporting Jews. I never understood why my grandfather didn't immigrate to Israel.

20. Joe Berkofsky, 'More than a quarter of French Jews considering emigration, poll says', *Jewish Telegraphic Agency*, 25 March 2003.

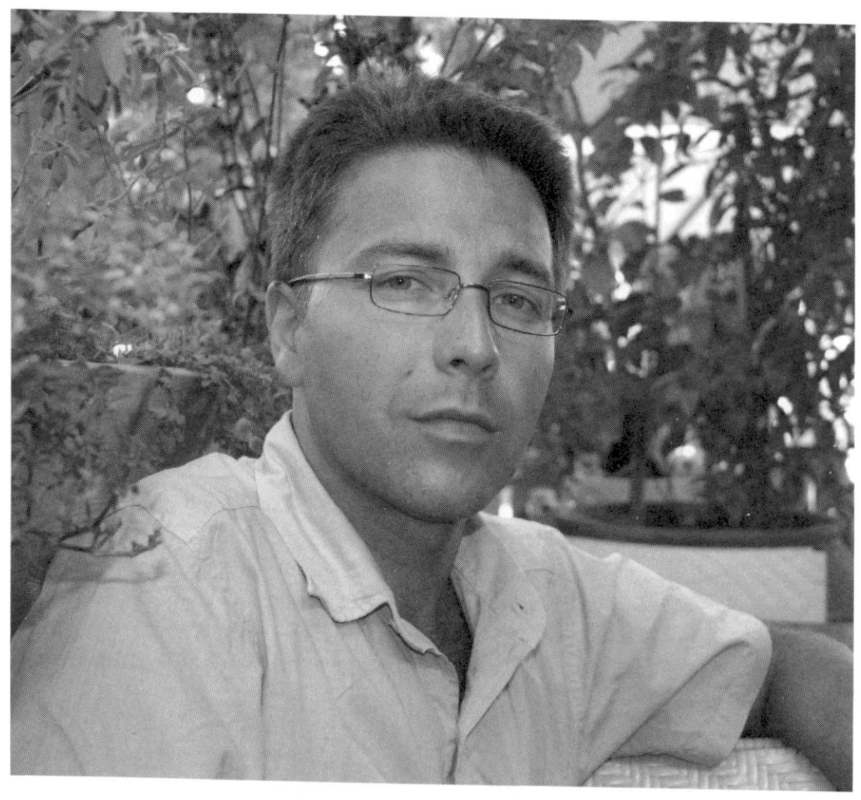

David Weizman. *Photo by Arthur Neslen*

There's a Yiddish expression, 'happy as a Jew in France'. In the Yiddishkeit (Eastern European Diaspora), they were all dying to immigrate to Paris even though it was the country of the Dreyfus Affair.[21]

As a young boy, I dreamt of coming to live in Israel. At school I fought with classmates who told me that the Jews should all have died in the camps. I was taught at home not to fight but I learned that you couldn't live that way.

When I was 17, we were talking about the Vichy regime in a philosophy class when, suddenly, someone threw a chair at my head. He said: 'Marshall Petain was an honest man and you Jews are treasonous!' There are two types of people in France: the French of the resistance and the French of the collaboration.

Today, Muslims in France are changing the political landscape. The fathers of the community went there to work but their sons and daughters consider themselves to be citizens with full rights. They are going to university and some of them are very brilliant, just like any community. Their fathers were used as workers and suffered a lot from racism. So they want to send a message.

The message is this: the Jews are not the only ones who suffered. We were the victims of colonialism. We want to be free but we also want to make the world understand that we have our own historical consciousness, just like the Jews. There is a strange and imaginative mental competition between Jews and Arabs. One expression of it is anti-Semitism.

In response, one Jewish tendency says, 'We have to defend Israel whatever happens'. The other says, 'We're independent enough not to accept everything Israel says'. After the Second Intifada, some influential Jewish intellectuals started to criticise Israel. This was a big change. Four years ago, they would never have dared. We have to watch out because some among us are responsible for Israel's bad image in Europe.

Ben Gurion said in the 1950s, 'What is important is not what goyim think, but what the Jews do.' Today it's important to understand what the non-Jews

21. Alfred Dreyfus was a Jewish captain in the French army who was found guilty of treason in 1894 for passing information to the Germans. In a secret military court martial, Dreyfus had been denied the right to examine the evidence against him. He was stripped of his rank and sentenced to life imprisonment on the Devil's Island penal colony. The incident led to an outpouring of anti-Semitism among the political right and Catholic establishment. However, the subsequent chief of army intelligence, Lt. Col. Georges Picquart, a self-proclaimed anti-Semite, after examining the evidence concluded that the guilty officer was a Major called Walsin Esterhazy. When he tried to reopen the case, the army transferred him to Tunisia. A military court then acquitted Esterhazy, ignoring convincing evidence of his guilt. In 1898, the socialist author Emile Zola published a famous denunciation of the cover-up called *J'accuse*. He was convicted of libelling the army and forced to flee to England. Finally, in 1899, Dreyfus was pardoned by the president and in 1906 was exonerated of all charges and allowed to return to Paris. The affair solidified a long-lasting alliance between French Jews, radicals, socialists, communists and republicans.

think and to try to improve your image. The foreign ministry's communications budget is one of the lowest in the world. They're focused on North America and are neglecting Europe. I'm trying to show them that if they want more Jews from England, Belgium and France, they have to improve their image.

For example, we now know that nothing special happened in Jenin. But they didn't show the world that it wasn't a slaughter.[22] People from the foreign ministry and Jewish Agency have told me they're so far behind in PR terms, they don't know where to begin.

Did you agree with Ariel Sharon's comments about France?

Anybody can understand Sharon. Israel is still a very young country, they need people here, and Sharon has done everything possible to encourage the French *aliyah*. You have more than 500,000 Jews in France so it's a big tank for emigration.

French Jews don't want to choose between being Israeli and French – and they don't have to. They can be both. Maybe telling people to choose a camp was a strategic mistake. In France I worked in PR for leftist parties and ministers. Some leftists are anti-Semitic but in France they generally advocate principles of tolerance, and for that reason, I could never have voted for the right.

Here, I don't know. The right and left in Israel are based on different principles. Menachem Begin promoted social justice and universal enfranchisement. He wanted to give the Arabs more civil rights. He made peace with Egypt. I've only been here for a year though and I'm still trying to understand this new world.

Why did you decide to make aliyah*?*

Because I believe that Israel changed the nature of Jewish identity. Israel is a miracle and I didn't want to consider it as a summer camp or final resting place. I wanted to be part of it. I believe in this country's values, I believe that Israel is the solution for Jewish security and I wanted to raise my three kids here.

My parents have also made *aliyah* now and I've explained to my non-Israeli friends that if you want to be part of Jewish identity today, maybe you have to be Israeli. There are 13 million Jews in the world and 5 million in Israel. The

22. In April 2002, a suicide bomb in Netanya killed 28 Israeli civilians. A few days later, the Israeli army invaded the Jenin refugee camp in an offensive against Palestinian fighters there, which killed 59 people. For days, the Israeli Defence Forces refused to allow press access to the camp. An AFP news report quoted the Palestinian minister Saeb Erekat as claiming that 500 civilians had been killed in a massacre there. Media organisations were unable to verify the story but the claims were widely reported. Less widely reported was the fact that a tenth of the camp – housing approximately 13,000 refugees – was levelled. These inhabitants were made homeless with no compensation from the Israeli authorities.

theological, spiritual and cultural moods that make Israel today are progressively changing the Jewish identity of the Diaspora.

Israel and Jerusalem have been at the centre of our prayers for centuries and now we have the opportunity to live our prayers. It's also an answer to anti-Semitism. In France your neighbour can tell you 'hey Jew, this isn't your country'. In Israel, no-one can say that. I don't feel insecure here.

Does the wall make you feel safer?

The wall? I don't think a wall ever made anyone feel safer. Let's talk about the fence. I'm idealistic and I believe it would be better to live without walls and fences, but the statistics show that there really have been less terrorist attacks. I have the feeling that they're drawing a border and it's very strange because the left in Israel was in favour of separation from the Arabs but the right is going to do it.

If a Palestinian said to you, 'This was my family's land for thousands of years, and yet you as a Frenchman just come here and take it from us?' how would you respond?

I would say, 'Listen, it's been your land for hundreds of years and it's been our land for thousands of years. Let's not compete. You have to build your future and you're not going to build it against ours.'

The Zionist founders wanted to create a 'new Jew', who would be different to the Diaspora Jews who they said walked willingly into the gas chambers…

A Jew proud of his identity.

A strong Jew.

A proud Jew. You have to be strong to want to keep your identity and difference in a very hostile world.

Is strength part of that new Jewish identity for you?

I believe strongly that the Jews are strong, and were strong, so the question today is what are we going to do to keep the strength in our people? Ben Gurion believed that we had to build a new Jew and we had to cancel many parts of our identity. But he wanted to keep Hebrew. The Jews who came to Israel from the ghettoes and the camps had the strength to build the country. That's maybe the main reason I wanted to be part of its history. It's a state that's been created on strength.

Do you feel at home here?

I feel at home everywhere but outside Israel, you're the Jew. Here, I'm the French (laughs). I don't have a problem with that. I mean the Jew has to speak many languages and that's very good for the brain. I speak also German, French, Hebrew and Polish.

Yiddish?

No, in fact when I arrived in my *ulpan* class, on the first day, I couldn't understand a word of Hebrew. I just looked at their black and white pictures showing scenes of Israeli history, saying to myself, 'What kind of immigrant are you?' The first word I learned in the *ulpan* was *milchama*, which means war. I arrived in the context of the second Iraqi conflict and that was nothing special. Sometimes I ask myself, 'Are we in a state of war here or not?' You can't tell.

But Israel is a very tolerant place. I arrived here and they gave me an ID and some money and help. I learned the language for free. I lived in a central apartment for $200 a month, and if this is not tolerance, what is? I also think about the help that Israel gives to the Arabs. They give them everything, I think.

Today, I'm the representative and PR man for the Menachem Begin Heritage Centre. Salaries are what they are here but I want to bring something to this country. I know I can do it. Kennedy said in 1961, 'Ask not what your country can do for you' and I think that if you want your *aliyah* to be successful, you always have to ask yourself what you can bring to Israel. The day my daughter said, 'Daddy, I feel like talking in Hebrew rather than French,' I told myself, 'Whoah, David, you made it.'

DIMITRIS AND OLGA

They teach them to hate us

Israeli commentators agree that the country's demographic balance has been forever changed by a wave of *aliyahs* from the former Soviet Union. But there is less consensus about its implications. The first Russian *aliyah* in the 1970s often involved political dissidents, and was very different in character to the '*Great Aliyah*' when the Soviet Union collapsed. As the Berlin Wall crumbled, the Jewish Agency opened offices from the metropolitan Ashkenazi heartlands to the Sephardic bastions in the Caucasus, doing all they could to facilitate mass migration. Fearing economic catastrophe and the revival of pre-Soviet anti-Semitic movements, around a million Russian Jews made *aliyah*. Today, Russian-speakers constitute some 20 per cent of Israel's population. Up to half of them are not considered Jewish in the traditional sense of having had a Jewish mother or of having converted to Judaism. More critically for a society as implicitly tribal as Israel's, many of those who were Jewish had no sense of Jewish religious, political or cultural roots. Dimitri, 30, and Olga, 26, both came to

Dimitris and Olga at home in their apartment. *Photo by Arthur Neslen*

Israel in the *Great Aliyah* hoping for a better life. Today they live in a small flat in a housing project on the outskirts of Netanya. Their precondition for this interview was that it take place on Shabbat evening, a religiously charged occasion in Israel on which it is forbidden to work or travel.

Olga: I was born in Zaparosha in the Ukraine to a Greek mother and a Jewish father. When my parents separated 25 years ago, my mother remarried and my father came to work as an engineer in an Israeli factory. In 2001 I came to get closer to him – not Judaism. My dad himself only made *aliyah* because he couldn't immigrate to the US. But when we met we were like strangers and after a few months I found myself alone. I suppose I'd also wanted to try a different culture after some Jewish friends told me about Israel. I became interested in learning more and met the Jewish Agency.

Dimitris: I made *aliyah* in 1993 during the Jewish Agency's biggest campaign. They opened synagogues and offices in every city in the country. They had weekend schools which taught you about Jewish traditions, religious holidays and Hebrew. They sent rabbis to encourage people to make *aliyah*. All the campaigns and activities were a means to that end.

The Agency arrived in Russia in 1990 at the moment that the regime changed, after 70 years of Communist rule. Life was becoming harder in economic terms and they told people, 'If you go to Israel, your life will be better in every way. You will be rich. You will find a job. You will own your own house, cars – lots of cars – you will be paid better for the same job because Israel is a rich country. There are great opportunities.' Most Russians came here for a better life, not because of Zionism. Most had no connection to the Jewish religion or people.

I was a 19-year-old university student. I'd chosen a bad career path with few prospects. I didn't see any future and I didn't want to serve in the army – it's not a respectable occupation like here – so coming to Israel was a spontaneous move. I hardly knew anything about the place. I just thought it was a great opportunity.

Olga: The Jewish Agency didn't say anything to me. I only thought that life here would be interesting and better than this.

Dimitris: I know exactly how the Jewish Agency behaves. They tell you to bring documents to prove that you're Jewish but even if you only have a Jewish father, they say, 'Yeah yeah, you can get citizenship immediately, automatically'. And one person can bring all his family to Israel, even if they're not Jewish.

Olga: That's what happened to me. At first, it was tough because they didn't consider me Jewish. But when I started to speak Hebrew, learned how to behave and what to eat, it became easier. I feel very Russian here but in Russia now, I'm more Israeli.

Dimitris: I'm 'pure Jewish' but in my heart I don't feel Jewish. Before I made *aliyah*, I'd never heard of Chanukah, Pesach or Rosh Hashana. I'm working as a Jewish nurse in a Jewish hospital in Tel Aviv but I still feel Russian.

Olga: My surname here is 'Hayat' but in Russia it was 'Hayit'. Everyone asked me where my father came from because it's an unusual name. It's not like Ivanov or something.

In my music college, I studied piano for 15 years but they told me that because my father was Jewish, I had to be rich. So if I wanted to pass the exam, I had to pay them a large bribe. I was shocked because I'd thought that people who taught music were more humanitarian.

Did you pay?

Olga: No. I passed all my exams and gave up music. You can't make a living teaching piano in Israel anyway.

Dimitris: My father was a very senior manager in Rostov but here he's working as a security guard. In Russia we were defined by nationality. We were a small community who looked different. But we didn't leave because of anti-Semitism. In fact it made me feel proud that I was different. At school, other kids would say that Jews killed Jesus, or we were the world's richest people because we stole the Christians' money. My mother told me it was because of the way their parents had educated them. She said that because of that, we had to be better students than them; the best in society. In Russia, Jews succeed more in science, education and every other field.

Russia is still my homeland, my culture, my language. We brought Russia to Israel. Today I watch Russian TV channels, read Russian books and newspapers, my friends are all Russian and so is my wife. I'm not a real Jew. I was just born to a Jewish family. I don't feel that I belong to this community. I tried very hard to become part of it and I didn't succeed so now I'm part of a Russian community in Israel.

What did you do to assimilate after you arrived?

Dimitris: I joined the army. It was an opportunity to become part of Israeli society but in the end I still didn't feel part of it. There's a different mentality. The values aren't the same. For example, I grew up believing that friendship was a holy thing, that it meant loyalty and commitment. You shouldn't have many friends, just two or three best mates. In Israel, it's not like that.

I was a fighter in dangerous places where you had to trust your friends 100 per cent. I thought some of my best friends were Israeli but it was only because of the army. We didn't keep in touch. Today I don't have any Israeli friends and I don't miss them.

How did you both meet?

Dimitris: Through a phone-dating service which had a Russian language section. I picked the nicest voice that I heard and it was Olga's.

Olga: All my life, I never thought that I would need to use that kind of service. But I worked in Haifa University's cleaning department and the night after the US attacked Iraq I found myself bored, so I called. On our first date, I felt that I had arrived home. I just knew that Dimitris had a big and open heart.

Dimitris: We went out together for six months, and then Olga moved in with me and my parents. After a while we found another apartment near Hadera.

Olga: But we decided to get married while we were at Dimitris' parents' place. I was so shocked when he proposed to me that I fell over! We got married in September 2004.

Dimitris: The first problem was to have a Jewish wedding because Olga is only half-Jewish. It was hurtful because we were citizens trying to be part of this society and they made getting married a problem for us.

Some friends told us about a 'wedding tour' in Varna, Bulgaria, where about 250 Israeli couples come to have civil marriages every year, even Sabras and couples from Mizrahi backgrounds. Most of them had the same problem as us but some just went because they were against the Rabbinate being allowed to police weddings, funerals and *aliyahs*. In a modern country, religious institutions should be separated from the state.

Olga: I feel bitter about it. You see, I'm working here, I'm living here, I pay all my taxes and it's a shame that this country doesn't give a damn about me.

Why do you think the state doesn't allow civil marriages?

Dimitris: For political reasons. We don't have enough people who resist these norms so, through religious parties, the Rabbinate takes control. Israel is more authoritarian than Russia ever was. They enforce laws more strictly, even traffic laws. If I get a fine here, I have to pay it. In Russia it's different.

Olga: Dimitris, you must obey the law! This is a Russian mentality – to find ways not to pay. But I don't agree with laws about transport on Shabbat, what to eat, or how to get married. My children won't be Jewish and I know it will be hard for them to grow up here.

Personally, I feel closer to Christianity because I was born and raised in a Christian culture. I never thought about converting to Judaism. I don't believe in it. In terms of having children, my life experience has taught me that it's not always better to be Jewish and I don't know where I'll live in the future.

Dimitris: We're thinking about migrating to Canada. It has a special law to accept immigrants and the economic and security situations will be better there. Also, Israelis are prejudiced against Russians. They don't appreciate this *aliyah*, and what we have to give. Zionism is just a fake. It's like a blur. The reality is an economic question. They put it like, 'We want you to help the Jewish state to grow', but then you're even denied loans to buy an apartment.

I think the government realised that we had the potential to change this society. They were afraid and so they tried to stop us, by denying us opportunities. 'Zionism' is an empty phrase. It's like a soup balloon. When I hear people talking about it, I don't believe them any more. In the early twentieth century it was an idea for people to come here and build the country. But today it's nothing.

How safe do you feel in this country?

Olga: I don't feel any security at all. It feels like a state battling for its existence. Everyone is nervous and aggressive to each other in the street. The pressure is never-ending. It's a small country and everything goes to wars and security so the country doesn't have any time or energy left to take care of its citizens.

Just after I arrived, I was in an *ulpan* in Haifa studying Hebrew and through the window I saw a bus explode. I immediately called my mother and said 'Mum, I don't want to be here, it's not good. I want to come home.'

Our teacher knew that we were from Russia and she tried to tell us it was just a car accident but we knew it was a bomb attack. Everyone went outside. We stood there, feeling shocked and very afraid. We realised just what sort of place we'd come to.

I feel sad that in Russia and other parts of the world, they blame us for treating the Palestinians badly. It's sad for me that they don't understand the situation.

Dimitris: I saw for myself how poisoned the atmosphere is against Jewish people in the territories. They teach them to hate us. It's aggressive. I have a friend in a hospital emergency room that treated a 12-year-old Palestinian who needed a heart transplant. When the boy woke up, he called his father and said in Arabic, 'I'm afraid. There are Jews here and one of them has given me his heart!'

I know what happens in the territories. That is why I voted for Sharon and the far right parties. The Palestinians only understand the language of force and power. I believe the army should show them no mercy. They should take radical measures. It's like Chechnya. We don't have a negotiating partner. They should use all means to fight the terror.

2
Soldiers and Sabras

A 'sabra' (or 'prickly pear') is Hebrew slang for a Jew born in Israel, someone 'tough on the outside, sweet on the inside'. The fruit grows on a cactus. The 'sabra' self-concept is the flipside of traditional Diaspora stereotypes. Where the European Jew was thought compromising, weak, passive and rootless, the sabra was dynamic, robust, pioneering and tied to biblical land. Where the Diaspora was believed to have gone like sheep to the gas chambers, the heroic Sabra took the initiative and against all odds carved out a Jewish homeland, regardless of world opinion. In Israel today, defending one's connection to the land is still the measure of moral authority and legitimacy. The mechanism for doing so is the gun, and the army's motto celebrates its 'purity'.

To the outside world, Israelis are often viewed as aggressive and truculent Middle Easterners, uncompromising in their mindset and vengeful in their actions. Most Israelis however, view themselves as cultured and secular westerners, tolerant of a primitive Islamic enemy that would annihilate them and patient in the face of a hypocritical and anti-Semitic world that closed its eyes during the Holocaust. The disjuncture in these perceptions stems from, and is most acute within, attitudes towards the country's most important institution: the Israeli Defence Force (IDF).

Israelis see their army as a great leveller. All teenagers are drafted, and those who serve undergo a rite of passage that forever links them with the national struggle and the national state. International observers may blanche at a logic that is unable to connect settlements, blockades, assassinations and land seizures in the occupied territories with terror attacks in Israel. But without denying the real fear such attacks provoke or the failures of Palestinian leadership, there are other possible explanations for the disconnect. Raised in a permanent war economy with zero-sum produce, the recognition by Israelis of injustices they and their children have committed, or that their silence has made possible, would imply culpability. Normalisation requires reconciliation with history and neighbours, and the tackling of several crucial identity issues that war has postponed. Rapprochement could also leave Israelis wrapped in the shadow self of the Sabra self-concept: the ghetto Jew, scurrying to do deals with implacable and terrifying foes that would annihilate his race. However war weary they may feel, most Israelis prefer being cacti.

Writing in *Ha'aretz*, Yossi Sarid tried to explain why the deaths of Israeli soldiers were so much more disturbing to public opinion than those of civilians:

> Soldiers are not only soldiers in our eyes but symbols of the state, and when a soldier is hurt the symbol is also hurt. Here soldiers are not just private people, like those blown up on a bus, each one to himself. Soldiers are also the collective that sheds blood from the national reservoir… When soldiers are killed, it's as if our protective gear has come undone and we are all more exposed… Soon there will be no one to protect us.[1]

Israel is a young country but the civil identification with army culture within it has been grounded in four major wars and two Intifadas. While the victories of 1948 and 1967 led to triumphalism and occupation, the partial defeats in the Yom Kippur War and Lebanon sparked reflection and withdrawal. In November 2004, a British correspondent favourably relayed to me a line on the Al Aqsa Intifada that a senior government official had spun thus: 'Just like in 1948, the Arabs declared war on us during negotiations and just like then, they will get less than they would have done otherwise.' Of course, an Israeli 'victory' in this context would simply lay the groundwork for the next war. But then, a cynic might say, the consequences of anything else could be far worse.

MAJOR YA'ACOV 'KOOKI' BAR-EL

Sometimes you feel as if you are the lord of this country

Few Israelis have publicly criticised the Israeli army's behaviour during the Second Intifada but there have been sporadic bouts of soul-searching, particularly during lulls in the daily body counts. In August 2004 for example, Shmuel Toledano, a former deputy head of Mossad, accused the IDF of having 'lost its morality'.[2] A few months later, the repeat shooting of a Palestinian schoolgirl by an IDF commander and pictures showing a Palestinian forced to play his violin for soldiers at a checkpoint sparked a wider debate. Shortly before these incidents, I interviewed Ya'acov Bar-El, a career military officer who I had been told was leaving the army to lecture because of war-weariness.

1. Yossi Sarid, 'The More Painful Deaths', *Ha'aretz*, 1 June 2004.
2. Ha'aretz service, 'Ex-deputy Mossad director accuses IDF of losing its morality', *Ha'aretz*, 1 November 2004. During a lecture at the Council for Peace and Security, 'Toledano asked "How can you like the IDF the way it operates today?" He then turned to the Chief of Staff [Moshe Ya'alon] and said, "What do you intend to do in order to return our IDF and not your IDF, which is soulless and merciless. There is a feeling among the public that the IDF under your command has entirely lost the sacred value of military ethics following the death and destruction the IDF is spreading at checkpoints."'

Major Ya'acov 'Kooki' Bar-El. *Photo by Arthur Neslen*

If you call me Ya'acov I won't answer. Call me 'Kooki'. That's the nickname my mother gave me when I was born. I was the first son after four girls and they said I was cute (laughs). Kooki is like 'cutie'. Moroccan families like to have an older son and when I was born it was a special occasion; not just another girl. That's pretty stupid but it's how it was. I was spoiled.

We were a typical Eastern family – very warm, close and involved with each other. My father came here in '53 and my mother in '55. They were Jews, this was the country of the Jews and you just came here. They came to a kibbutz but were sent on to what they were told was a city half an hour from Tel Aviv. Actually, it wasn't half an hour away and it wasn't a city (laughs). It's very funny. But they liked it.

My father was a construction worker but I always knew I wanted to be a warrior. It's like giving something back to the country. I wanted to be in the Seals[3] but at the test, they told me to jump into the sea. There were high waves and it was cold and raining, with freezing water up to your shoulders. The commanders were walking on the shore with umbrellas. I thought, 'What the fuck are they doing? They're supposed to be leading me!' So even though I passed the test, I joined the paratroopers and then the officer corps.

All my life, it was obvious that there were no other options for me. When I was 16 or 17, they used to ask us in school 'What are you going to be?' Most of my class said an electrician or something. But I said, 'No, this is the country where everyone who can be a warrior must be a warrior.' I mean people died to build Israel. Six million people died in the Holocaust just so I could be a Jew, right? It's immoral not to be a warrior when you can be.

There is no real discrimination against Mizrahim in the army. Anybody can be anything. I passed a test to be a pilot but I didn't want to do that because I thought it'd be boring. It wasn't 'in' and I wasn't from a highly respected background. I was from a regular family in Kiryat Gat and I had no connections. But I really believe that discrimination is just an excuse for people who don't get on with things.

My first tour of duty was in Lebanon in '87. I'd been in the army for half a year and I was sent to an ambush as a sniper. I killed two people. This was highly respected because everybody wanted to kill the bad guys. It's something very prestigious. I came back as a hero. But now I feel bad that I killed people. When you become a father, it's different. They had families and kids maybe. They had brothers and friends. I mean it's not so glorious.

How old were they?

I don't know. I killed them from 800 metres and just saw them fall.

3. The Navy Seals are a special forces group in the Israeli army.

You knew they were Hezbollah?

Yeah. Well we saw them with guns and they were on the way to our place and the intelligence knew all the details so we just shot them. We had a lot of respect for Hezbollah. If you don't respect them you can find yourself in big trouble. They were a guerrilla force but when you have belief, you're halfway to winning.

They believed that we had to leave Lebanon and they had to conquer Jerusalem. It was a saying more than a belief really, because they'll never conquer Jerusalem. For me, the West Bank or the 'Gada' is also Israel's country and our people must have security. They believed that this state belongs to the Arabs. You can dress that up as occupation, struggle or discrimination even, but it was really a struggle of beliefs.

But then their belief was stronger than yours. They won, Israel left Lebanon and Hezbollah is stronger and more popular than before, isn't it?

Yeah, they're more popular and stronger but since 2000, there have only been minor events on the border. They're not shooting on our cities as they did before 1982,[4] and they're not infiltrating into Israel or murdering civilians. Israel wanted security and we got it.

I think the war was fought ethically. Our motto is 'the purity of the gun'. We don't kill people we don't have to, even if by law, by definition, they must die. In Gaza, a girl of 17 or 18 tried to stab me with a knife but I didn't shoot her. I'd just arrested her brother and she was desperate and very angry. I just grabbed her hand and took the knife and that was it. By law I could have killed her but I just kind of thought, 'She doesn't have to die.' She was upset. She didn't really want to kill me. I hope not, anyway.

Did anyone in your units ever harm people unnecessarily?

Maybe they hit people but it's not the way, even though they were told, 'You can hit people.' When you treat riots, you hit people, all over the world. Soldiers sometimes cross the line. You know, you have so much power in your hand. You're the big boss, the ruler. But if commanders do that, they'll be court-martialled. The authorities won't close their eyes.

4. Noam Chomsky, *Hegemony or Survival* (Owl Books, 2003), pp. 167–8. Israel's official justification for the invasion of Lebanon in 1982 was actually the attempted assassination of its ambassador to London by the Abu Nidal group. However, Abu Nidal had been condemned to death by the PLO and was at war with the organisation for years. Officials subsequently claimed that the war had been launched to prevent 'unprovoked' shelling of Israel's northern border but this *casus belli* was disputed. 'Chief of Staff Rafael Eitain echoed the common understanding in Israel when he at once declared the 1982 invasion to be a success because it weakened the "political status" of the PLO and set back its struggle for a Palestinian state.'

But around the world, don't people see images of soldiers firing bullets at teenage stone throwers in the West Bank?

Most of the time they're rubber bullets, they're not really shooting them. How many riots did you see on television, a hundred? How many riots do you think there are in a day in Gaza? I'll tell you, more than a hundred.

I served in Nablus and Gaza but Rafah[5] was the worst place in the world. They're at the very end of the Gaza Strip and they've lost everything economically. They suffer from depression and I can understand why they take all their aggression and depression out on the army. They're more desperate because they have nothing to lose so they're pretty hard to fight against. I mean, you're really struggling to find things they can lose. We tell them, 'Listen, you have family, you have kids, what are you going to feed them with?'

Were you ever given any orders to carry out that you were unhappy with?

No. What do you mean?

Like using human shields.

How many times do you think that happens?

I don't know, did you ever see it happen?

I think it's 99 per cent rumours and maybe one of the commanders was afraid and put somebody on his jeep and drove out. But we have armour, we have vehicles and shields, we don't need a young boy to protect us.

So you never saw that happen?

No. Well, I'll be honest with you. It's not like that. It's like, you take somebody and start walking out of a crowded market, ok? Everybody can shoot you. So we take one of their leaders and start walking, say 20 metres behind him. It's a way of saying if something happens, we will shoot him. If you shoot us, we shoot him. But no-one declares that.

Some people did it. I saw that. But it only happened a few times, mostly with young squad commanders who were afraid or inexperienced. I told you, you get so much power in your hand, sometimes you feel as if you are the lord of this country so you just do things. But it's really out of perspective to say that Israel uses human shields.

The Palestinians use human shields all the time! There would be six or seven lines of children, women, old people and all the armed Hamas and Jihad people

5. Rafah is a Gaza Strip town containing a refugee camp on the border of Egypt. It had been a prosperous frontier region but since the Intifada it has sunk into extreme poverty.

shooting between them, above them, hiding behind them. They can put six or seven kids in front of them and shoot us – and they know we won't shoot back. Hundreds, thousands of times they do that.

We'd try to go round their back or else we'd just let them shoot us... In a way, I can understand them. They have no armour, no shields, less money than us but morally, how can you do that? If you care about your kids, even if you don't use them like this, how can you let them go to riots? Why?

Was it an accumulation of these sorts of experiences that led you to leave the army?

I didn't leave the army. I'm now an academic lecturer teaching military strategy, the basis of war and academic strategy. I'm going to Sandhurst. I was always fascinated by teaching. It just so happens that this way I can spend more time with my family. I think it's pretty important that the commanders come and teach but I'm still a major, a captain actually. In fact, you could call me Captain Kook.

DOV YIRMIYA

The era of the wall and the tower

The War of Independence or 'Naqba'[6] is venerated by almost all Israelis as a heroic episode in the founding of their nation. In the last two decades, though, 'new' historians have questioned many assumptions about the Israeli army's conduct which were formerly taken for granted. Dov Yirmiya, 88, was a deputy battalion commander in the war who tried to court-martial one of his officers for mass murder. He was expelled from the army after publishing excerpts from a diary detailing atrocities committed in Lebanon in 1982.

I took the name 'Yirmiya' from 'Yormanovic', the old name that my father brought with him from Irkutsk in the early 1900s. Before Ben Gurion asked the Israeli army's officers to change their foreign names into Hebrew ones in '48, I cut the 'ovic'.

My father came from a Zionist family in Siberia but he was unusual. He was one of the SR terrorist revolutionaries[7] against the Tsar. Several times he was

6. Palestinians talk of the events of 1948 as the 'Naqba' or 'catastrophe'. As this book deals with the self-identity of Israelis, the term 'War of Independence' is used throughout.
7. The Party of Socialist Revolutionaries (SR) was a populist revolutionary group focused on Russia's peasantry. It was very active in the 1905 revolution, in which it was the leading advocate of terrorism as a political tactic. It suffered greatly from

Dov Yirmiya plays the accordion. *Photo by Arthur Neslen*

arrested and he only escaped a bad end because his family were of good standing. When he turned 18, they sent him to Israel.

That's where he met my mother. He liked the life of the *halutzim* (pioneer farmers) in the Galilee and they settled in a small village called Beit Gan. I was born there two months after the declaration of World War I. In 1921, we moved to the first Moshav, Nahalal.

The country was quite wild then. The Turks had some sort of administration but you needed a local landlord or a Bedouin sheikh to rule the area in a partisan way, with violence. So when Baron Rothschild established the first colonies,[8] they were based on cheap Arab labour and run on typically capitalist lines.

In the Moshavim,[9] they wanted to build a new life for Jews on idealistic grounds but there were no Arabs involved at all. The co-operatives were for Jews only. So when Zionists bought land from Arab landlords, whole families had worked for them would have to go over to working for the Jews, or become landless and move on. This created some friction. But they benefited from colonisation, even ours.

The *fellachs* (peasants) had lived a poor life in their villages for generations, while their landlords lived like landlords anywhere. Some of them didn't even live in Palestine, they lived in Jordan or Lebanon or Syria. The *fellachs* may not have been allowed to work on our farms but we bought vegetables from them and we used their mills to grind our wheat into flour.

What ideas inspired you?

It inspired me that if the Arabs attacked us, we would know how to defend ourselves. In 1922, the first Arab pogroms and riots were beginning. Even as small children, we knew that our fathers were hiding English and German rifles around the farm. Our blacksmith was making blades for bayonets. When I turned 15, we all joined the Hagana and began training with revolvers, sticks and bayonets. It was a national Jewish organisation, which in time became the embryonic state – in a way we were the state. But it was all underground

---

the subsequent repression but revived briefly in 1917, when it entered Kerensky's provisional government and briefly became the largest party in Russia. However, most of the SR opposed the Bolsheviks and were defeated in the Civil War, while the Left SR which allied with the Bolsheviks was soon crushed by them afterwards.

8. Morris, *Righteous Victims*, pp. 18–22. Between 1883 and 1899, the French millionaire Baron Edmond de Rothschild donated £1.6 million to various Zionist charities and enterprises. He was made honorary president of the Jewish Agency in 1929.
9. Moshavim were conceived as rural co-operatives in which each family would maintain its own farm, while participating in the collective marketing of produce. Kibbutzim by contrast were intended to be democratic communes in which property would be collectively owned and decisions collectively taken.

and illegal. In 1929, when the second – much more dangerous – Arab uprising began,[10] we went into action, guarding the Moshav.

Would you compare the Arab 'pogroms' you mentioned to events in Russia?

What's a pogrom? It's when armed people kill defenceless men, women or children, whether Jews or others. There were such cases. With us, they knew we were better organised so they didn't attack us. But in Hebron, there was a pogrom.

Were there Jewish pogroms against Arabs?

Never! There are pogroms now in the Gaza Strip and other places but that's another story. In the 1930s, things were always changing rapidly.

Many Jews were coming to the country despite British limits on immigration. There was speedy social and economical development. The Arabs benefited because they were working, hewing stones and building our houses with them. The British, as usual, used the imperial principle of divide and rule but there were enough good reasons for Arabs to oppose the Zionist colonial tide. They had worked on their land for generations and here come the Jews to take it away.

By 1934, like many of my peers, I was attracted to the new kibbutzim which were sprouting up around our village. I left the farm to join one with my younger sister. I was a violinist then and I decided to study music in Tel Aviv. There, I found Hashomer Ha'tzair.

Meanwhile, my kibbutz, Eilon, had to wait until 1938 to get 1,000 acres of cultivatable land from the British authorities near the Lebanon border. By then, the 1936 uprising against the British government and the Jews was under way. Maybe you've heard about the system of 'a wall and a tower'? A kibbutznik invented it to deal with Arab resistance.

The area where groups planned to settle would be cleared of Arabs, and within 24 hours a wall of about half an acre would be built. It would have a wooden frame filled with chips so that bullets couldn't penetrate it, and in the middle a ten metre-high electrified tower would be erected with a 'projector' lighting up the surroundings. This was the era of the wall and the tower.

Things were moving fast. The 'Palmach' was formed as a conscripted unit of the Hagana, to train for a higher phase of war with the Arabs. As a Hagana activist, I was made a military commander. When World War II broke out, Ben Gurion decided that we should co-operate with the British army, in case the Germans broke through from Egypt.

10. The 1929 uprising began with a series of demonstrations over worshippers' rights at the Western Wall and ended with a massacre of 60 orthodox Jews in Hebron, and 18 Jews in Tsfat. Many more Arabs died at the hands of the British army and Hagana fighters during the fighting, but there were no comparable Jewish massacres.

Wasn't Ben Gurion's slogan, 'Fight the war as though there is no white paper [restricting immigration] and fight the white paper as though there is no war?'

Yes, because the white paper even then was hampering our settlement projects. But the British were clever. They wouldn't train us in fighting units because they knew that one day they would have to fight us. So they took us only into service units, carrying water and goods. In time, they also appointed Israeli officers. I myself became a sergeant and went all the way from Syria to Egypt, where I joined up with Montgomery's army. From Alamein we went up to the River Po in Italy and joined the invasion at the war's end.

Sometimes the British officers teased us. One corporal said, 'Why are you so ardent about your work? The war isn't a rabbit. It's not going to escape.' I told him, 'If you were a Jew and knew what the Nazis were doing to your brethren, you would act as I do'. We were near Tobruk and rumours about the Holocaust were starting to get through, even though Montgomery's army newspaper never reported them.

We were very eager to go forward but mostly we were kept in the second echelon. We were very efficient and the British knew it. They'd established a powerful Jewish brigade with an English-born Jew called Benjamin as the brigadier. He was loyal to the king, but he was a Jew so they held his brigade on desert guard duty, until the last three months of the war. Our applications to join his unit were all turned down.

When the war ended, we joined up with the brigade on the Austro-Yugoslav border. Its soldiers were roaming around Europe trying to discover what had happened to their relatives. At the same time, the remnants of the Holocaust heard about our brigade and started finding their way to us. We illegally smuggled Jews from Tripolis to Palestine – along with as many discarded Italian and German weapons as we could find.

As transport company, we also had to ship thousands of German POWs to camps in southern and middle Italy. Some Hagana soldiers tried to kill German prisoners so I warned all my men that I would shoot anyone I saw maltreating a POW. Nothing that happened in the war changed my basic ideas about human rights in Germany, or Palestine. My party maintained until the last moment that we shouldn't have a Jewish state but a bi-national one with equal rights and power-sharing.

Why then did you fight in the 1948 war to establish something you disagreed with?

I had no hesitation about fighting because the Palestinians were not a factor in the war. They were very weak. I am still convinced that if the Jordanian, Egyptian, Iraqi, Syrian, Lebanese and Egyptian armies had captured Palestine, they would have left no Jews. We found out later that very bad things happened – although the Arabs were much worse in this respect.

Were you aware of Plan Daled?[11]

Only later, I never heard from my commanders 'Dov, drive them away', not once. But there was a case where an officer of mine killed about 35 civilians[12] in Hula, a village near the Lebanese border. It was on the last day of the war and the 'Liberation Army' had run away to Lebanon and Syria. There was no shooting, nothing, and as deputy battalion commander, I came up to see the situation. The commander told me the night had been peaceful.

Most of the village had fled but about 70 civilians stayed behind because they were friendly with a nearby kibbutz and wanted to live under Israeli occupation. I told them I'd have to convince the brigade first. I went back to see the brigade commander. He said, 'We don't want the Lebanese in our place.' We had an argument and I returned to Hula with orders to send the villagers away. It was very quiet there. I met this officer and asked him, how the night had gone. He said, 'Very quiet, no problem whatsoever.' Then, a corporal jumped up and said, 'He is he lying to you! What quiet? He killed all the men during the night.'

I asked him, 'Why did you do it?' And he answered me cold-bloodedly – and he was a good officer – 'I killed them to avenge my friends who were massacred in the Haifa refineries.'[13] So I said, 'Show me the place.' We went there and I

11. Walid Khalidi, 'Plan Dalet: Master Plan for the conquest of Palestine', *Journal of Palestine Studies*, issue 69, Autumn 1988. Benny Morris, *The Birth of the Palestinian Refugee Problem* (Cambridge University Press, 1989). As many as 900,000 Palestinian refugees may have fled the country during the 1948 war. Israel has always maintained that they left voluntarily, expecting to return victoriously under the banner of Arab armies. But in 1961 Walid Khalidi revealed the existence of Israeli army documents, which appeared under the aegis of Plan Dalet to give official approval to the ethnic cleansing of the refugees. In section 3b, it talked about how to deal with 'enemy population centres': 'Destruction of villages (setting fire to, blowing up, and planting mines in debris), especially those population centres which are difficult to control continuously… in the event of resistance, the armed force must be destroyed and the population expelled outside the borders of the state.' Pro-Zionist historians contend that the plans were only intended for use in battle situations. However, the opening pages of Morris's book *The Birth…* lists the reasons for departure of the population of 369 Arab towns and villages during the '48 conflict. In 41 cases, they were expelled by military force; in 228 localities, they left under fire from Jewish troops; in 90 cases, they fled in a state of panic following the fall of a neighbouring town, fear of an impending attack or rumours such as those spread by the Israeli army after the 9 April massacre of some 250 civilians in Deir Yassin.
12. Wikipedia. <http://en.wikipedia.org/wiki/Hula_massacre>. Lebanese sources put the number of dead at 58.
13. *Middle East Journal*, April 1948, p. 216. In December 1947, 41 Jewish workers were massacred by their fellow workers at Consolidated Refineries Ltd (CRL) in Haifa after Stern Gang or IZL militants threw two bombs into a crowd of Arab employees, killing six workers and injuring 48.

found that not only had he killed them but he'd exploded a house on top of them. It was a mass grave. On the spot I told him, 'I'm putting you under arrest. I'm putting another officer in your place and I'm going to put you under court-martial.' And this I did.

I reported to the brigade commander and he and all his officers started to argue with me. Why should I put such a good fighter, renowned for his bravery, on court-martial? So he killed 35 dirty Arabs? So what? The most you can say is he made a misjudgement. I went to the General who was a friend of mine, also a kibbutznik, and said, 'I'm not going to let it pass.' He agreed and it went to court-martial.

To cut a long story short, he had the best lawyers in north Israel and he changed his version. He denied telling me that it was revenge but his lawyers said that his force was too small to hold prisoners and prevent a counter-attack. Still he was sentenced to seven years' imprisonment.

In the brigade, everybody turned against me and that month I was transferred to Jerusalem. Within a year, there was an appeal. They shortened the sentence to one year and as he'd already been in the camp for 12 months, he went free. Twenty years later, I read in the paper that this young officer – who by now was a successful lawyer – had been made secretary of the Jewish Agency. His name was Shmuel Lahis.

I wrote a letter to the chairman of the Jewish Agency, asking how he could appoint a murderer as head of the Jewish Agency. He said that Lahis was pardoned by the president of that time, on Independence Day. He was, as he put it, 'innocent as a newborn baby'. I got it in the papers but it didn't change anything.

The deterioration of Jewish and Israeli morals after '48 went so far that I fear we reached the abyss. Unfortunately, the Nazis – and here I say a dangerous thing – seared the evil of the German soul on to people here. Hatred comes usually of hate. There was a recent opinion poll saying that 65 per cent of Israelis want Arabs to be transferred.[14] We were transferred once. How can we utter that word?

In human history, the oppressed often become the worst oppressors if conditions allow. It's human nature, and I have a very bitter feeling that the Jews, the ablest people on earth for doing good, can also easily become the opposite. After what we went though, to become racists, how can that be? That's bitter.

14. Amnon Barzilai , 'More Israeli Jews favour transfer of Palestinians, Israeli Arabs – poll finds', *Ha'aretz*, 12 March 2002. Opinion polls in Israel have often discovered large reservoirs of support for the 'transfer' of Arabs from territories controlled by Israel. In 2002, for example, a Jaffee Centre for Strategic Studies poll in *Ha'aretz* found that 46 per cent of Israel's Jewish citizens favoured transferring Palestinians from the occupied territories while 31 per cent supported the transfer of Israeli Arabs.

Do you feel no pride in having helped to bring a Jewish state into being?

But I have to weigh the other side, and that is much heavier. As long as there is no justice, how can I be proud? I am an Israeli. I don't feel very Jewish because Jewish for me is also the extermination of seven nations, while Jerusalem was under King David. It started long ago. We've shown in many ways that we are no better than anyone else. In the Zionist movement they wanted a new sort of secular Jew in an idealistic nation of justice, mercy and well-doing. That was the basis of kibbutz thought, and this has failed also now.

We have become one of the worst countries in the world. I don't compare us with Ghana and Uganda but with those countries we pretend to be a part of: Europe; the West; America. I wouldn't say the Arabs are better than us. But in Israel they are the underdogs and we treat them as dogs.

I've got very good connections with my Arab neighbours and I'm always active in trying to improve relations, but then my education taught me that the grassroots is always more important than the high roots and trees.

I started playing this accordion 20 years ago in Bedouin villages, which were then unrecognised. At the time, I didn't have one Arabic song so I had to learn from a Bedouin teacher. But I looked around and found about 200 Arab children's songs on Syrian cassettes. They sing of the things that children all over the world sing about.

Too many Israelis think that Arab children learn only how to kill Jews but I didn't find one song about killing. Around Acho and Carmel now, I go to kindergartens, teaching the children to sing. I always wanted to be a musician and I will do it for as long as I can carry the accordion. It is getting heavier now from year to year.

ROMAN RATHNER

Defence of the motherland is absolute

Despite constituting some 20 per cent of Israel's population, ethnic Russians only make up around 5 per cent of Israeli Defence Force personnel. However, in the autumn of 2001, many Soviet-era veterans took umbrage at a letter sent by Matan Kaminer and five other 'refuseniks' to the Israeli prime minister and defence minister. In the missive, the five vowed to 'obey our conscience and refuse to take part in acts of oppression against the Palestinian people, acts that should properly be called terrorist actions'. The 3 September letter called on other conscripts and reservists to do the same. However, what had been intended as a stand of conscience appeared to some an act of narcissism and petulance

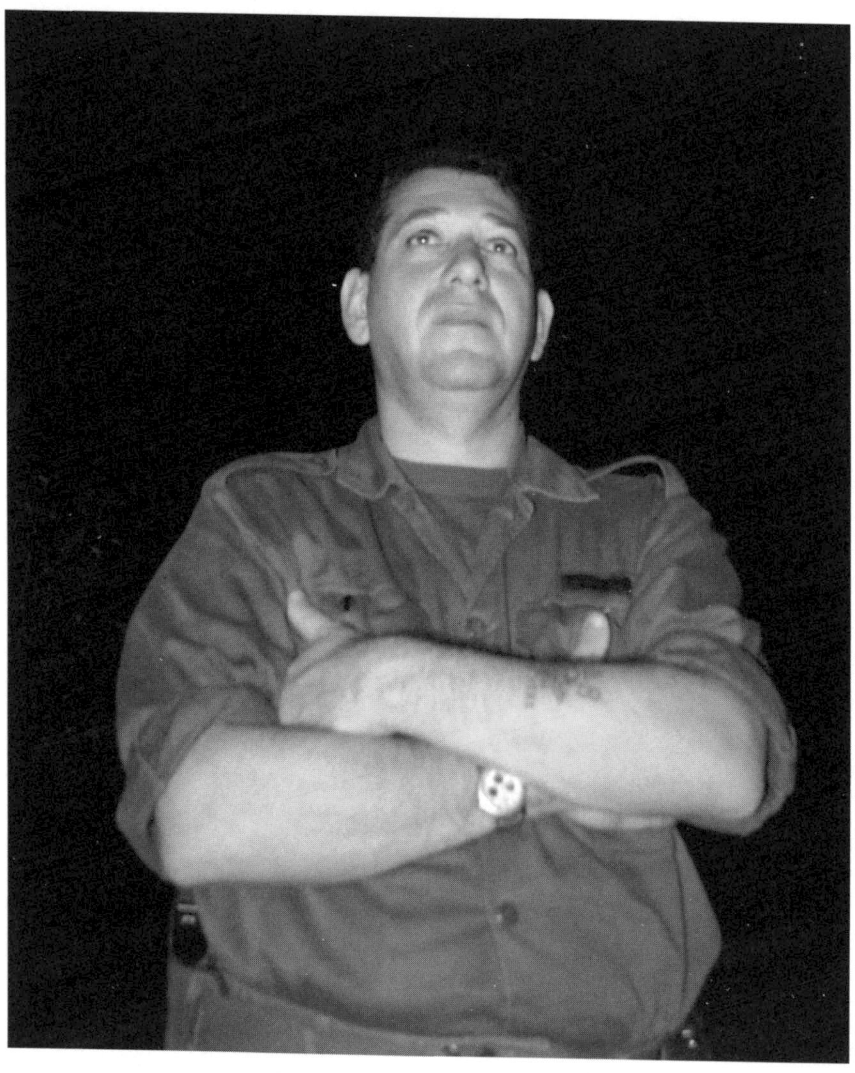

Roman Rathner. *Photo by Arthur Neslen*

by a privileged Ashkenazi elite. Some ethnic Russians were outraged at the appropriation of the word 'refusenik', which they felt had a specific historical meaning to them. Out of the discontent, Battalion Aliyah, a unit of Soviet army veterans who had fought in Chechnya and Afghanistan, was formed. It was said that they were forced into unpopular missions that regular soldiers turned down, like guarding West Bank settlements and assassinating Palestinian militants. Journalists wrote that more than half of them were not even Jewish. Nonetheless, they achieved cult status in the Russian-speaking community and praise from the highest echelons in Israeli society. Roman Rathner, a trained sniper, is the group's founder.

I always felt a special closeness to my grandfather. My father fought at Stalingrad but my grandfather was a general in the Soviet army and his life was an example of service for me. I was born in 1960 in Nabruisk, Belarus, which was then the centre of Jewish life in the northwest of the Russian empire. I joined the Soviet army when I was 18.

My father was a member of the Communist party and my family saw the army as a protector. One result of the Russian revolution was that for the first time a military career became open to Jews. My grandfather enlisted in 1917, and fought in the Civil War and World War II. In the book *Heroes of the Soviet Union*, Jews occupy fourth place for the sacrifices they made during the conflict, despite making up a small percentage of the overall population.

There were times when we felt discrimination in the 1960s. Jews were prohibited from serving in the air force and some rocket units. Many colonels left the army then, but I had no problems. I started my career in Spetznaz, a unit similar to the British SAS, and went on to serve in Afghanistan until 1988.

The Mujihadeen were excellent fighters for their motherland. But their methods of war were cruel beyond human comprehension. Afghanistan was deeply unpleasant for me. I always felt that my life was in danger. Fighting there changed me, and when I came back to civilian life, I started to evaluate people differently, to think about the opportunity they had to stab or hurt me. After Afghanistan, when I decided to do something, I knew I must do it whatever the cost.

Why did you make aliyah?

The collapse of the Soviet Union in 1991 triggered a personal crisis for me. I didn't agree with it. I didn't want to live in an independent Belarus under a strange regime, and migration to Russia was complicated so I decided to come to Israel. I felt closer to Israel than any other country. But there was always a problem between my identity as a Jew and as an Israeli. I was born in a country where Jews were the intellectual elite of society: musicians, doctors, engineers, scientists. Here, it may be a Jewish state but they have an awful education system and a very poor culture. We came from a country with a great cultural tradition, yet Israeli society pressures us into believing their culture and education are best. It's absolutely wrong.

Some Israelis assume that Russian-speakers are not Jewish...

I am Jewish! See my nose? The problem between Israelis and Russian Jews is the same as between American Indians and the first immigrants from Great Britain.

Who are the Indians?

The Russian Jews. I believe that a cultured society could be built here, mixing ancient Jewish traditions with the Diaspora cultures of Shakespeare, Dostoyevsky and Molière. This is my idea but a more primitive cultural level currently forms the basis of this society. It's very sad.

How did Battalion Aliyah come about?

One problem of the Great Aliyah was that nobody expected soldiers and policemen to come. Many mixed families – where the lady was Jewish but her husband was not – also made *aliyah* and such people were often military men. They had problems integrating.

We know that the army is one of the best ways to integrate into Israeli society because you meet local people, speak the same language and fight for the same land. Also, these people had rich experience of fighting terror in Afghanistan and Chechnya. Yet the army told them – and the army is society – that they weren't needed.

So how did the letter of refusal by anti-occupation activists galvanise you into action?

Citizens of the state – any state – do not have the right to refuse to serve. If you refuse to fulfil your obligations as a citizen, you should be stripped of your citizenship. After their letter was published, I made an appeal on a Russian-language radio programme for volunteers to come forward and take the place of those who would not serve. Some of the Hebrew-speaking community understood it was real Zionism. Others thought we proposed a paramilitary structure. We found negative attitudes to us very strange because we wanted to risk our lives to protect Israel.

Five hundred people came forward initially and today, I have 1,200 volunteers, aged from 25 upwards, from soldiers to colonels. A third of them served in Chechnya and the vast majority are Russian-speakers. About 60 per cent are Jewish.

Don't you find it ironic that you're risking your lives for a motherland which doesn't pay you, discriminates against you, and wouldn't even let 40 per cent of you get married here?

We don't feel any discrimination. The terrorists fight against the people as a whole. I feel the threat from terrorism constantly, there could be a suicide bombing at any time. So we are ready to do anything that the army or security services ask.

I personally participated in anti-terror operations in the Gaza Strip between autumn 2003 and May 2004. My unit searched for terrorist groups and their networks. They were well-trained, highly skilled fighters and I was wounded by a Palestinian sniper who shot me in the shoulder.

Soon, the Palestinians will be very good fighters. The Israeli army helps them. They enter their territory then retreat, enter and retreat. This is good training for them. It's not on the same level as Chechnya or Afghanistan yet but I see a tendency in that direction.

You can't compare the Israeli and Russian armies. Their doctrines and moralities are too different. In the Soviet army, it was accepted that a soldier should give his life to protect the country. Here, the most basic principle is to protect soldiers and return them home alive. In the USSR, a soldier killed during a clash was a very sad incident. Here it's a national tragedy, on TV and in the papers. There are different concepts. Nonetheless, for both, defence of the motherland is absolute.

Do you see Islam as a threat to European values?

I think that the responsibility for the current situation rests with the Soviet Union, Western Europe and the USA. If the Soviet Union hadn't trained the Palestinians on its bases and Britain and America hadn't trained Islamist terrorists in Peshawar for Afghanistan, the situation would be different. I think that Western Europe, Russia and America face the situation which they themselves prepared 15 or 20 years ago.

Do you ever miss Belarus?

I have no nostalgia but I miss the place. The town has changed. You know the saying, 'Everything is lost'? Well Nubraisk was a Jewish city, but all the Jews have left. It's another city now, another people, another country. In my dreams, my city and country are still there. But if I visited today, it wouldn't be the same place. This is my home now.

'SAMMY'

Just a good soldier

More than a thousand Israelis have refused to serve in their country's army since 2001. Some have wished to totally dissociate themselves from an army whose behaviour and ethos they consider immoral. Others have refused only to serve in the occupied territories or, in some cases, to follow orders they consider illegal while serving there. Certainly, many tens of thousands of young Israelis – perhaps as many as 30–50 per cent – exercise a 'grey' officially tolerated refusal, in which 'medical' or 'psychological' reasons prevent service. Some say the *haredim* and Ashkenazi elites are disproportionate beneficiaries of this unofficial policy. 'Refuseniks' are thought to suffer in the job market after leaving the army. But many soldiers have been traumatised by the experience of fighting an enemy often indistinguishable from the civilian population it lives among. 'Sammy' is one of them.

It was like a routine. Everyone in school went to the IDF. You want to be the fighter of the school, and most of the good guys are going to the front. Maybe I can say I wanted to learn how to be a man?

I remember the Saturday before we left, we sat in a friend's house and his father asked us 'why are you going?' The question shocked me because I hadn't thought about it. It was an automatic thing to do, a good thing to do, the best.

It usually takes eight months to learn how to be a soldier. But in my case it took a year, as I was in shock at leaving my parents. It wasn't easy. I'm not one who has the good shape. Also they make you feel like a very small man so you lose your will.

You have your commanders, who are everything. They are God for you. You can't do anything without their permission. You have to run and run and shoot and run again for very long distances, carrying heavy weights. You have to reach their limits.

My company was an old ground forces unit that was reactivated after the Yom Kippur War. We were stationed in the Rafah refugee camp in the south of Gaza, which was one of the most problematic towns.

Rafah is three times worse than Jenin and uglier, I think, than any place in the world. Every morning, you would go into the town on foot or in a jeep, to catch the young people who throw stones at you or if there is a demonstration, to disperse it.

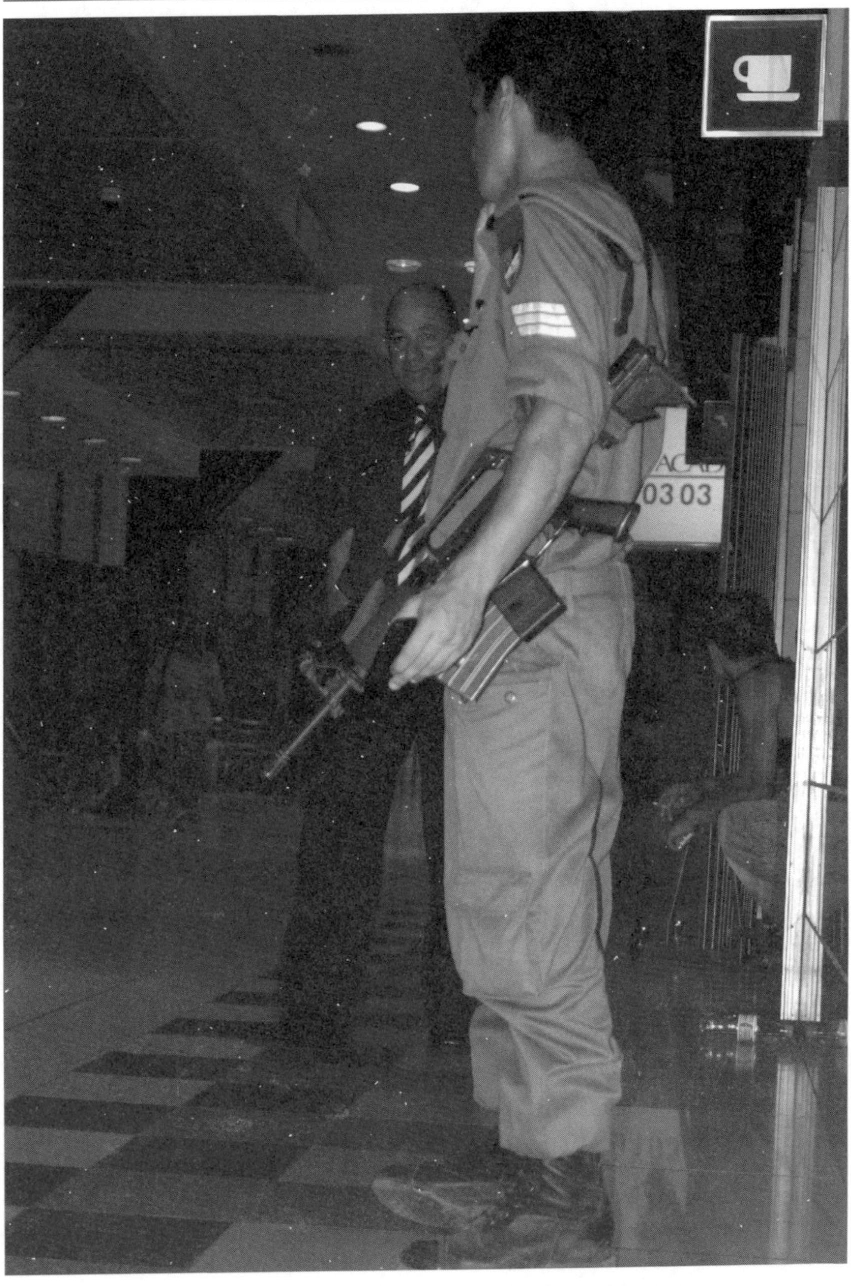

Anonymous soldier. 'Sammy' asked not to be identified. *Photo by Arthur Neslen*

If someone wrote in Arabic on the walls 'We are Hamas' or 'Hamas will kill the Jews', you had to go inside the – you cannot even call it a house – and take the person out and make him whitewash over it.

They direct you not to use violence but, actually, it's an everyday routine. You are the strong one. You are the one who's in charge and they are weak. Sometimes, you are not even looking at Palestinians as human beings. This is what is so cruel.

The Palestinian boys would look at you with hatred, such hatred that it reminded me of how the Jews in the concentration camps in the Holocaust looked at their prisoners.[15]

You are the most evil thing on earth right now for them, like it was during the Holocaust. You are the persecutor. As a boy who grew up with stories of the Holocaust, this was something that stayed with me. I became an angry man, an unrelaxed man.

As a medic, I tried to save one Israeli whose car had gone into Rafah by mistake. They killed him, of course, in two minutes flat. I was the one who got to him first and tried to help.

But they had smashed his head in with stones, until his brains were on the pavement. After that, I just hated the Palestinians. I thought of them as evil in essence. They don't take prisoners. They are not western moral people. They are animals, and I became like I wanted to kill them.

There were moments I found myself crying. I saw something that was really cruel or something – but you are thinking of another reason.

Everybody understood that after two and a half years in this unit in Gaza, you might become violent, that you might not handle the situation in the rational way. You have patience for nothing. Every small thing annoys you. It was common knowledge.

They used to put soldiers on the third floor of a tall building for five or six hours at a time. After two and a half years, they would be shooting at stray cats.

Every week or two, you'd arrest someone and take him to your vehicle, and from the moment he was in the vehicle, four or five other soldiers would be kicking him.

You are supposed to take him to the big base. It's a five-minute ride but you have a man – it doesn't matter the age – you can do whatever you want with him. All the tension was taken out on the Palestinians.

Maybe you stand on the side because you are more humanistic. Maybe you don't want to be involved but you do nothing because it's a friend, or a bigger

15. Of course, the Jews were the prisoners in the concentration camps, and the Nazis were their guards.

soldier than you and you are a platoon, with all the implications that has. You are supposed to defend each other, brothers in arms and all that.

And even if he is human, he is a Palestinian human and you won't say nothing. You won't even think about the need to say something. It's not you. You're not the one who does it.

I saw things that you cannot imagine how evil they are, across the spectrum of humiliation. Maybe I don't want to talk about those things.

But it's even the small stuff. You arrest someone. You put them in a big camp south of Gaza, cover their eyes and tie their hands behind their backs. Every soldier that walks past can punch their heads.

We were in a refugee camp one evening – in a shielded vehicle – but they were throwing stones at us, which is not so nice. So when a friend saw a little kid, about four years old, who he thought had thrown a stone, he went down and punched the kid in the throat with his rifle.

I crossed the line from being on the outside. I didn't think about it; it wasn't me. This was the line that I broke in me. These are the things I can't forget.

Around this time, they brought some trainee soldiers from a special unit, the Golani Brigades, to help us. The Golani are the most respected unit in the IDF but I took charge of five of them, because I was the most experienced of the non-officers.

All the camps in Rafah are on one side of the main road and we would drive down it very fast. But one 50-year-old man had made a small bumper to slow the cars because he was worried about his children. This, of course, was not allowed.

We gave him one hour to remove it and, when he didn't, we went into his house. The oldest son, who was about 16, shouted, 'Leave my father alone' or something like that but it was in front of these young officers.

So I dragged him outside and shouted, 'With what right do you shout at an Israeli officer?' I took his face and very gently, [forced it] into the windscreen of the car. 'I am arresting you' and then: bang, boom, inside the vehicle.

That incident happened because I wanted to say to the soldiers I was commanding, 'You may be a special unit but you are young and you don't know nothing about this area.'

I was in a very grey unit. It didn't have a reputation. We were the black sheep but I had the opportunity to give them a message:

'We are the masters of this place. Look and learn. This may be hell but I am responsible for everything that happens here. I know how to rule this place. I know the Palestinians. I know how to speak to them so give me some respect.'

'You may be the special ones but remember that you met someone from this grey unit who knew how to treat those Palestinians.'

I became what I became. It was not what I wanted. I was inside the garbage can of the world during those very crucial years of 18 and 19. I don't know if you can understand what that does to you.

My decision to go to jail rather than to the territories at the beginning of the Second Intifada was a moral position. I didn't want to take a part in this crime.

One major reason for going to jail was the feeling that in jail, I would cover my sins. This will be the price.

When I see news on TV about Gaza today, I feel sad. Sometimes it makes me crazy inside. I feel bad that I'm not doing something to help and sometimes I feel very desperate or helpless.

If there was a reunion for people who served in my unit, I wouldn't go to it. This was the most terrible period of my life.

I didn't humiliate Palestinians most of the time, but I stood by and did nothing while it happened. A very few soldiers in my unit were critical but I wasn't one of them. I was just a good soldier in the most banal sense of the phrase.

I didn't think I was someone evil. I had become the essence of the evil without even thinking about it.

YEHUDA TAJAR

From the depths I call out to you

Perhaps no Israeli military mission has been more darkly viewed than the one that began in Baghdad in the 1940s. In 1951, several Mossad agents in Baghdad were arrested and convicted of bombing Jewish targets – and killing Jewish civilians – in a bid to spark a mass flight of Iraqi Jews to Israel. Some of the Israelis were executed. However, their alleged goal succeeded. All but a handful of Iraq's estimated 130,000 Jews fled the country. Three years later, the 'Lavon affair'[16] in Egypt proved to many that Israeli agents and local Jews they had hired were indeed capable of such subterfuge. But doubts about what really happened in Iraq remained. Prior to this interview, Yehuda Tajar, one of the arrested Iraqi Mossad agents, whose court testimony was often cited as 'proof' of his guilt, had never before spoken to a non-Israeli journalist about the events of 1951. He is an urbane, slightly mischievous man,

16. Morris, *Righteous Victims*, pp. 281–2. When Britain and Egypt signed an agreement for the removal of British troops from their bases in the Suez military canal in 1954, Israeli strategists began a black operation in Egypt. 'At the beginning of July

Yehuda Tajar. *Photo by Arthur Neslen*

now living an anonymous existence in the suburbs of Tel Aviv. He is still associated with the Mossad, whose motto is: 'By way of deception thou shalt do war.'

My first memory of life is of being evacuated from the Jewish quarter of Kiryat Moshe in 1929, when I was six. Kiryat Moshe was the village adjacent to Deir Yassin.[17] My grandfather was the quarter's rabbi.

It was a Saturday morning and they attacked us with gunfire. We had almost no defences. Just a few people from the Hagana tried to do something. I remember my grandfather taking the Sefer Torah[18] in his hand as we travelled to a hospital in Jerusalem. This is my first memory of life.

My family had lived in Israel for more than 25 generations, since they were expelled from Spain in 1492. My mother comes from the Meyuhas family, who led the Jewish community in Spain and established a synagogue in Jerusalem in 1510. My father's side were comparative newcomers. They arrived in 1712.

I was born in 1923 or '24 – we don't know the exact date – in Mishkenot Sha'ananim which faces the Old City in Jerusalem. Mishkenot's residents were known as 'the old people', because Jews used only to come to Jerusalem to pray and die. My family had lived for such a long time under Muslim domination that they accepted it as natural. The mayor of Jerusalem was always an Arab, the responsibility for your life lay with the government, and the way to deal with any injustice was to petition the authorities, as all Jews did in the exile. My family were not Zionists.

1954, Unit 131, a psychological warfare department of IDF intelligence, launched a long-dormant Egyptian–Jewish network on a bombing campaign in the streets of Cairo and Alexandria, targeting American and British cultural centres and other sensitive Western sites.' The agents involved, mostly young Egyptian Jews who had been recruited by Israeli intelligence, were arrested, tortured, and in two instances, executed. Israel initially denied any involvement in the operation but the incident eventually led to the ousting of the defence minister, Pinhas Lavon and the director of military intelligence, Col. Binyamin Givli. It came to be known as the Lavon affair.

17. Menachem Begin, *The Revolt* (rev. edn, New York: Nash, 1977), p. 164. On 9 April 1948, Jewish fighters of the Irgun and Stern Gang massacred more than 250 Palestinian civilians in the village of Deir Yassin. Palestinians charge that the killings were an act of ethnic cleansing, intended to provoke a flight of surrounding villagers. Begin, the IZL's leader, and future Israeli PM, wrote of the effect of Deir Yassin: 'Arabs throughout the country, induced to believe wild tales of "Irgun butchery", were seized with limitless panic and started to flee for their lives. This mass flight soon developed into a maddened uncontrollable stampede. The political and economic significance of this development can hardly be overestimated.'
18. The Sefer Torah is a scroll containing the Five Books of Moses. It is kept in a synagogue and read publicly on holidays and the Sabbath.

But Jewish immigration was beginning – and so was a revolution for the old people. Jews were starting to move outside the Old City and work in agriculture. My family were one of the first to go. What became known as the 'Medina Bederech' – the state *in situ* – was beginning.

When the disturbances started again, there were no evacuations because we had the Hagana and Etzel[19] to defend us. In 1937, I joined the Hagana, while I was still in school. In 1941, I joined the Palmach in Jerusalem and in 1943 I worked for Aliyah Bet, helping illegal immigrants come to Israel.

At times I admired Jabotinsky[20] and the Etzel people who were ready to sacrifice their lives for their ideas. But, unlike, the Hagana, they were outside the national consciousness. Yitzhak Shamir[21] had even taken the underground name of 'Michael' after the Irish leader Michael Collins who argued against any compromise with the British.

The Holocaust changed everyone's attitudes. After the war, a UN resolution called for the establishment of two states because the world felt that nothing had been done to help the Jews. We accepted the resolution, the Arabs rejected it, and Arab armies attacked us from every border. It was very hard. We at the time were hardly 600,000 people and more than 6,000 of us were killed.

The Arabs were very cruel. When Gush Etzion was cut off from Jerusalem, a platoon was sent to reinforce it. They were ordered to kill an Arab shepherd they found on the way but the commander was a humane man and he refused. The shepherd let out a 'tsfaza' [warning cry] and thousands of villagers descended on the platoon and massacred all 35 of them. Their bodies were slashed open and their testicles were cut off and stuffed in their mouths.

19. Avi Shlaim, *The Iron Wall* (New York: Norton, 2001), p. 21. The April 1936 Palestinian uprising was sparked by a series of tit-for-tat sectarian killings but directed against the Jewish settlers who were agitating for statehood. It lasted three years and, though unsuccessful, provoked the Peel Commission in London to conclude that Jewish and Arab nationalisms were equally intransigent and Palestine should thus be partitioned into two separate states.
20. Shlaim, *The Iron Wall*. Lenny Brenner, *51 Documents* (Barricade Books, 2002), pp. 10–14. Vladimir Jabotinsky (1880–1940) was the founding father of revisionist Zionism and former leader of the Irgun. He saw Jewish culture as being an offshoot of western civilisation that would have to be implanted into a primitive and backward Middle East. Jabotinsky was not uninfluenced by the rise of Mussolini, and in his 1904 'Letter on autonomy', justified his credo thus: 'It is impossible for a man to become assimilated with people whose blood is different from his own… A preservation of national integrity is impossible except by a preservation of racial purity.'
21. Yitzhak Shamir became the Lehi director of operations after splitting from the marginally less extreme Irgun in 1940 and was involved in the planning and execution of numerous terrorist attacks. He went on to work for the Israeli security services after the founding of the state and succeeded Menachem Begin to become Likud prime minister from 1983 to 1992.

How did you feel about Jews who stayed in the Diaspora during such carnage?

I was a company commander in the sixth brigade at the time and I was so busy fighting that I didn't even pay attention to the declaration of independence. I admired Churchill's speech, 'You give us the tools and we'll do the job'. At the time, we didn't want fighting people. We wanted assistance in other respects.

Yet you risked your life going to Iraq to help Jews there...

In August 1950, I was sent on a mission by the state of Israel, by the Mossad. I am very proud of the Mossad – I am still connected with it – but back then we were taking our first baby steps and mistakes were made. We had three objectives. First, to bring the Jews of Iraq to Israel because we were only 600,000 people and we had to increase our numbers as fast as possible. There were 130,000 Jews in Baghdad. Second, their situation was very bad. There had been a pogrom in 1941 and the Hagana had set up a self-defence branch there after that, trained by Israeli instructors. Thirdly, we wanted intelligence because during the war the Iraqi army fought in Israel. But my preparation was very bad and I was recognised twice.

To improve my Arabic, my last posting had been as area commander of Acre. But an Arab who worked with us there became one of the refugees. In Iraq he got a job with the Tacticat (CID) and we came face to face one day. He recognised me.

The second time was after I had been in Iraq for eight months. I had to go back to Tel Aviv for the Passover and I went via Paris. My girlfriend of the time was working as an air hostess. All she knew was that I'd disappeared from her life. Well, it just so happened that as the Iraqi group I was with marched through the terminal, an Israeli group with her in it walked straight past. She saw me, ran over and tried to kiss me. I kind of threw her back but the whole Iraqi group saw it.

What happened to you?

I was arrested, I think on 25 May 1951. There had been three big explosions, concentrated in a short period – I think Masauda Shemtov was the last and biggest.[22] I was in Baghdad then but it was the Muslim Brotherhood who did it, not us Israelis. The reason given – that it was done to frighten Jews into making

22. Naeim Giladi, 'The Jews of Iraq', *The Link*, vol. 31, issue 2, April–May 1998. 'On January 14, 1951, at 7pm, a grenade was thrown at a group of Jews outside the Masouda Shem-Tov Synagogue. The explosive struck a high-voltage cable, electrocuting three Jews, one a young boy, Itzhak Elmacher, and wounding over 30 others. Following the attack, the exodus of Jews jumped to between 600–700 per day.' Before this attack, Jews had been wounded in bombings at the US Information Office and the Dar-el-Baida coffee shop, among others.

aliyah – doesn't hold because more than 120,000 of the country's 130,000 Jews had already registered for exit visas. There was no need to encourage anyone.[23] Still, myself, Mordechai Ben Parat and others in our group were sent to prison for the bombings.

Now, I cannot prove it but it was confirmed indirectly to me that one Israeli was responsible for later bombs. In my cell in Baghdad Prison, it became a tradition that when prisoners were to be hanged, they'd call me in to be with them on their last night. I asked one man, Yosef Basri, whether he threw the bombs. He said, '*I* didn't'. I asked, 'Maybe other friends?' He kept quiet. So after I was released ten years later, I spoke with the wife of a man who had died. She said she'd asked him [if he had thrown the bombs] and he'd replied that if a bomb were thrown while we were in prison, it would have proved that it was not us who bombed the Masauda Shemtov. She implied that he on his own initiative, without orders from Israel, did it in order to save us.

What was the man's name?

Yosef Bet Halachmi. His name there was Josef Habaza.[24]

And which was the incident where he threw the bomb?

(prays) I know of what I know.

And he didn't throw the bomb at Masauda Shemtov?

No! Not Masauda Shemtov. Yosef threw one or two small explosions. I don't know where or when. I'm afraid if you ask others they will say we Jews did not throw anything. I cannot confirm my story. I think it is the way I presented because I knew this young man, Josef Habaza's way of thought. He was an activist. He always wanted to do things. Thinking that it would help us, I believe that he did it.

23. David Hirst, *The Gun and the Olive Branch* (Futura Publications, 1977), ch. 5. Hirst posits that the rush for exit visas was a direct result of the panic that swept the Iraqi Jewish community in the aftermath of the bombings. He says that 'about 10,000' Jews signed up for visas after the Dar-el-Beida bombing and cites an Iraqi government newspaper quoted in 'the Black Panther' (a Hebrew journal) of 9 November 1972, to show that travel restrictions on Jews was not a key issue. 'The encounters between the police and the emigrant groups showed that some Iraqi Jews do not want to live in this country. Through their fleeing they give a bad name to Iraq. Those who do not wish to live among us have no place here. Let them go.'
24. Giladi, 'Jews of Iraq'. 'Yosef Basri, a lawyer, together with Shalom Salih, a shoemaker, would be put on trial for the attacks in December 1951 and executed the following month. Both men were members of Hashura, the military arm of the Zionist underground. Salih ultimately confessed that he, Basri and a third man, Yosef Habaza, carried out the attack.'

You're saying that he was responsible for throwing minor bombs which were never publicised and had no practical effect?

The first three explosions were also small. The media only made a big noise out of it because the government wanted them to. I don't recollect that there was any public notice or reaction to the other two.

Some people think that all the bombings were carried out by Mossad...

I'll tell you what. Recognising how things work in Iraq and knowing what followed in the time of Abdul Salaam Arif,[25] when Jews were sentenced to death for no reason at all, I wouldn't have minded at all – I mean, knowing that I, personally, in order to save Jewish lives, or at least to decrease their numbers [in Iraq] – I wouldn't have hesitated to put a bomb in order not to kill, but so that people would [leave]. Not that I did it. But years after, I do say that openly.

A columnist once wrote something similar. 'If I had the power as I have the will, I would select a score of efficient young men, intelligent, decent, devoted to our ideal and burning with the desire to help redeem Jews... and I would send them to countries where Jews are absorbed in sinful self-satisfaction. The task of these young men would be to disguise themselves as non-Jews and plague Jews with anti-Semitic slogans and similar intimacies... I can vouch that the results in terms of considerable immigration to Israel from these countries would be 10,000 times larger than the results brought by thousands of emissaries who have been preaching for decades to deaf ears.'[26]

He puts it very nicely. But anti-Semitism in the world is so strong that Jews will come [to Israel] wherever they have the chance. Things would have happened the same. All the Jewish community would have come.

Did you have a fair trial?

On the surface it was a regular ordinary trial, but everybody knew what the outcome would be. Believe it or not, I should only have been sentenced to five years according to Iraqi law. The confessions were obtained by torture. For the first ten days, I said nothing. I was hung from the roof by a chain and beaten by two gorillas with *sjambols* and clubs covered in blankets. The blows would make you fly but then the chain would suddenly stop so you were torn to the other side. And they put your fingers in a machine which took your nails out. They also shoved a club up the backsides of prisoners in front of me and said, 'This may happen to you'.

25. Abdul Salaam Arif came to power in a military coup that ousted Abdul Karim Qassem in 1963. While he was president, Iraq was swept by a bloody wave of revenge attacks. In 1966, Arif died in a mysterious helicopter crash. His prime minister, Dr Abdul Rahman al-Bazzaz, was nominated as his replacement but prevented from taking office by sections of the military.
26. Abraham Spadron, *Davar*. 11 July 1952.

Little by little, I stopped denying. 'You are Israeli.' 'No, I'm not Israeli.' Little by little, I kind of kept quiet. You may say in a negative way I confessed that I'm Israeli by not denying it any more. I decided to hold to red lines that I would not cross. We were in contact with Israel at an active station in a respectable Jewish suburb and until the last moment, I would not endanger any other Jew there.

But I had to give them something. I told myself: 'Never get to the stage where you're broken because once you confess, you'll become so angry with yourself that you'll lose control. You won't know what is important or not and you'll tell them everything. When the time comes, retreat under control.' In other words, try to win time.

One of us, Rodney, was a British citizen, and I thought he'd left because only the British could leave the airport without a permit. So I spoke about Rodney in order not to speak about Mordechai Ben Porat who, as a local Jew, would have been hanged. Rodney as a British subject would get a short jail sentence and his conditions would have been much better.

You say what you have to, in order to protect those who you need to.

(coughs and nods)

Did you find any solace in prison from religion?

I was from a religious family. As a youth, my father wanted me to become a rabbi and I studied in a yeshiva. The Communists dominated life in jail but they fought with me and even staged a mock execution for me. They had a big library but I was boycotted so I could only get a Bible. I read it from the artistic and ethical perspectives. I knew the psalms of David by heart, but the story of the prophet Jeremiah in prison had particular resonance for me. Then there is the psalm, 'from the depths I call out to you'.[27] I repeated it to myself. I'm not a religious man but these things comfort.

I was thinking of Jonah and the whale…

Strangely enough, now that you say it, I wonder why I didn't. It is also set in Babylon.

In any case, I was sentenced to life imprisonment – 25 years – with hard labour. The first seven years, I got no reduction at all. After the revolution, the

27. Psalm 130: 1–8, King James Bible. 'Out of the depths have I cried unto thee, O Lord. Lord, hear my voice: let thine ears be attentive to the voice of my supplications. If thou, Lord, shouldest mark iniquities, O Lord, who shall stand? But there is forgiveness with thee, that thou mayest be feared. I wait for the Lord, my soul doth wait, and in his word do I hope. My soul waiteth for the Lord more than they that watch for the morning: I say, more than they that watch for the morning. Let Israel hope in the Lord: for with the Lord there is mercy, and with him is plenteous redemption. And he shall redeem Israel from all his iniquities.'

government pardoned all nationalist and Communist prisoners. Gradually, they reduced our sentences too. I was released after ten years. Iraq under Abdul Karim Qasim was by then fighting for its independence against Nasser's Egypt. Syria and Egypt were old allies and they were facing Iraqi units on the border. Israel was then on friendly terms with Iran and through its contacts, it informed Iraq of many things. As an act of grace, we were released.

In prison, I met a famous Iraqi nationalist, Abdul Rahman Al-Bazaz. He was a former Dean of Law at Baghdad University and he'd always preach. I'd stand outside his salon listening because I'm a permanent student. When he saw me one day, he said I was his most faithful listener. Others came and went but I stayed there. He told me, 'Outside I will kill you but here you are under my protection.'

Later he was sent to England as the Iraqi ambassador, while I was at the Israeli embassy in London doing my PhD at the LSE. One day, at an embassy reception for the Queen, he passed by in the other direction with a group of Arab ambassadors. I didn't want to embarrass him but he saw me and I smiled. He gave such a big smile back that all the Arab ambassadors looked. After he left London, he was appointed as Iraq's prime minister.

But during a coup, he was tortured to death in the basement of a palace. One of his eyes was gouged out with a finger. That's how things work in Iraq. There is nothing democratic in the Arab world.

3
Strangers in the Land of their Fathers

The Hebrew word 'Mizrahi' ('Eastern' or 'Oriental') is a strange term for Jews to use negatively. Ashkenazi Jews in Europe were historically viewed as Orientals or, as the German philosopher Johann Gottfried von Herder put it, 'the Asiatics of Europe'.[1] From the late eighteenth century, some in the Ashkenazi Diaspora idealised the 'Oriental' label. Reacting to popular imagery of the 'noble Orient', for instance, Benjamin Disraeli, the British Tory prime minister of Jewish descent, once described Jews as an 'Arabian tribe' and Arabs as 'Jews on horseback'.[2] In the post-Enlightenment period, the Orient was reconstructed as an inferior value system in such a way as to justify European imperial ambitions. Anti-Semites, such as Adolf Wahrmund, morphed the noble Orient into a 'nomadic culture of the desert [that can] only interact with settled peoples such as the Europeans by robbing and enslaving them'.[3] Zionism developed as an 'authentic' late-European nationalism in this period.

By the time of the first mass Mizrahi migrations to Israel in 1949, a popular image of the Orient as illiterate, wild, despotic and pre-modern was prevalent in Ashkenazi society. Arye Gelblum wrote in the liberal *Ha'aretz* newspaper:

> This is immigration of a race we have not yet known in this country... we are dealing with people whose primitivism is at a peak, whose level of knowledge is one of virtually absolute ignorance, and worse, who have little talent for understanding anything intellectual. Generally, they are only slightly better than the general level of the Arabs, Negroes and Berbers in the same regions ... These Jews also lack roots in Judaism, as they are totally subordinated to the play of savage and primitive instincts... As with the Africans you will find card games for money, drunkenness and prostitution. Most of them have serious eye, skin and sexual diseases, without mentioning robberies and thefts. Chronic laziness and hatred for work, there is nothing safe about this asocial element.[4]

1. Ivan Davidson Kalmar and Derek J. Penslar, *Orientalism and the Jews* (Waltham: Brandeis University 2004), Introduction.
2. Ibid.
3. Ibid.
4. Arye Gelblum, *Ha'aretz*, 22 April 1949.

Such characterisations were not uncommon. David Ben Gurion described Mizrahi immigrants as 'without a trace of Jewish or human education' and stressed, 'We do not want Israelis to become Arabs. We are duty bound to fight against the values of the Levant, which corrupts individuals and societies, and preserve the authentic Jewish values as they crystallised in the Diaspora.'[5] Politicised Mizrahim believe that the Kur Hitukh ideology was aimed at separating, 'de-Arabising' and disadvantaging them.

Mizrahi immigration in the 1940s was needed to make up the shortfall of European and North American Jews who had not made *aliyah*, especially with regard to cheap manual labourers.[6] Arab regimes in which the Mizrahim lived also had political and financial interests in their departure. However, integrating a non-Zionist community that had lived relatively peaceful and integrated lives among Arab societies posed particular challenges to Zionists, for whom Jewish history was a European or Biblically Middle Eastern affair. Four decades after Arye Gelblum's diatribe, Ashkenazi intellectuals like Amnon Dankner were still using racist language in *Ha'aretz* to justify stone-walling dialogue with their co-religionists:

> These are not my brothers, these are not my sisters. Leave me alone, I have no sister... They put me in the same cage with a hysterical baboon running amok and they tell me, 'OK, now you are together, so begin the dialogue'. And I have no choice, the baboon is against me and the guard is against me, and the prophets of the love of Israel stand aside and wink at me with a wise eye and tell me, 'Speak to him nicely. Throw him a banana. After all, you people are brothers...'[7]

By 2002, Dankner was editor of the popular right-wing newspaper, *Ma'ariv*. While he was avoiding empathy and understanding in 1983, though, the Mizrahim were en masse being taught Ashkenazi history in sub-standard schools, suffering routine discrimination and living in decrepit accommodation with few life prospects. Ashkenazim had on average three years' more schooling, an academic high school attendance rate 2.4 times higher, and a university attendance rate five times higher than Mizrahim.[8] Real change did not begin until the 1970s when a Black Panthers movement emerged in Jerusalem's

5. Quoted in Ella Shohat, 'Zionism from the standpoint of its Jewish victims', *News from Within*, vol. XIII, no. 1, January 1997.
6. Segev and Weinstein, '1949', p. 172. In a secret record in October 1948, Berl Locker (chairman of the Jewish Agency Executive) wrote to the American-Jewish politician, Henry Morgenthau, saying: 'In our opinion the Sephardi and Yemenite Jews will play a considerable part in the building of the country. We have to bring them over in order to save them, but also to obtain the human material needed for building the country.'
7. Amnon Dankner, 'I have no sister', *Ha'aretz*, 18 February 1983.
8. Shohat, 'Zionism'.

Musrara neighbourhood, which linked Mizrahi and Palestinian oppression. It was ultimately gobbled up by Menachem Begin's Likud party but to some extent it changed the nature of public discourse.

Mizrahi Jews constitute perhaps the majority of Israel's population yet, by the late 1990s, 88 per cent of upper-income Israelis were Ashkenazi while 60 per cent of lower-income families were Mizrahi.[9] According to researchers such as Ya'akov Nahon, the socio-economic gap between the two groups is continuing to widen despite intermarriage and absorption efforts. While Mizrahim as a bloc have tended to vote for right-wing parties, individual voices are still struggling to have a voice heard in the national debate.

RABBI SHLOMO KORAH

I am nothing and nothing that hurts me counts

The airlift of Yemenite Jews to Israel in 1949 is revered in Israel as one of the country's finest hours. Many Mizrahi Jews had been killed during riots in Aden, and the mission to save an apparently helpless and desperate community was hugely costly to the fledgling state. Yemenite Jews, though, were more ambivalent about 'Operation Magic Carpet'. Many felt a particularly acute sense of dislocation in Israel that few Ashkenazim could empathise with. In the 1970s, the first claims surfaced that hundreds of Yemeni children had been abducted for forced adoptions within Ashkenazi families between 1949 and 1954. Two public inquiries exonerated the authorities but Mizrahi hopes were raised when a third National Commission of Inquiry was established in 1995 under the retired Supreme Court Justice Yehuda Cohen. A *Jerusalem Post* editorial argued, 'What was done cannot be undone, but after half a century, the least the government owes the victims of such outrages is to come clean. The whole truth may never be found, but more must be done than to bury the problem with partial conclusions based on suspect documents.'[10] However, this, Mizrahi campaigners say, is what happened. The issue had already become symbolic of a greater loss that had not been recognised and could not be assuaged. Shlomo Korah, the Rabbi of Bnei Barak, was then and remains now one of the Yemeni Jewish community's most articulate, capable and respected spokespeople.

Time, in Yemen, was measured according to the sun. It was better that way, you were more relaxed. Here, you have to run from place to place, looking at your

9. Shlomo Swirski and Etty Konor-Attias, *Israel: A Social Report* (Tel-Aviv: Adva Center, 2003), p. 10; Chetrit, *Hamaavak Hamizrahi Beyisrael*, p. 218.
10. Editorial, 'Time to come clean', *Jerusalem Post*, 28 August 1997.

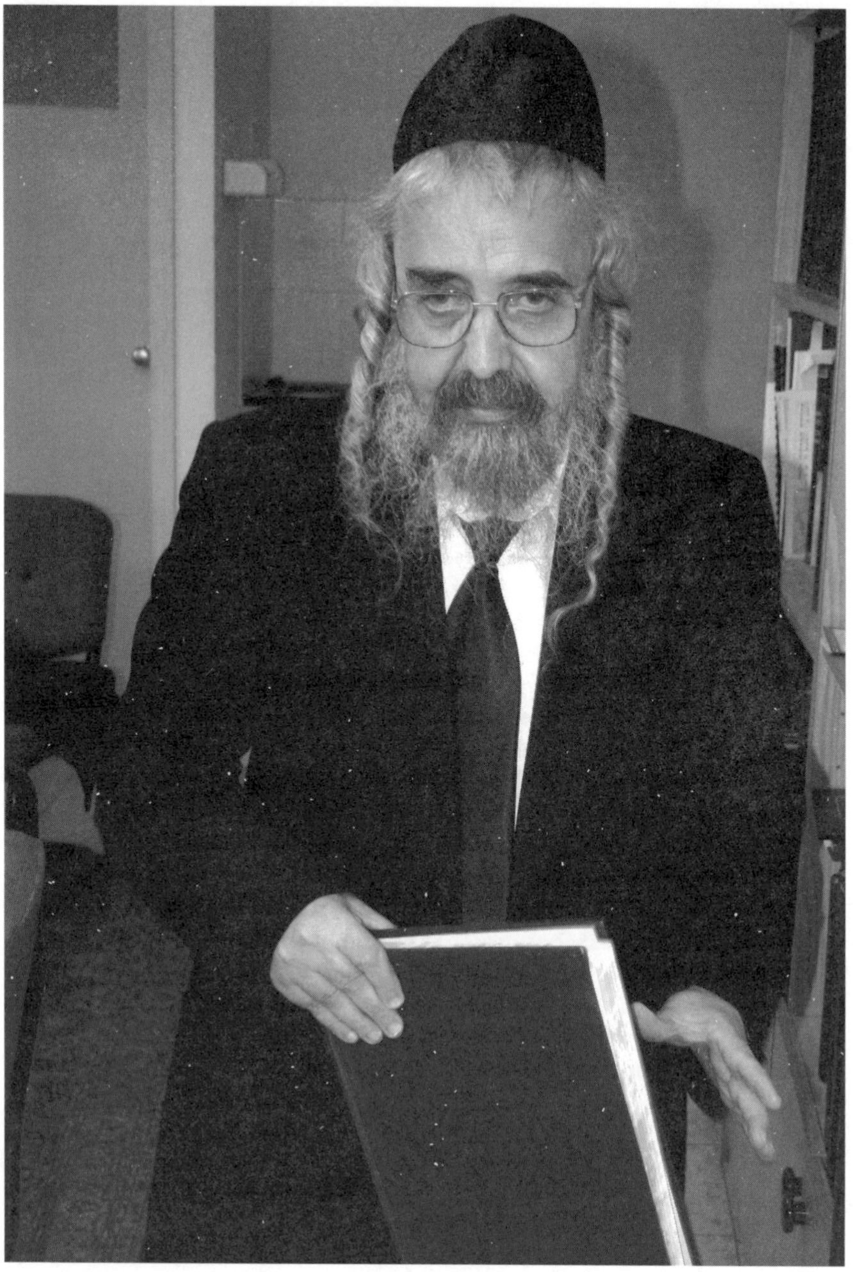

Rabbi Shlomo Korah. *Photo by Arthur Neslen*

watch every other minute. I was born in Sana'a, in Yemen. My family migrated there from Tiberius [in Iraq] in 1260. We had documents to prove this but they were stolen from us by the Jewish Agency when we arrived.

Jews in Yemen faced a similar situation to Jews in Poland before the Haskala.[11] Our synagogues were the social centres of life. We spoke Hebrew when we didn't want anyone else to understand us and a Judaeo-Arabic language which mixed Aramaic, Hebrew and Arabic at other times.[12] We're still the only community to translate the Bible into Aramaic every Sabbath morning. It's an ancient tradition. Our Hebrew accents, religion and prayer books are all different to those of other Mizrahim. In fact, our accent is recognised as scholastically the most accurate. But today you won't hear one news broadcaster using a 'het' or 'aiyin'. It's become an obstacle to getting on.

In political and economic terms, we were freer in Yemen. We didn't need licences to import or export or open a shop. All the government demanded of you as a Jew was that you paid a yearly Jewish Tax – assuming they knew you existed. We had some autonomy. My grandfather was the head of the Jewish court in Yemen – which was like the Supreme Court here. He could put people in jail or exile them if he wanted, but he never had to. We were a God-fearing community. The only real problem we faced was poverty, and that wasn't a specifically Jewish problem.

We didn't want to come to Israel[13] but after the state was created, Bedouins started moving into our neighbourhood, our neighbours started selling their apartments and the situation became intolerable. In 1949, we decided to go. Around 50,000 Jews had already made *aliyah* but another 50,000 were hesitating. My grandfather was a spiritual authority who people looked to for guidance so when he decided to leave, the 50,000 who'd hesitated went with him. Only a few hundred stayed behind.

Some Jews had donkeys or horses but most went by foot. There were hardly any automobiles in Yemen but the King did allow my family to use his car. For

11. The Haskala or Jewish enlightenment encouraged secularisation among European Jewry and gave birth to phenomena as diverse as Zionism, Reform Judaism and the revival of the Hebrew language.
12. Yemenite or Temani Hebrew is the dialect most closely related to biblical Hebrew. However, its phonology has been influenced by Yemeni-spoken Arabic.
13. Diaspora Jews have a long and rich history in Yemen. Some trace the first Jewish settlements back to the time of King Solomon, 42 years before the destruction of the First Temple. According to oral history, some 75,000 Jews first travelled to the region under the Prophet Jeremiah. When Ezra the scribe commanded them to return to Jerusalem, they refused and Ezra retaliated by banning them from the city and cursing them to forever be a poor people. As a result, 'Ezra' is the one biblical name no Yemeni Jew will give their child.

most Jews it took weeks of walking to get to Aden[14] and many died on the way. Little groups of people would march together, carrying their family manuscripts in their hands. There was no printing technology in Yemen then so people kept manuscripts from their ancestors.

The two largest libraries belonged to my family and the al-Shech's. They covered 700 years of Halachic law, Kabbala, history, philosophy, court protocols, astronomy, poetry and the writings of the Rambam, Maimonides. We also had original documents from the age of Rabbi Saadia Ga'on of Babylon, 950 years ago. They were priceless.

My family put our manuscripts in wooden boxes and sent them to the port of Tel Aviv. When they arrived, the port authorities wouldn't let us collect them for four months. Then they said the documents had been destroyed in a fire. It was a lie. I found two of the manuscripts which were supposed to have been burned in a shop in Jerusalem afterwards. We also have testimony from people in the port that there was no real fire. Several times, we went to the police but they insisted that there'd been a fire. We couldn't fight the police and the government.

Some of the manuscripts were sold abroad. They're now in the Vatican Library, the Baltimore Library, the Schechter Institute, and the Rabbi Kook Institute here in Jerusalem. The really rare manuscripts like Saadia Ga'on's, you will never find anywhere. But I saw manuscripts which once belonged to my family – with our signatures on them – in the basement of a synagogue in Haifa. They weren't important ones but still we weren't allowed to take them. Personally, I think that we should go to the synagogue, break down the door and take them by force.

After 950 years of looking after those manuscripts, it's a racist *chutzpah* to suggest that we were incapable of taking care of them.[15] Should the government take the paintings of Chagall from the collectors? And what about our wealth that was also stolen? Some big families in Sana'a deposited their money with an English bank and got it to Israel via London. But those who took their money with them were robbed in Aden by the Jewish Agency. Sometimes, immigrants were told that airplanes wouldn't be able to fly with gold on board. Yemen was

14. As the waves of Jewish migration to Palestine accelerated in the early twentieth century, so did anti-Jewish feeling in the Arab world. In the slums of Aden, 82 Yemeni Jews were killed in riots that followed the announcement of the UN Partition Plan in 1947. In September 1948, the British authorities said that they would allow Yemeni Jews to travel to Israel. However, it was not until June 1949 that they decided to do so, and 'Operation Magic Carpet' began.
15. Yemeni activists say that Yitzhak Ben Tsvi, the second President of Israel, defended the theft of their manuscripts and scrolls on the grounds that they were national treasures, which could not be entrusted to the care of the Yemeni Jews themselves. Activists claim that the same logic was responsible for the abductions of their children.

at the technological level of the Bible, and people seeing an airplane for the first time could be told anything.

I think part of the reason for the thefts was to rob us of our distinct cultural identity. A power system rules over our culture and they wanted to weaken us culturally. In 1948, the Yemenite community was 50,000 out of 600,000 people and it had much political power. We could have prevented Ben Gurion becoming prime minister if we'd wanted. So there was political fear, cultural fear, a demographic fear and racism all mixed up in the state's reaction to us.

Just talking about it makes me feel 100 years older. After we arrived in Israel, my family spent a month in Rosha Ein before moving to Jerusalem. Two days after we got there, my eight-month-old sister Bracha caught a cold. She wasn't too sick, but we called a nurse and she took Bracha to the camp's infirmary.

The next day, we went there to pick her up. They said 'come back tomorrow'. They kept saying this. One day we came and they said they'd taken her to a hospital and she'd died. We went there and tried to make noise and protest but nothing helped. We went to the police and they wouldn't even log our complaint about what we believed was a kidnapping.

We were weak. We stood in front of the government bureaucracy and nobody would take us seriously. The authorities didn't want to show us the body. They said she underwent surgery and seeing the body would distress us. We wanted to believe them. Still, we were never given Bracha's body to bury. The authorities said they buried it. Only a fool would believe them. They took us to the 'grave', a place with no other graves and said, 'It's here'. They put a wooden stick in the ground but it was just a piece of land like your backyard. Their disrespect and contempt was much worse than a physical beating.

So we went to the press, and asked for a public inquiry. There were three. The Yemeni community staged demonstrations but we had no power to fight the system. I believe that my sister was abducted and sold. I wonder how her new mother can embrace her and love her after inflicting such cruelty on her biological parents.

I don't want to say the state is my 'enemy', but our disappointment was enormous because we came here expecting to meet our brothers and we met something else. The state broke our leadership, stole our children, attacked our cultural values, discriminated against us and deliberately ruined our society. At first, we wanted to mix in the Kur Hitukh and be one nation. Now many of us want to turn inwards and deal with our problems alone.

No political parties represent us. If I had the time – if I were an Ashkenazi – then I would consider the Palestinians' problems. As it is, nothing I express will be important in Israel. My existence here feels meaningless. Since I am nothing and nothing that hurts me counts, nothing that I say counts and nobody will listen. Someone else decided these things, so someone else should deal with the problem.

I feel a connection to Israel but not to the state. The land of Israel – and the Bible – is home. Its not like land, it's a spiritual home, a holy land. But the quality of life was better in Yemen in every way. If you're looking at poverty, we have poverty in Israel. If you're talking about second-rate citizens, we're second-rate citizens here. When we immigrated to Israel there were almost no criminals amongst us. Now there are many and it's a result of the destruction we went through in the country's early days.

At least in Yemen, we were called Jews. Here we are 'Yemenites'. If Jews were free to travel to Yemen – without fear of Muslim extremists – about 20 per cent of us would return. I know people who were so disappointed with Israel that they had heart attacks in their first year after arriving.

Rabbi Al-Shech and the elder ones have said that we are now living in exile in Israel because, before 1948, we were all Jews. Now we are Moroccans, Yemenites, all the nations of the world. I would add to that: Before, when we were apart, we loved each other. Now, we are physically close but we feel only hate.

LIMOR

The fear that someone will recognise me

Betar Jerusalem Football Club is an icon for young Mizrahis in Jerusalem. In the days of the Yishuv, the football team was one outcrop of the wider Betar movement[16] founded by Jabotinsky's Revisionists (the forerunners of the Likud party). A rival football team, Hapoel Tel Aviv,[17] emerged from the Labour party. Competition between the two teams was fierce. More recently, Betar supporters have become associated with racist chants at visiting fans and players, and crowd trouble. In one incident in 2004, supporters even stoned their own team's bus. However, it was the relentless racism at the team's Teddy Stadium that prompted Limor, a diehard Betarnik, to start providing report-backs for The New Israel Fund on their behaviour. I spoke to her a few days after the death of Yasser Arafat.

16. Betar was the Revisionist movement formed by Vladimir Jabotinsky in Latvia in 1923. It called for the subordination of everything towards a movement for Israeli statehood within biblical borders. 'Betar' was the scene of Bar Kochba's last stand in the uprising against the Romans in 135 CE.
17. Hapoel Tel Aviv means 'Tel Aviv Workers'.

Limor. *Photo by Arthur Neslen*

I was born into the family of Betar Jerusalem fans 31 years ago. It's something you grow up with. You have to be on the right side of the political map. I got it from my parents, along with my religion. My brother even played for Betar as a child. It's something in your blood. I was nine when my father took me to my first Betar game at the old YMCA stadium. All I remember is the crowds and the singing. It was such a warm atmosphere. Betar has a national meaning here. Because our logo is the menorah,[18] people identify with the Israeliness of the team.

On my father's side, I'm seventh-generation Israeli, a real Sabra, although my mother's family are from Morocco. Most Betar fans are Mizrahim. They sit in the Mizrahi (east) end. Ten years ago, you couldn't be an Ashkenazi and support Betar. It's different now, but I still wouldn't tell someone that I liked Betar right away. I'd want to introduce the thoughtful me who has a life outside football first. Betar fans have a real stigma.

I was raised in Jerusalem in a right-wing family but my aunts were from a kibbutz and I wanted to be like them. I wanted a better life for myself and I knew that my parents didn't have money so I decided to go to the kibbutz alone. There weren't many other Mizrahim there. But I was never very Mizrahi-looking, so people assumed I was a kibbutznik. I just never felt that it was my place.

It must have been a bit like leading a double life?

Yeah, I remember the first time the teacher asked us what political parties we knew, everyone said 'Likud, Marach…' and then someone shouted 'Kahane.'[19] The teacher said 'I'm not going to write *that* on the board.' I stood up and asked 'WHY?' I didn't know who Kahane was really but where I grew up, they didn't say anything against him. The kibbutz taught us to see other people's rights as equal and there was anger at what Kahane represented. Coming back to Jerusalem was hard for me. I had to hide my personal thinking about the Israeli–Palestinian conflict from my parents. They didn't understand. When I got married, I had to cover up my feelings again because no-one would have wanted me, thinking the way that I did.

I also had to stop going to football games. When I was 18, I used to see every Betar match, home or away, but my husband said that a woman didn't belong at the football stadium. So after I got divorced, I decided to take my two boys there, to teach them that a woman can do anything – and that you can be on

18. A menorah is a seven- or nine-branched Jewish candelabra used specifically at the festival of Chanukah. It has been appropriated as a Zionist symbol, to symbolically represent Israel's mission as 'a light unto the nations' outlined in Isaiah 42:6.
19. Before he was assassinated, the New York Rabbi Meir Kahane formed a racist, perhaps neo-fascist party, 'Kach' (Take!), which called for the ethnic cleansing of Arabs from Israel. After the Kach supporter Baruch Goldstein massacred 29 Palestinian civilians in 1994, the group were proscribed in Israel.

the right and still be against racism. I live in the territories and almost every day my boys were coming home from school saying that Arabs stink or they can't be friends with anyone black – even Ethiopians. They didn't know they were Jewish.

When I heard about this project – *A new voice on the field* – I thought I could do something to help change society. For 12 years, I'd worked as a payroll clerk in a factory. Now, even though I don't get paid, I go to matches and note what the fans are saying, using SMS or tape. Then I help collate statistics for a weekly online racism and incitement table that the fans discuss every Saturday. It was hard for me when Betar topped the table last year.

If we stand for a minute's silence after a suicide bombing, you'll hear them saying, 'Death to the Arabs'. Whenever Salim Tuama[20] touches the ball, they'll chant, 'You have to know, we hate Arabs, we want the country without any Arabs.' It's horrible. Also Baruch Dego, an Ethiopian-Jewish player, gets abuse from his own fans at Maccabi Tel Aviv: 'Monkey, black man, go to the zoo.' It scares me that my own kids might join in. Now, when the fans sing racist songs, I tell them 'Shhh'. They know we can't say that.

It's only the teenagers, not the older, harder fans from way back, just poor kids with nothing else in their lives and they're treated like second-class fans by the police. The cops search everybody on the way in and they have a special 'blue area' for the women where they touch you. It's so embarrassing! The guys also get beaten though. They never do that to Hapoel Tel Aviv fans.

Aren't Hapoel Tel Aviv associated with the left and Peace Now?

That's true, but they yell 'Arab!' and 'monkey' at Salim too. If the player is from Maccabi Tel Aviv, they can do it. In the last few games, everyone, in every crowd, was shouting 'Yasser Arafat is about to die.'

Was it like cheering on his death?

Look, he didn't die. I don't know what will happen this Saturday but I think they'll happily shout 'Yasser Arafat is dead!'

How did you feel when he died?

I was happy because now we have a chance for peace. That's what I want to believe anyway. Arafat was a terrorist. He didn't do anything for peace but the Palestinians got tired from the fighting just like we did and they want peace now.

I live in a settlement near Ramallah but I want to give my house to the Palestinians, and so do other families there. Hopefully, we can have peace with two states and a border and I can go back to Jerusalem. I never held settler beliefs.

20. Salim Tuama is an Israeli Arab football player who suffered high-profile racist abuse in 2003 while playing for Hapoel Tel Aviv. He currently plays for Petah Tiqva.

We just wanted a cheap, big house, in a quiet street and the government gave us money to buy the house eight years ago, before the Intifada. It's got less pleasant to live in since then, but I still like my house and my neighbours.

Do you have any Arab friends?

Yeah, Layla, who's my best friend ever. She lives in Jerusalem, so it's kind of hard when you ask her, 'How was it in the Mall yesterday?' and she didn't get in because she's an Arab and she didn't have the right ID. She can't even come to my house. Everyone else came to my party four months ago but I was too embarrassed to invite her. I told her the truth, that I wanted her to come but I understood that the territory where I live is really hers. I'm on the Palestinian side of the wall.

Would you call her an Arab or a Palestinian?

An Arab (laughs). I don't know what I would do if I was an Arab. They have no money, no jobs, no future, all they have is to fight the Israelis who they blame for their situation. I think they still have to do a lot to fight terrorism but I can't judge them. No-one would want to live like they do. Yasser Arafat took all of their money and their hope so they went to the Hamas, where you can be a *shahid* and do something for your country.

You're still on the political right.

Well, the right used to protect the Mizrahim but now no-one takes care of anyone except themselves anymore, certainly not the single mothers, the weak or those on the margins. I don't trust anyone. But I do believe in Arik Sharon – because he looks like a big father.[21] He stands there and no-one can move him. He might be the only one who can bring peace.

What would happen if a team from Jenin played Betar?

Well, we'd have to win the game but I think the fans would have half of a war. There's crowd trouble even when we play Sakhnin.[22] Sakhnin's fans are

21. Matt Rees, 'The man who turned Sharon into a softie', *Time Magazine*, 23 May 2005. The cultivation of the 'Grandpa Sharon' image was a deliberate campaign strategy by the advertising guru, Reuven Adler. He told *Time Magazine* of Sharon: 'He's a warrior, he's quite fat, he stomps along, we had to give him some feminine appeal.' Rees added, 'On a scale of 1 representing the extreme left and 5 the far right, Adler figured Sharon was a 4.7... TV ads with soft music showed Sharon strolling the fields on his farm and hugging his granddaughter... Suddenly the 'unelectable' hard-line general had turned into... Grandpa Sharon. He won easily.'
22. In 2004, Bnei Sakhnin became the first predominantly Israeli Arab team to reach football's Uefa Cup after winning the Israeli Cup. Despite having a Jewish coach and several Jewish players, the team are reviled by many Israeli Jewish football supporters.

worse than Betar's. They wind the Betar fans up, so they shout 'Ha'rabait' – which is the Muslim quarter in the Old City. They mean, 'We have the most holy Muslim place in our hands.' Israel has everything and you have nothing. When the Sakhnin fans shout back, we all go 'Ooooooohhh', so no-one can hear them.

How has Betar FC reacted to the problem?

You didn't hear anything from the management or politicians until the fans started throwing rocks at the players. Now they've put up signs around the pitch and they're making pre-match appeals for calm. But they don't really deal with it. The coach is like a god to the fans. Why doesn't he say something? Ehud Olmert was the Mayor of Jerusalem. People would listen to him. But he's staying quiet because the fans are his constituency. He doesn't want to mess with them because they are the future. They are also the Israeli mirror.

What do you think would happen if your identity was revealed?

They'd kill me (laughs). Some of them can get really crazy, I'm not kidding. They'd see me as a traitor, or a secret policeman. It's really dangerous. I'd like to believe they wouldn't hurt me in front of my kids but the fear that someone will recognise me is always there. You know, someone looks at you funny and you get scared that maybe he saw you somewhere. Jerusalem is a big city, but everyone knows everyone else here. At first I used to go to the Betar game one week and a Hapoel Jerusalem game the next. I had to stop because the Hapoel sandwich-seller guy said, 'Hey, I know you' in front of everyone. I told him, 'No, you're mistaken', but he said, 'Yeah, I know you. You were here last week with your kids.' That was when I realised that I had to stick with Betar.

SHARON REGINIANO

I am the actor

Given the dramatic possibilities the last 30 years have gifted Israeli society, the possibilities for a renaissance of Israeli film should be manifest. Yet Mizrahi actors often complain about a racial stereotyping among Ashkenazi directors that confines them to playing gangsters in daytime soap operas. Sharon Reginiano starred as an Israeli army colonel in the critically acclaimed gay Israeli soldiers epic, *Yossi and Jagger* and played alongside 'A' list names such as Jean Claude Van Damme and Charlton Heston in 'The Order'.

I was born in Holon. My father was an industrial worker and I was an only child. I first decided I wanted to be an actor while I was in the army. I served in a small, stinking fuel base in Ashdod. If the Arabs had known we were the Israeli army, they'd have come with knives and forks! It was a lousy place, a joke. I was the chef. I was put in jail for 35 days because I ran away (laughs). Jail was better than the base.

My parents came here in the 1940s, my mother from Persia and my father from Libya – two countries that hate Israel. They came because they were Jews and this is the place for Jews, praise God. Although my father was from Libya, he was deported to Bergen-Belsen when he was three years old.[23] I was always aware of my Mizrahi heritage. I liked it because it was a warm way to live but when I went to study acting, I felt the difference between the two 'races'. The Mizrahim are primitive sometimes – like all warm people – but respectful. They don't patronise you. I'm proud that I'm Mizrahi.

For me, being Jewish means turning back to see the first line of light that built the world.[24] I have a lot of Kabbala books but I'm a simple Jew. I go to synagogue every Saturday. A hundred years ago, all of our grandfathers were rabbis. Now, even among Mizrahim, the cracks are showing. I believe in the Jewish people.

23. The Simon Wiesenthal Centre. In 1942, the Italian rulers of Libya began deporting Jews with British passports to Italy, where they were interned. Some were subsequently sent on to the Bergen-Belsen concentration camp.
24. Cantor, *Jewish Women*, pp. 40–42. In the sixteenth century, the Sephardic Kabbalist Rabbi Isaac Luria (originator of the Lurianic Kabbala) described how, to make creation possible, God 'contracted' inwards before sending out a ray of light from the *ein sof* or infinite. However, the vessels that were supposed to hold the light shattered into fragments from which evil emerged. When good and evil are separated and the damaged vessels repaired – by means of performing *mitzvoth* – then cosmic harmony will be restored and the Messiah will come.

Sharon Reginiano. *Photo by Arthur Neslen*

You can say I'm racist but I know we have the most beautiful way to live. To be a Jew is to be a man – or a human being – I went to school with women as well as men, Ashkenazim as well as Sephardim…

Israeli Arabs...?

No Arabs. I know a lot of Arabs now. I can't say they're my friends but I say hello on the street. This is a difficult period to be friends with Arabs in. I hate everyone who hates Israel and Israeli Arabs hate Jews. Don't imagine it any other way. This is Jaffa, man. If you see how the Arabs look at Jews here, you'll see the hate. If I took Ahmed or Abdullah and gave him $50,000 to kill two Israelis, do you think he'd do it? If you don't know, there's a chance and so these people are not good for the Jews.

Maybe Ivan or Vladimir from Russia would do the same thing...?

Yes, but the Arabs would do it with a smile. They hate us because they think we hate them. But I don't like to make war. I love them. For me 'bitachon' [security] means the joy of being able to say 'Shalom' to Abdullah and he will say Shalom back. And that my daughter will grow without fear that anyone will hurt her in any way.

Who were your heroes when you were growing up?

Al Pacino and gangsters, you know? A gangster is like a Rabbi because he has a lot of power. When I was a kid I saw *Scarface* and I met real-life gangsters. I love them. I love doctors too. I love people who walk on the edge and search for what's on the other side of the abyss. I wanted to be like them but I couldn't so I decided to play them. There are a lot of gangsters in Holon. I chose to be with them. I saw their robberies and I thought about them when I acted some parts.

Are Mizrahi actors often stereotyped?

Yeah, particularly in soap operas. Muuuhhh (adopts deep slow voice). He has this way to walk and talk. He's not so clever. He's primitive, strong, a gangster, a joke. The Ashkenazi (adopts British accent) is very clever, very clean. It's clear what I say, yes? I'm big and tall and strong and black, so they try to put me in their box. But if you have a backbone, you'll go your own way.

Do you ever try to subvert stereotyped roles?

No. I turn down roles that are too simple, that laugh at God, or which I have to do naked. Israel is not Hollywood. We are an eastern society, trying to be western. We are not. Walk down Jerusalem Rd [in Jaffa], It doesn't belong to the west. It doesn't even belong to the east. It doesn't belong anywhere. It's a garbage place.

You see the pipe going down the middle of the avenue? You know what it is? It's shit, squeezed shit that's coming from [Tel Aviv in] the north. They don't want to deal with it so they pump it to the sea through this neighbourhood. This isn't a western way of thinking. I want to be eastern because that's who I am, but it is hard in Israel.

If you were directing Othello in this country who would you cast as the lead?

Myself, because I like the role and I think I can do it. You know, he's like an animal but really he's a little kid. The part I'd most like to play though is Cyrano de Bergerac. At the moment I'm working on a version of *It's hard to be a Jew* by Shalom Aleichem. I started a non-profit theatre group called Ha'makom [The Place] and it's our first production. It was a dream of mine to own a theatre and now I'm educating people to love Israeli identity, our roots and culture.

What would happen if an Israeli Arab wanted to act in the play?

You know, I'm not a racist but if he wasn't a Jew, it'd be a bit of a problem. If we had an Arab part, an Arab would do it, probably. Israel is racist. It's a fact that Mizrahi actors are better than Ashkenazis but they often don't succeed unless they fit the *shtanz* [stereotype].

There's one Sephardic theatre group who always seem apologetic. They have no pride. You always have to hide your Judaism and ethnic origin here. 'You're in Israel now. You will be like America. Forget yourself!' Sometimes I feel like an outsider. I can't tell you how much of myself I put on show. The actor is me and I am the actor. It's always me. Sometimes I'm making a show for you, even now.

ELISHEVA BAR YISROEL

No fear in Dimona

In 1966, a Chicago foundry worker called Ben Carter had a vision that his African ancestors were descended from one of the lost tribes of Israel. Three years later, Carter – now renamed Ben Ammi Ben Israel – travelled to Liberia with around 30 disciples for a two-year 'cleansing period' before heading on to the Promised Land. When they arrived, they were quickly directed on to Dimona, a desert absorption town famous for its nearby nuclear plant. The Black Hebrews – or Hebrew Israelites as they call themselves – believe they are the true inheritors of the Old Testament and cite biblical evidence that Abraham, Moses et al. were black. The group has grown exponentially in the last three decades despite official harassment. Israeli attitudes towards them softened after one of their community was killed in a Palestinian attack on a barmitzva in Hadera in January 2002. A team from the

Elisheva Bar Yisroel outside her home in Dimona. *Photo by Arthur Neslen*

community subsequently won the Israeli baseball trophy and, in 2003, Whitney Houston visited Dimona and sang with their famous soul, gospel and R'n'B choirs. Elisheva Bar Yisroel was one of those she performed with.

This is the village of peace. We are a Hebrew Israelite community of over 2,500 people. We're vegans and we're very close. You could almost call us a kibbutz. We own everything collectively. Why, we put everything in the pot so everyone gets a share. If one brother or sister goes hungry, we all go hungry. The majority of the village is children. I have 10 children and several grandchildren. I'm a musician and a singer. I came here with my husband from Detroit, Michigan, 33 years ago. I love Israel, despite the fighting and religious strife.

When I left America, my friends and family thought I was crazy. My mother said, 'Why go way over to a foreign land that really doesn't want you there?' But to serve God and find my roots I had to. I'd had a Methodist upbringing and I sang gospel in spiritual churches. My father died very young from leukaemia. He was from the South, Georgia, and he worked on the trains.

After I arrived, I changed my name from Elisabeth to Elisheva, which means 'the promise' or 'the covenant'. In Hebrew, your name always has a meaning. I learned about my Hebrew roots because, in the Bible, it's stated that Abraham's children would go into slavery and bondage for 400 years. Well, Israel has suffered several slaveries since but it was said that we would be taken away in ships. There's only one people who was done like that, we just happened to be Africans who were shipped to America and lived for 430 years in slavery.

Today, you can't spot out a Jew from the tribe of Judah because we're all different colours here. You see Ethiopians, white Europeans, Moroccans, it's like a skin that's coming together after a flesh bite. You know, when I was growing up, my mother used to say 'la swanee', whenever something happened. In Israel, I learned it meant 'to the river' and (sings) 'I'm going to lay down my burdens down by the riverside'. In Detroit, when we saw a friend, we used to say, 'Hey! Kol basedit!' like 'See, everything's alright'. Here it's, 'Ha kol beseder' ['everything's alright'].

You believe that Abraham and Moses were black?

Yeah, you have to consider where they came from. Egypt and Israel were landlocked and Egypt is a part of Africa. The annex of Israel by the Suez Canal was only done recently. This is really the eastern part of Africa. Abraham moved all over, ok? From the Nile to the Euphrates. The truth is that we are still one family.

Did you come into much contact with Jews in Detroit?

I worked as a receptionist for a white Jew named Schumacher for a while. He ran a cleaning supplies company. I liked him, he was ok. There was a very negative spirit toward Jews in the US though. The feeling was that you couldn't trust them. I grew up in a mixed middle-class community on Detroit's east side. My first experience of racism came in the early '60s, when I was playing with my next door neighbour, Joey. His father shouted at him, 'Why are you playing with that nigger?'

I studied classical music until the age of 16 when I started doing background vocals at Motown. I was a substitute singer for the Marvelettes and I worked with Stevie Wonder 'cause we were friends. I did background vocals for Martha Reeves and the Vandellas too, studio work. Stevie was magnificent, very special, very talented. Out of all the musicians I met, he inspired me the most with the soul and spirit that he possessed. The last time I saw him was at a show with the Fantastic Four in New York in '69 or '70. Not long after that, I came here.

How did you discover the Black Hebrews?

It was my husband. He didn't believe in nothing before he went to the army, but he came home a changed and bitter man, with his eyes opened to racism in America. He met some brothers in Detroit, who were visiting from Israel and, one day, he amazed me by asking for a Bible. I said, 'What you want a Bible for?' He said, 'This is a history book and I'm in it somewhere.' Two months later we came to Israel. I had a round trip ticket. Never went back.

My daughter was an epileptic but she went on a strict vegan diet when we got here and she hasn't had another seizure. They said she'd never live to see five years old. She's 35 today. When I go back to the US now, I see the changes, the crime, the community that has been run down by drugs and I run back here, believe it or not.

We don't have citizenship but we can work now. When we first came, the brothers had to work illegally and a lot of them were deported. Difficult times, some bitter times, but we stood our ground and now we have Israeli ID. Yes, and our children are entering the army. My nephew Uriahu recently became the first Black Hebrew soldier, and my son will be going in a few months too. He just turned 18 and he's one of ten going. I feel a little nervous, but proud too. This is another bind between our kids and this society.

Doesn't it bother you that you can die for Israel but you can't vote in its elections?

We can vote in Dimona. We can't vote in the national elections yet, but until we break down racial and religious misunderstanding, things won't change. There's a lot of racism here so we have to tolerate and educate. A lot of times you hear the word 'Kushy'. Kush is Ethiopia but the way it's used, it's really calling you a nigger. When I hear it, I educate people about the Kush, and our history. There's as much racism here as anywhere, I wouldn't say more, I'm not going to say it's so much less. It's getting better.

Much as we love this land and want to be a part of it, it's sometimes felt like they didn't want us here. But things changed. The arrival of the Ethiopian Jews made it more common to see black people on the street. We've made links with them. I teach Ethiopian children Hebrew songs twice a week. Ariel Sharon helped get us permanent residence status. The Mayor of Dimona helped us too with houses that were gutted in and bombed out (laughs), no windows, doors, sinks, toilets... We rebuilt them.

How does your home here compare to your house in Detroit?

Oh *please*! I had a beautiful home in Detroit with furniture and everything but I gave that up to come and sleep on the straw mat, so to speak. Marcus Garvey was the first black leader who said 'Come out of America.' We didn't go exactly like he said, but I'm not in America now, and I'm glad. I think the original decision to send us to Dimona was an act of God. He was in on this thing. Even though they sent us to this absorption town maybe hoping that we wouldn't like the conditions, we've made it into a blessing.

Have you experienced more cancers here because of the nuclear plant?

There's a lot of foods that come back irradiated but because we're strict vegetarians and we use kelp and exercise, our cells are constantly replenishing themselves. Most of the cases of cancer we've had have come out of America. But we're still planning to move to a *moshav* in the Negev. Things are in process. Paperwork always seems to get in the way but with the help of Jah it will be very soon.

What does being an Israelite mean to you?

Being a part of the 12 tribes of Israel. No-one can really say which tribe they're from. But I feel – and my spirit tells me – that I'm from the tribe of Judah. It's not based on religion. This is a way of life. It's very close to orthodox Judaism but we don't celebrate Purim or follow Talmudic commentaries. We do fast on Shabbat and we only wear pure materials that are written about in the Bible – linen, silk and cotton – and we don't mix them.

We have divine marriages. Abraham had two wives, ok? A brother can have up to seven wives, though the most a man has taken here is four. In the Bible, seven women would cling to one man and share the work. So it wouldn't be *my* child or *your* child, but *our* children. My husband has three wives. We work together so I have less cooking and cleaning to do. That's why I'm able to sing. We're like sisters.

Why can't a woman have three husbands?

Well, that's also a physical thing because a man carries the seed. It would be very strange for a woman to have the seed of three men in her, ok? That would be balagan. Confusion, ok? Because how will she know whose children are whose? When a man has three wives, you can figure that one out. We're not changing laces here. And I'm definitely opposed to birth control too, I've seen too much cervical cancer.

What about the allegations of cultish behaviour and even child abuse?

We're not a cult. That was a phrase the media put on us. We're not doing any crazy unnatural things in our community. When I was growing up, if I did something wrong, my mother whooped me. It wasn't child abuse. We don't beat our children to physically harm them but to punish them so they know right from wrong. There has not been any child sex abuse. That's a right out lie. We don't have any paedophiles. There are no homosexuals living in our community. We've had a few people who became bitter or chose to become our enemies more or less, because of what they believed or understood or didn't want to do right according to the laws of God. But a lot of our children who left the community feeling certain things have now come back because they saw there was nothing wrong here. But rumours are rumours. What do you do? You have to take things with a grain of salt. See the children? They run free here. I have no fear in Dimona. I don't even lock my door. All day long, children can come and visit. We're just one big happy family.

RAFI SHUBELI

The sun had to reverse

In 1970, a group of Mizrahi teenagers, frustrated by the poverty and racism they faced, decided to form a version of the US 'Black Panthers' movement. In the next two years, they mobilised thousands of young Mizrahis to confront the police on demonstrations. On one Panthers demo in 1972, more than 60 Panther-supporters were arrested after chanting against the annexation of Arab lands. The movement declined after the 1973 war in the face of organisational repression and political co-option. Menachem Begin's Herut (now Likud) party fashioned an electoral alliance with alienated poor Mizrahi voters that won him election in 1977. The Likud never mounted any serious challenge to Ashkenazi power structures in Israel but has maintained its Mizrahi alliance to this day. Rafi Shubeli, 44, was one of those politicised in the 1970's tumult. Today, he sits on the board of the Keshet

Rafi Shubeli. *Photo by Arthur Neslen*

Democratic Mizrahi Rainbow, a civil rights group. Our first conversation in July took place on his birthday but he would not accept congratulations. In Yemen, there are no numerical measurements for time and birthdays are not celebrated.

I am not a Zionist Jew because I understand that Zionism is racism directed at me, and the Arab world. This is why there can never be peace, while the Ashkenazim rule Israel. I opposed Oslo because it was a racist agreement between the rich and wealthy from both sides, the Ashkenazim in Israel and the Ashkenazim of Palestine. Peace could never have come from such a miserable process and I, as a Hebrew-speaking Arab Jew, will never be at peace with the likes of Shimon Peres.[25]

I always voted for Likud even though I'm on the left in economic and social terms and I support a Palestinian state, but I stopped supporting them when Netanyahu made their economic policy radically more capitalist. I might vote for Shas if Aryeh Deri would run.[26] I'd never vote for the left-wing parties because they're the most racist. They say we are part of the West. For God's sake, they are only 30 per cent of the Israeli population! The Middle East will never accept them as the frontier of Europe.

My parents came here from rural Yemen in 1936 after my grandfather, a coffee 'saher' [merchant], lost a court case. Muslims and Jews had separate religious courts in Yemen but in a dispute between the two, there was no equality for Jews. My grandfather was sent to jail after one of my grandfather's workers falsely claimed he owed him money. He was released on appeal but he had to flee Yemen, without his wealth or property. The sun had to reverse.

We were victims of Zionism. The situation for us in Yemen had become impossible because of Zionists here. There was no going back, and our money to go elsewhere had been stolen when we left Yemen.[27] In those days, if you were a Mizrahi in Israel, you joined the Etzel. In the Hagana and left-wing parties, you were pressured to be secular and disrespect your parents' culture. But all Yemenite culture and heritage was religious.

So my parents suffered discrimination. Even during the Yishuv, Yemenite immigrants were treated as a different class by the left parties. We were the

25. Shimon Peres, the current leader of the Israeli Labour party is considered one of the chief architects of the Oslo peace agreement, and also of Israel's nuclear weapons programme.
26. Aryeh Deri was a founding member of the religious Shas party, who was jailed for three years in 2000 for accepting $60,000 in bribes. He blamed the Ashkenazi left establishment for his downfall. He variously served as the Shas secretary-general, a MK (member of the Knesset) on several occasions, and interior minister.
27. Jews exiting Yemen were obliged to leave all their property to the state, following a ruling from the highest Yemeni Imam.

'quantity' element. The Ashkenazim were the 'quality' element. The Arabs got the worst salaries, the Ashkenazim got the best and the Yemenis had to work harder for less money.

Here in Rehovot, women were beaten by farmers for 'stealing' fallen branches to cook with. One was tied to a horse and dragged through the main street so all the other Yemenis would see. In the Tel Aviv cleaning agency where my mother worked when she was nine, the Ashkenazi ladies used to pick them, like they were slaves in America. They had to eat their food off the floor too.

My father joined a Jewish police force when he arrived here but he left because of Mizrahi pay differentials and the police's orientation on hunting down Etzel members, who were his brothers in the neighbourhood. My dad was a Herut man. He hated the left-wing parties so much that he told my brother he wouldn't be welcome in our house if he voted for Meretz.

He sold clothes in the Yemenite neighbourhood. He never got a good schooling but he read books, even Karl Marx's. He thought I should become a labourer because the Ashkenazim would never let me get an education.

The establishment in Israel is Ashkenazic and left-wing. The left is the right here. We and the right are underdogs. The settlers support us on issues like the kidnapped Yemeni children and I've given them talks in the West Bank. I think they should be evacuated but I don't believe in humiliating them. They're our brothers. Left-wingers say that the occupation corrupted Israel. I think that we were corrupted before then. Maybe we even corrupted the occupation.

As I grew up, I saw that the schools, media, courts and academia were all controlled by the Ashkenazim. When you went to a disco, you'd be stopped at the door because as a black, you might be violent. You'd go to an Ashkenazi home and feel uncomfortable but you wouldn't know why. In school, you'd learn how the Ashkenazim established Israel. You'd be brainwashed into becoming ashamed of your parents. At night, I dreamed of metamorphosising into a blond-haired, blue-eyed Ashkenazi.

There was a window between the ages of 13 and 15, when I was an Israeli but now I can't be. If you're ashamed of who you are, you're weak inside and out. You become offended when they remind you that you're a Yemenite because it's so negative. It's a thing of yesterday you should have thrown away. I was so ashamed of my parents' culture that I chose to learn French rather than Arabic at school! Now I know who I am. I am not a third grade Israeli. I'm a first-grade Yemenite.

Do you see any parallels with the way that Yiddish culture was suppressed in 1948?

No, because that was an internal Ashkenazi dispute. They did it to themselves. They had no right to force this on other populations. Hatikva [the national anthem] is an Eastern European song. Our national poet, Bialik, wrote about

Eastern Europe. They didn't give up their culture. The national theatre even came from Moscow. Our culture was stolen and the Israeli identity we were offered was folk songs, folk dances, writers like Amos Oz and Ashkenazi yeshivas (religious schools) where Mizrahis had to learn in Yiddish.

Despite everything, I feel closer to Ashkenazi Jews than Israeli Arabs. I want Israel to be a Jewish state, not a secular one. But I want Arabs to have equal rights and I want a Palestinian state too. I want to connect with Europe – but also with our neighbours.

How did you become politicised?

It was a process. The most crucial point was the election of '77 when Likud won power for the first time. The political defeat of the Ashkenazi establishment was our victory. In high school, we were suddenly proud of our identity. I remember writing two pages about Yemenite history and asking my teacher to give it out to the students. We hadn't been taught about Yemen before. Begin didn't ask to be our representative, we made him our representative. He's the only prime minister who wasn't a racist. Before '77, a Mizrahi could only be minister for something like the post office. Likud appointed the first Mizrahi treasury minister, foreign minister, security minister and head of the army.

I remember I was about ten when the Black Panthers were marching and Golda [Meir] said they were 'not nice boys'. I read a lot about them. They were outside parliament and they're a good example of how the establishment can break a radical organisation. They bought some of them off with good jobs and pushed the others to the margins of society.

My first political activity was with a Yemenite paper called *Afikim*. I wrote articles about the transfer of Yemenite Jews from Kinerret and Migdal. In the '90s, I became outraged by the case of a Yemeni rabbi called Uzi Mishulum who'd been researching the Yemeni abductions story. His house was surrounded by the army's anti-terror units. They murdered one young person inside and wounded another. The newspapers then turned people against Uzi with false claims that he was a terrorist. If the state was taking this trouble to suppress his activities, I thought they must have something to hide. I started campaigning to get the false graves of Yemeni children exhumed. They opened ten graves and found there were no skulls inside. There were pieces of something they said were bones but an English lab found no traces of DNA in them.

Did you support Oslo?

No, it didn't do anything about Palestinian poverty. They only made peace with the Palestinian upper class. That's why the process never got a majority in Israel. When Rabin and Meretz signed Oslo, they brought foreign workers into Israel to work for lower wages than the Palestinians. It lowered the salaries of the poorest Mizrahis. Then they moved the factories where Mizrahim worked to the Palestinian authority, Jordan and Egypt where people would work for even less. The Mizrahim were hurt economically by the Oslo process. Why should they support it?

Tell me about your group, the Keshet.

We're involved in legal battles over land issues involving kibbutzim and we're organising to get more Mizrahi material into school books. We have hundreds of members and a lot of support among Mizrahi communities. I'm one of the board members who think we should take a position against the occupation. The problem is that the Mizrahi street here votes for the right – for cultural reasons – and that's where we draw our power from. We can't distance ourselves too far from it. We might use the same words as left activists but if the Keshet ever joined with them, I'd resign. We shouldn't deal with them until they deal with the Ashkenazi hegemony.

You believe the Mizrahim have suffered a 'cultural holocaust'...

Yes. We are suffering it still. I see kids poisoned in schools and I can do nothing. My nephew told me 'I don't like studying Arabic because Arabs are bad people.' I replied that his beloved grandmother's first language was Arabic! It surprised him and at the next Shabbat supper, he proudly told me that he knew how to count from one to ten in Arabic. And then he counted.

4
Strange Orthodoxies and Quantum Secularities

Israel was created by a movement of non-believing Jews. When the UN voted to partition Palestine on 29 November 1947, much of the world's orthodox community opposed the move. One of the most powerful groups, Agudat Israel, actually appealed to the UN General Assembly to vote against the motion. For centuries, orthodox Judaism had held that an 'ingathering of the exiles' in biblical Israel would be heresy before the Messiah's return. One of Agudat Israel's leader, Jakob de Haan, was assassinated by the Hagana in Palestine in 1924 after making the same argument there.

However, within months of Israel's establishment, Agudat Israel's opposition to Zionism folded. In retrospect the turning point was a letter sent to the organisation by the executive committee of the Jewish Agency on 19 June 1947. In it, David Ben Gurion and others outlined what was to become known as the 'status quo' agreement, a historic compromise between religious Judaism and political Zionism. It proposed that in the new state the Sabbath be made a legal day of rest, kosher food be guaranteed in all state kitchens, the rabbinical courts be granted effective jurisdiction over marriages and full autonomy be guaranteed to religious schools.[1]

Such a compromise was needed because, from a religious standpoint, Zionism was irredeemably assimilationist. In 1893, the movement's founding father, Theodore Herzl, even proposed a mass conversion to Christianity:

> I wanted to solve the Jewish question, at least in Austria, with the help of the Catholic church. I wished to arrange for an audience with the Pope and say to him: Help us against the anti-Semites and I will lead a great movement for the free and honourable conversion of Jews to Christianity. 'Free and honourable' inasmuch as the leaders of this movement – myself in particular – would remain Jews and as Jews urge a conversion to the majority faith. In broad daylight, at twelve o'clock on a Sunday, the exchange of faith would take place in St Stephens Cathedral with a solemn parade and the peal of bells.[2]

1. E. Marmorstein, *Heaven at Bay* (OUP, 1969), pp. 86–7.
2. Orr, *Israel*, p. 16.

Such betrayals of faith alienated secular Jewish leftists as much as the religious. After the Kishinev pogrom in 1903, Herzl had gone to Russia to try to negotiate a deal with Vyacheslav Von Plehve, the Russian interior minister, and instigator of the pogrom. Herzl boasted afterwards, 'I have an absolutely binding promise from him that he will procure a charter for Palestine for us in 15 years at the outside. There is one condition, however: the revolutionaries must stop their struggle against the Russian government.'[3] The revolutionaries in question, the Bund, who had organised Jewish communities to defend themselves against the pogrom, denounced the Zionist strategy afresh. Vladimir Medam, for instance, wrote:

> [The Zionists] speak of a national home in Eretz Israel, but our organization opposes this thinking absolutely. We believe our home is here, in Poland, in Russia, Lithuania, Ukraine, and the United States. Here we live, here we struggle, here we build, here we hope for a better future. We do not live here as aliens. Here we are at home! It is on this principle that our survival depends.[4]

The Holocaust changed the terms of the debate but not so much that Israel appeared a desirable residence for a Diaspora establishment scared of charges of dual loyalty. When David Ben Gurion instructed a meeting of American Jews in 1950 on the need for more *halutzim* [pioneers] from the US, Jacob Blaustein, the president of the American Jewish Committee, angrily retorted: 'American Jews vigorously repudiate any suggestion or implication that they are in exile... To American Jews, America is home!'[5]

Only the blessing of the religious institutions could endow the Zionist project with the legitimacy it needed. Failing that, Israel would have struggled to attract immigrants, to attain international credibility as a self-proclaimed 'Jewish state' and provide an underpinning for its citizens' self-definition and the state's own *raison d'être*. However, the price exacted by the Rabbinate was a heavy one, and it continues to be felt across a largely secular society, which would most likely reject large swathes of the status quo agreement, were it ever to be put to a referendum. After 1967, religious Zionism became a powerful political phenomenon in its own right as Messianism melded a faith-based Jewish identity to secular Zionist security-consciousness. The trend is discussed further in Chapter 9.

3. Henry J. Tobias, *The Jewish Bund in Russia* (Stanford, 1972), p. 248.
4. Vladimir Medam, *Neyer Felt*, 2 July 1920, p. 12.
5. Erik Shachter and Amotz Asa-El, 'The Anglo difference – contributions of English speaking Jews to Israel', *Jerusalem Post*, 2 October 2003.

RABBI SHMUEL ELIYAHU

Like a switch had been clicked

After the Spanish Inquisition of 1492, large numbers of religious Jews sought refuge in Tsfat, a mixed Arab village in the Galilee. It quickly became one of the world's centres for Kabbala and Torah study and remains one of the four holiest cities in Judaism. For the last 14 years, Shmuel Eliyahu, the 47-year-old son of the former Sephardic Chief Rabbi of Israel, Mordechai Eliyahu, has been the town's rabbi. On 28 November 2004, *Ha'aretz* reported that he had been questioned by police on suspicion of inciting hatred against Arabs in the nearby town of Akbara. A fly posting campaign there had falsely claimed that Jewish girls were being held captive by local Arabs. Four months previously, he had told a local paper, *Kol Ha'emek* of 'another form of war that the Palestinians are waging against us. We must know how to defend ourselves against it. It involves Jewish girls aged 15–25 that are seduced by young Arab men ... We must save them.' Eliyahu supports the 'transfer' of Palestinians from Israeli territory and was a leading opponent of the disengagement plan.

Throughout history, the enemies of the Jewish people – Hitler, Saddam Hussein, the Palestinians – have been the enemies of humanity. The world suffers when the Israeli people suffer and it benefits when we benefit.

My father's family came here from Spain in the fifteenth century, but the story of the Spanish Inquisition has not been a big influence on my life. I relate more to the stories of the destruction of the First and Second temples, the Exile and the Bar Kochba war.

The Spanish Inquisition was very important to the Jewish people. It happened at the same time that America was discovered, the beginning of a new and better age and a global revolution in human spirit.[6] Dogmatic and blinkered ways of thinking began to fall to the more open-minded American way, and the people of Israel started to return to their homeland.

Some say that before 1948, Tsfat was a model for peaceful co-existence.

Only if you ignore 200 years of Arab violence. You can see what happened in 1929, the Jews never dared to raise a hand or stone in defence against their Arab

6. Eliyahu believes the Inquisition and *aliyahs* of the fifteenth century changed the Jewish spirit by paving the way for the Shulchan Aruch or 'set table', a codex of Halachic religious injunctions that was composed by Rabbi Yosef Karo of Tsfat in 1560, and subsequently used by Sephardim as a guideline for material and spiritual values.

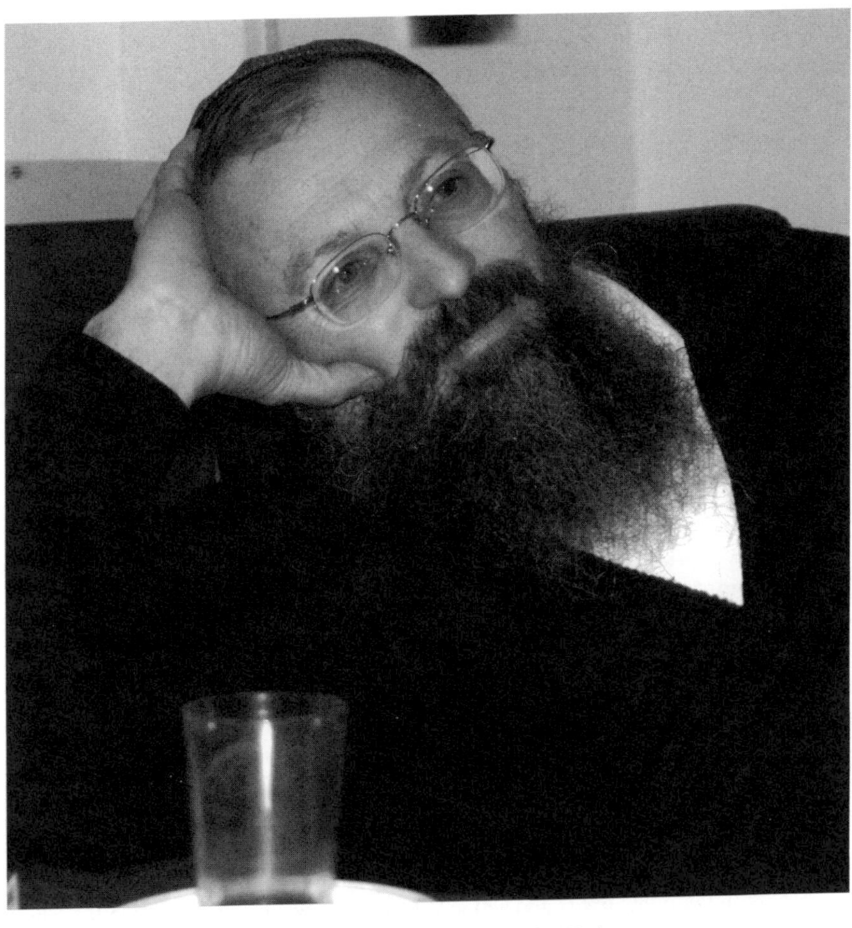

Rabbi Shmuel Eliyahu. *Photo by Arthur Neslen*

attackers. The old people here can tell you how the Jews were weak. They never resisted rapes, massacres, torture or murder. They never did anything.

It's the same as what happened in Europe. These events were exactly predicted in the Bible and the Torah. When we were in the Diaspora, we were weak and we ran away from everyone. In 1948, something changed in our mind, it was like a switch had been clicked. We became strong.

Why don't you differentiate between the experiences of Mizrahis and Ashkenazim?

It's become less of a problem. People live together, are educated together and marry together. Most now identify themselves as Israelis, so it's not as important as when I was growing up. Talking about it wouldn't bring anything positive to bear, just divisions.

My secretary once told me her family had been in Israel since the fall of the Second Temple but she was confused because she didn't know if she was Ashkenazi or Mizrahi. I told her: 'You are neither, you are a Jewish woman.' Recently I told some teenagers that although they'd come from Romania, Bulgaria or Yemen, they were still Jews. They had just been guests elsewhere for a while.

Why is a Palestinian whose family lived here for 2,000 years a guest, while a Jew whose family lived for 2,000 years in Yemen is an exile?

Because God says so. This is *Eretz Yisroel*. The land belongs to God and He decided the answer. Mark Twain once described coming to Israel and finding that the land was empty of people.[7] Palestinians living here for 2,000 years is just a nice story. The Arabs are our guests here and if they understand that, it will be ok. If they think that they're the owners of this house, we'll have a problem. In October 2000, they were very violent.[8] We cannot have scenes like that. Too many of them have been involved in terror attacks. This does not give us hope. We can donate all the Palestinians to England or Europe (laughs).

7. Mark Twain, *The Innocents Abroad* (1881). Twain visited Israel in 1867 and described it as a 'desolate country whose soil is rich enough, but is given over wholly to weeds – a silent mournful expanse...A desolation is here that not even imagination can grace with the pomp of life and action...We never saw a human being on the whole route.' However, as 650,000 Arabs had been estimated to be living in the country by the Second Zionist Congress in Basle, 1898, Twain's words are open to interpretation. Twain was himself unashamedly racialist towards Jews. In 'Concerning the Jews' (1898), he described the 'Jewish race' as having an 'unpatriotic disinclination to stand by the flag as a soldier'. He continued, 'If that concentration of the cunningest brains in the world was going to be made in a free country . . . , I think it would be politic to stop it. It will not be well to let that race find out its strength.'
8. Thirteen Israeli Arabs were shot dead by soldiers during anti-occupation protests in Sakhnin.

Isn't that what Spain said to the Jews in 1492?

Maybe. So what's the problem?

That Rabbi Hillel said to do unto others as you would have others do unto you.

It's true. But the Inquisition was held until 1830 and it involved stealing Jewish properties and setting fire to those who wouldn't convert to Christianity. We haven't done that to Arabs – and Jews in Europe didn't behave as Arabs do here. We didn't bomb cities, hijack buses or shoot families. We didn't smash heads with stones, throw Molotov cocktails at families in cars or try to throw Europeans into the sea. We never said we wanted to either. If we had tried to overthrow the king or queen and seize power it would have been justified to throw us out.

Is that why you forbade the sale of property to Arabs in 1995?

It's written in the Bible. It was true in 1975, in 1995 and throughout history. It's true now. The land belongs to God and he gave it to Abraham, Isaac and Jacob for so long as they would not sell it to anyone else. You can't break this law. These are not my words. I quoted them but they were said by God in the Bible. If you behave like a guest here, ok. If you want to throw us out, please find another place. Go to the desert.

What if you want to be not a guest, but a citizen?

In another country. You have the right to live, to exist, to respect, but you must know that this is a Jewish country. How would you feel if Muslims in England tried to take over your country and throw people into the Atlantic? Here, as a community, they declare that they want to throw us into the sea. If it happened in England, it would be legitimate to expel them. We are dealing with people who support terror and if you even slightly support terror, then you don't have a place here. You should be expelled not to Gaza but to Saudi Arabia. I can give them to England if you want them. Do you want?

What else do you think Israel has given the world?

Everything. Everything that Moses, Jeremiah and the others wrote has come true today through us. The Bible has been translated into more than a thousand languages and more than 3 billion copies have been printed. It's the most important book in the world's history. It teaches the world that we have one God and we live this book today.

Why are so many Israelis turning away from religion?

It was predictable. A pregnant woman is going to give birth but from the outside she looks very weak. So the people of Israel are coming back to life but from the outside they look weak. Fifty per cent of Jews are religious people, schooled in the religious educational system. You won't see this in the media but the fact that you are here means that you are home. It's a long process. We believe that in the end, you [addresses me] will come back. I'm not bothered even if we disagree and argue. We love each other. Even if I am right and you are left, in the end we will be even closer.

Did you feel any sympathy for the posters warning about Arabs in Akbara?

There are problems with young Arabs who start with some young Jewish women. I think it is unhealthy for Jews and Arabs to marry each other. The Arab villagers told me they think it is wrong for them too. I would never allow a son or daughter of mine to marry an Arab. It would never happen, though, because they're educated people with well-rounded personalities.

All the residents here are like my sons and daughters and when it has happened, it's hurt me very deeply. It hurts the groom and the bride. We can see it. We know it. It is destructive and it always ends in violence and pain. The children suffer the most. They are divided in their minds. When there is a terror attack, they don't know whether to be happy or sad. It is wrong to bring sorrow to so many people.

Would you feel differently if your son or daughter married a Christian Zionist?

Both cases are wrong but we haven't got a fight with the Christians. We have a fight with the Arabs.

Yet Christian Zionists would ideally see two-thirds of Jews killed and the other third converted to Christianity.[9]

You can find more than a hundred versions of Christianity and many different interpretations. It's based on the Bible so we have a lot of common ground, even if we don't agree on everything. Even the Pope now recognises Israel. What's important is that Christians have no problems with Jews today but the

9. The 'dispensationalist' credo of the 30 million or so Evangelical Christians in the US holds that Israel must expand to its biblical borders in order to bring on Armageddon and the Second Coming of Christ. Some believe they will be taken to heaven before the End of Days, others that they will be resurrected soon after. They are agreed that Jews who do not convert to Christianity will perish. The theological basis for the belief comes from a rather deliberate reading of Christ's last words on Israel (Matthew 24 and Luke 21). The 'two thirds' number is obtained from a prophesy by Zecharaia (13: 8, 9): 'And it shall come to pass, that in all the land [Israel], saith Jehovah, two parts therein shall be cut off and die; but the third shall be left therein. And I will bring the third part into the fire, and will refine them as silver is refined, and will try them as gold is tried.'

Muslims hate us. Throughout history, the Muslims have hated us. They just weren't sophisticated enough to build gas chambers.

My family didn't suffer in the Holocaust but I think its lesson is that we Jews should live in the state of Israel. Germany before the Holocaust was the greatest society in the world for poetry, science and art – but that wasn't a secure guarantee for humanity. You cannot trust human society, you must have a connection to G–d. Faith and security come from the same word. 'Emuna' or 'faith' in Hebrew comes from 'omenet', which describes the feeling of a little child in his mother's hands.

So faith and security are the same thing?

Of course.

RAHEL

There is a chain

The controversy over the Tsfat 'Arab abductors' poster campaign touched a raw nerve in Israeli society. 'Marrying out' has always been uniquely feared within Jewish communities, and Golda Meir spoke for a deep wellspring in Diaspora as well as Israeli thought when she described it as an existential threat to Jewish life.[10] Yet 25,000 Jewish women in Israel are estimated to have married Arabs.[11] The figure may not compare with an intermarriage rate of nearly 50 per cent in America,[12] but it is more religiously and racially charged. In a mainstream Israel National radio online op-ed in November 2004, Mayaan Jaffe wrote: 'The Arabs are trying to steal our land... and through their violence, eradicate the Jewish people. In the same way, the Arabs aim to steal our women... The battle against Jewish–Arab intermarriage is a war we cannot afford to lose... We cannot sit by idly and let Jewish women fall into Arab hands... Each woman stolen by an Arab abuser is a generation of children vanished.' Such a militant objectification of Jewish women runs counter to diasporic tradition in which the 'loss' through marrying out was something to be mourned and accepted rather than fought and avenged. In Jaffe's five-part series, a consistent narrative was presented of Arab lotharios seducing Jewish women with honeyed

10. Golda Meir, *Knesset Debates*, official publication, Jerusalem, vol. 13, p. 770, debate of 9 February 1970.
11. Mayaan Jaffe, 'Jewish wives are Arab husbands' prey', *Arutz Sheva*, Israelinationalnews.com, 22 November 2004, quoting from Lev L'Achim, an anti-assimilation organisation dedicated to 'bringing the lost souls of Israel home'.
12. National Jewish Population Survey, 1990.

A protestor takes a hammer to the Separation Wall in Abu Dis. 'Rahel' wished to remain anonymous. *Photo by Arthur Neslen*

words, only to imprison them in violent and abusive confinement. Rahel, 34, is one woman whose experience challenges this view.

I had a religious but tolerant schooling in Jerusalem. My mother came from a wealthy Turkish family, my father was from Romania and he had a survivor's attitude to life. He was on the extreme right. He died in 1995, the month before Rabin was killed. The Arabs were an unspoken issue in our house. We'd go to Abu Ghosh to eat humus but the Israeli Arabs were like the natives, they didn't exist. There was a feeling that you couldn't quite trust them. At school, we never learned that we made Arabs refugees in 1948. The teaching was like: there was a Holocaust, the Jews had to come here, they had no option, the Arabs didn't let them. Before I met Hayman, I only dated Jewish guys. When I joined the army, I became secular and my family tolerated that.

Is being Jewish still important to you?

It's complicated. It's important because it represents my family. There's an emotional connection. I still consider myself Jewish, I speak Hebrew and I know what Mishna and Talmud are.[13] I guess it's a loaded issue. It means being my mother's daughter. Do you know the American TV series *Thirtysomething*? Well, there's an episode about Michael – who's Jewish – and his wife who's not, where someone tells Michael, 'There is a chain. Will you dare to break it?'

I'm still a Zionist but in a very particular way. Obviously I believe that the Jews must have a place of their own, it's a legitimate right for every people. But if we're occupying the Arabs and there's no justice, then just having a state is not good enough reason for me.

How did you meet Hayman?

I was helping a friend look for a flatmate and we interviewed Hayman together. Months later, she reminded me that I told her after the interview, 'He's amazing! Too bad he's an Arab.' I thought he looked like a prince. He came from a poor but very proud Bedouin family and he carried himself with dignity. Anyway, a few days later I saw Hayman on the street and I just melted. I invited him and a friend round for supper and my friend left early. Two weeks later, it became obvious to us that we were in love.

I always used to say that I'd marry an Israeli guy from a religious background so that we'd have a mutual world. Hayman and I didn't have feminist issues

13. The Mishnah refers to the oral religious story-telling tradition, which orthodox Jews believe began with Moses, but was reformulated by rabbis in the first century and put down in written form in the second century. Additional commentaries added in the centuries that followed were called the Gemara. The two together constitute the Talmud, the entire collection of religious laws.

or TV in common, but actually we looked at the world quite similarly. It's something deep and intimate. He has a cynical sense of humour which I like, and he's emotionally intelligent. I can't say that about many Israeli guys.

Most Israeli men are so fucked up. They think too highly of themselves and they brag about all kinds of stuff. They're so pathetic. I think they suffer from severe insecurity and they hide it with machismo. I guess it's the same everywhere but especially here, you have to be the hero. It's like the 'new Israeli', the opposite of Jews in the Diaspora. It's very rare for them not to affect indifference.

My secular friends thought it was exotic and cool that I was dating an Arab, and in the elite neighbourhood where we live, nobody would dare say anything. It's PC, you know. But my brother's attitude was that I was nuts. He hasn't spoken to me for six years now. At first, my mother seemed tolerant but it was an act. A few days after I told her about the relationship, she called to say that she couldn't handle it. She was depressed and not sleeping. I started crying and after a few days I decided to just lie. I told them that we'd split up.

For two months, I had a perpetual headache. I hated the fact that my family were putting their ideological values – which were racist, basically – above my happiness. When I told my mother that I'd lied, she said, 'In that case, I can no longer be part of your life and you can't be part of mine.' That was it. She couldn't resist it. My brother was still in touch with me until the day we married because he kept hoping that Hayman would convert. But I couldn't be with someone who changed his beliefs because of pressure. I just let my brother think that it might happen.

During this year, my brother married and it was terrible. I went to the wedding and my mother didn't speak a word to me. It was such a chaotic situation. When I approached the civil rights association for information, they said: Don't marry him, he won't be able to live in Israel. So after four months, I tried to break up with him. I told him we had no future. We separated for two days and it was awful. It just didn't make sense. So we got back together and, after eight months, decided to marry. We went to the Interior Ministry, paid them and went to Cyprus for a civil ceremony.

None of my family came to the wedding. Our best friends were there so we weren't alone but you don't want to know what it was like. They were playing the wedding march on a tape and the weddings officer was so moved that a Jew and an Arab were getting married that he gave a speech about how important it was to build bridges and break borders, blah blah. He was thinking of the Cyprus and Turkey situation but I just felt lonely and upset because my family wasn't there. Then Hayman had to stay in Jordan for two months because of the Interior Ministry's rules. It was a very difficult time. I had to keep fighting to prove to them that it was true love. Finally he was given a visa and work permit and after a year I got pregnant.

There were issues around the *bris* [circumcision]. Hayman didn't want a Jewish *mohel* [circumciser]. But in the end, we found a gorgeous *mohel* who was sensitive and it wasn't bad. When our second son was born, we got the same *mohel* to just say the blessing with Abraham's name in it.

At first, Hayman's family tried to convince him not to marry me. But after we got married they accepted us. I think they believe that I became a Muslim. Hayman didn't correct them. Also I brought sons, which is very important to them. Every time, they butchered a sheep. The children are Muslim according to their beliefs because lineage goes by the father – Mohammed also had a Jewish wife.

Did both families feel that the child belonged to their religion?

Hayman feels that his children are Muslims with a Jewish mother. We were naïve and thought that love would solve everything, which it doesn't. It was hard for me to be apart from my family. But a month after my second son was born my mother collapsed and started to cry when she saw the children. She couldn't handle it. Three months later, she became the ultimate grandmother. The story has a happy ending basically.

A lot of Jewish women who marry Arabs tend to be uneducated and live in their husbands' villages. I know of cases where the husbands have restricted their behaviour. Even Hayman was raised to believe that women have specific roles and shouldn't dress in certain ways. His uncle has two wives and he was brought up with many double standards. But he knows that women should have equal rights. He's proud of what I do and, because he's not egotistic, I think it's exciting and flattering for him that his wife is successful.

Do you think that the Jewish attitude towards marrying out is racist?

Of course. They have the excuse about preserving Judaism but I think it comes from a racist point of view, that Jews are better than everyone else. If you see the way we look, Jews throughout history must have had sex with other people. Otherwise, we'd all look like Yemenites.

There was a time when it was difficult to establish the lineage of a child because the rape of Jewish women was so common.[14] *That's why Jewish ethnicity is inherited from the mother. But I was wondering how Jewish women appeared to Arab men?*

I think they represent the West, modernity and sexual freedom because most Israeli girls are not religious. So Arab men are envious but they probably consider

14. Cantor, *Jewish Women*, p. 87. 'The popular explanation among Jews of halacha's definition of a Jew as an individual born of a Jewish mother demonstrates how pervasive the expectation of rape was. The explanation is that because Jewish women were at high risk of rape by non-Jewish men, to determine and trace Jewishness

them as promiscuous too. And they're also the enemy. So it's quite loaded. I don't think that sex with Arabs is a common Jewish woman's fantasy. But there's something heroic or noble and mysterious in Arabic and Bedouin culture, and they're a foreign enemy.

I suppose I have challenged some ideas but I wasn't intending to. I don't think people say 'Oh, she married a Muslim, I guess they're not all monsters.' It was a totally personal choice, and if Hayman and I are able to immigrate that will be too. I assume now that the best place for my children won't be Israel. If I want a better life for them, the 'personal cost' for me will be giving up my home – I want to say abandoning Israel – but I feel that Israel abandoned me.

ARIK ASHERMAN

Then we're the oldest

Arik Asherman is the executive director of Rabbis for Human Rights. He has been arrested several times and prosecuted for trying to obstruct house demolitions and help olive tree harvests in the West Bank.

I was born into a religious family in Erie, Pennsylvania, in 1959. My father was a businessman, my mother was a teacher. I have two brothers and three half-brothers and sisters from my father's previous marriage. I'm the oldest of the younger family. Relations between the two sides of the family were usually pretty good. They lived in a different city, and in the '80s we had family get-togethers in South Carolina every summer for a week. Over the years it brought us closer. I played the role of ambassador at certain points.

I'm the first person in many generations to become a rabbi but my mother's side had one in the nineteenth century and my father's side had a vegetarian *magid*! By the time of my *barmitzva*, I was already dealing with the ethical Jewish tradition and commandments, what we now call *tikkun olum*. I didn't

through the father's identity could have been impossible; painful and humiliating for women and conducive as well to intra-communal conflict. It might have even led to the creation of a subgroup who like mamzerim [bastards] are forbidden to marry non-mamzer Jews. Frequent expulsions and migrations would have made it eminently difficult to have kept track of who was a Jew. Given the absence of a territory by which to define the nationality of group members, the only possibility left was to base it on the mother's identity.'

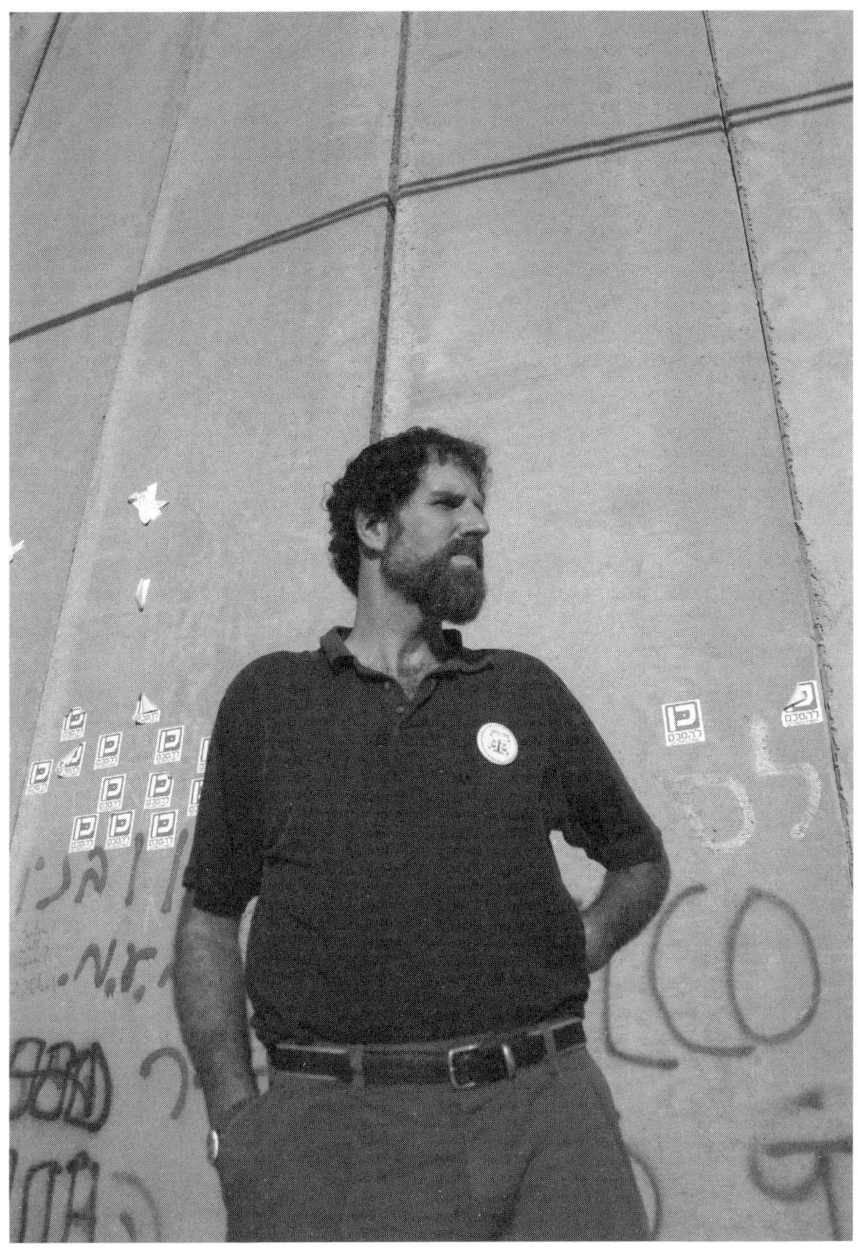

Arik Asherman. *Photo by Arthur Neslen*

call myself a Zionist back then. I got very involved in student anti-apartheid work and I saw myself [working] in South Africa. I never believed that all Jews had to live in Israel.

A basic part of my Judaism was concerned with universal human rights and social justice. It was a rude awakening after I made *aliyah* to discover that not everybody here saw those values as necessarily axiomatic. From the outside, people see us as one of the world's most powerful armies, the superpower in the region. But we see ourselves surrounded by a sea of hostile enemies and a battle for survival is our common denominator.

Has that sense of existential threat been used to solidify Israeli identity?

The period from Purim through Israeli Independence Day is used consciously or unconsciously to press that home. It's like the old joke that every Jewish holiday is, 'They tried to kill us. We beat them. Let's go eat'. You have Purim where Haman tried to destroy us, then Passover where it was Pharao, then you have Holocaust Remembrance Day and Memorial Day for the fallen soldiers, and then you get Israeli Independence Day and that's the solution. How much of that is intentional manipulation and how much of it is reality?

I don't believe I have more right than a Palestinian to live here but neither do I have less right. If you want to talk about the trump claim being the oldest, then we're the oldest. If you talk about by dint of expulsion, we too were expelled, and if you want to say that the expulsion of 50 years ago has more import than the one of 2,000 years ago, then I would say: what's the statute of limitations? Maybe someday we'll have a world with no borders but until then we have as much right to a place of our own as anyone. Full realisation of everyone's rights is impossible so either one side dominates the other, one side concedes, you're continually at loggerheads or you find a way to compromise.

Why are settlers opposed to compromise such a powerful minority?

They really believe that what they're doing is their G–d-given duty. I mean, not all of them are religious, but increasingly they are and in many ways it's an ideological steamroller versus a marshmallow. Secular leftists go out every so often to demonstrate but these folks are moving ahead with their plans day in and day out.

Right now, even people who disagree with them feel a great deal of sympathy because they see them under so much fire. If you take the Bible seriously, you can't deny the covenant between G–d and the people of Israel. You know, we accept the Torah and G–d gives us the land. In terms of Jewish values though, even Rabbi Ovieda Yosef, the spiritual leader of Shas has ruled that holy as the land is, human life is more important.

All human beings are created *B'tselem Elohim*, in G–d's image. He who kills one person, it is as though they killed the universe. The Ten Commandments are usually presented as two tablets with five commandments on each. The *Midrash* asks why does it say 'I am the Lord your G–d' opposite 'Thou Shalt not Murder'? The reason is that an attack on a human being – which is the one and only image of G–d in this world – is therefore dissing G–d too.

Another of my favourite *Midrashim* states that different people were chosen for different things. The Romans were chosen to bring architecture to the world, the Greeks to bring philosophy and the Jews to bring Torah. 'Chosen-ness' doesn't necessarily means the exclusion of everyone else. It imbues a responsibility which we can't ever necessarily say that we've fulfilled.

Can the wall around Jerusalem be morally justified?

The barrier is not a human rights issue, its route is. I'm for a barrier if you're talking about a kid asleep at night feeling safe. Outside Jerusalem, there is a simple solution, which is just put the barrier on the 1967 political border. It's a way of having your cake and eating it too: we have security and the Palestinians have their land.

I don't think that two states would stop the violence, but the occupation is a cause of violence and human rights violations. We're like two roosters put into the ring to fight. It's a kill-or-be-killed scenario, and ending the occupation is crucial to ending that. The occupation is eating away at our moral fibre. Things that before 2000 would have made headlines now just go by without a thought. To continue feeling good, we put ourselves in a bubble where even if we do something wrong, it's their fault. They started it and the world is against us.

But the Bible very clearly says that we cannot assume ownership of this land in all perpetuity. The land has a soul. The land is a living being that will vomit you out if you pollute it by shedding blood. There may be a paradox here in that the very activities needed to hold on to the land are the very ones that make us unfit to do so.

YOSSI BEN YOSHIM

Everybody is the Messiah

The mystical theory and practice of Kabbala has had a profound influence on the development of Judaism. From the Middle Ages onwards, it provided an explanation for the continuance of exile and oppression, namely that Jews were fated to be enslaved by gentiles of the world until they had uplifted the sparks of divine emanation that had fallen among them. Some see an institutional anti-gentile racism in the Kabbala that religious Zionist groups have exploited. Others see a defensive reaction to medieval anti-Semitism. Certainly, the practice invigorated traditional Judaism with theories that God was not wholly omnipotent, that he had an explicitly female element (the *Schechina*), and that human agency could hasten the Messiah's return and so end exile. What was needed was transformative repair by Jews to the world and themselves. The idea may have played a role in catalysing the Hasidic movement of the eighteenth century and influencing generations of revolutionary Jewish thinkers. But after the Shabbatai Ben Tsvi debacle in the seventeenth century,[15] Kabbala largely retreated into the occult shadows. Lately, it has been given a new lease of life by new-age acolytes of Rabbi Berg[16] in the US. There, as in Israel, the phenomenon has tapped the same reservoir of spiritual malaise associated variously with a growth in the popularity of eastern religions, self-help books and drug use. Yossi Ben Yoshim is a worshipper in Rabbi Berg's Kabbala Centre in Tel Aviv.

I'm a 36-year-old computer engineer. I have three children but I'm not married. My parents are from Iraq. I've been going to the Kabbala Centre in Tel Aviv for eight years but it's been a problem for my family. They have other goals in their lives. Money gives my sister a guarantee in life – the more she has, the more secure she is. It's ok.

15. Shabbetai Ben Tsvi was an eccentric Kabbala scholar who was expelled from seventeenth-century Salonica after 'marrying himself' to the Torah in a synagogue. He is notorious in Jewish communities around the world for declaring himself to be the Messiah, and whipping up mass hysteria. Tens of thousands of Jews followed his lead, but in 1666 he was brought before the Sultan of his native Turkey and given the choice of death or apostasy. He chose the latter and converted to Islam.
16. Rabbi Berg is a former insurance salesman called Feivel Gruberger from Brooklyn, New York who turned the Tel Aviv Kabbala Centre into a million-dollar franchise. However, it has been dogged by accusations of cultism, heresy and corruption. An investigation by the BBC journalist John Sweeney found that 'healing' water the Centre sold for roughly $8 a bottle came from a bottling plant in Canada. One devotee was allegedly advised to buy about $1,000 worth of the product to help cure his cancer.

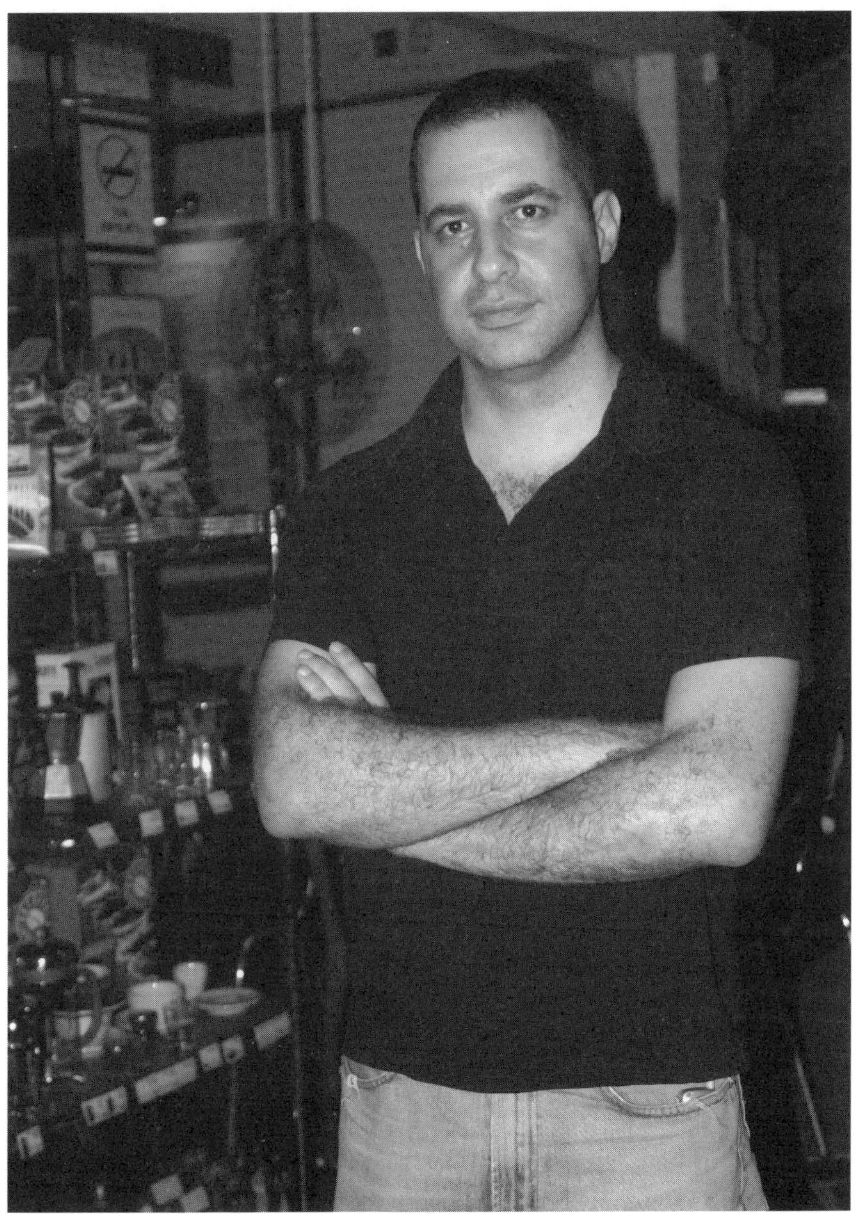

Yossi Ben Yoshim. *Photo by Arthur Neslen*

I found Kabbala through a newspaper guide. A friend of mine said, 'Let's try this' and we flipped a coin. The coin said to go. Maybe it was fate. It's the only way I've found to connect with Judaism. My father took me to synagogue on holidays but it was boring and I never understood what I was doing. With Kabbala I can work on myself.

The Centre includes Jews and non-Jews and mixes Buddhist rituals with traditional Judaism. Around 400 people go every week. The men and women sit separately. Nobody speaks when we're praying and a kind of homogeneous community is created, including a lot of Russians. Sometimes people go to meet members of the opposite sex. Many couples were created at the Centre.

Why do you think that Kabbala is becoming so popular today?

Because it's connected to our parents' Judaism and at the same time it's the new age. In a way it's a rebellion against what was there, because it wasn't enough. People are very confused in Israel today. We live in an environment of fear and I don't like it when they say that if you have a *Zohar*[17] with you, you'll be protected from suicide bombers.

I don't relate to Madonna either. I have a problem with instant spirituality. People who go because of Madonna won't really change. The idea that having more money brings you closer to Kabbala is a problem. But when I joined the Centre, we only had 100 people in Israel, and a few in the States. I remember Rabbi Berg saying that in a few years, pop stars will be standing in line to come, and it happened. Last year, I went to the States and there were 3,000 people from all over the world praying. There are 50 or 60 centres around the world with tens of thousands of people like me.

But is that more to do with spirituality or selling $500 bracelets and bottled water?

It's very commercial. I don't like the video screens during prayers and the way they over-charge for hotels on their US trips. But Kabbala has important aspects which are right for me, and I turn my eyes away from the other things. The prayers and Kavanot touch my soul and sometimes when you pay for something, you're more related to it. I know it's going to a good cause. They distributed 10,000 Zohars to the occupied territories and this from all the ear-rings the cynics laugh at.

17. The Sefer Zohar or 'book of splendour' was written in the thirteenth century and mainly theorised about the role of divine emanations in the creation of the universe. However, after the catastrophic exile from Spain in 1492, Kabbalists attempted to merge this theme with apocalyptic Messianism, most notably through the Zohar of Isaac Luria (see below). Luria believed that Jews could effect a cosmic reconstitution of the light shattered at the dawn of creation. In practice, this was a mystical injunction to reform the societies Jews lived in. Luria influenced Jewish intellectual thought for centuries.

The issue is not the status of the West Bank, it's like Rav Berg said, you do a good thing and the consequences will come. It's very strange, on Lag B'Omer,[18] they said they'd given enough Zohars to the West Bank to stop the violence there and for the last six months there's been quiet, I can't explain it.

It's been quieter in Israel, but a lot of Palestinians have still been killed.

I didn't think about this. You're right, but I'm sure Kabbala will help repair relations. It will break this wall. It can't stand. There is no other way than peace between the two nations. Any spirituality is a better way than violence. The way I see it, we are living on the generosity of God, because we don't behave right. The Kabbala says that actually everybody is the Messiah. You are the Messiah, I am the Messiah and everybody is the Messiah.

A year ago, the Haredim were burning the Zohar because it's not traditional Judaism. Kabbala is like the black sheep of the family but it has many streams. Sometimes this one doesn't teach deeply enough. But Kabbala also says that the Haredim are scared of losing their power. That's why they're against women freely studying the Zohar. You should only learn it if you're an honoured male *yeshiva boche*.

They would say Kabbala is too powerful in the wrong hands.

Well, we just do theoretical Kabbala. Practical Kabbala involves saying the names of God in different combinations to create reality. Still, I've seen people get so involved in Kabbala that they lose other aspects of their lives. You have to be constantly aware of what you're doing and thinking and what's happening around you.

Sometimes we don't see the connection between our actions and their consequences. But time is always getting shorter. Time is mercy in the Kabbala. When you make a mistake, you have time – and mercy – to repair it. But things are happening more rapidly now and the connection between action and consequence is becoming shorter. You have less time to fix your mistakes and the consequences of your actions will come more quickly than before.

Do you believe that time is speeding up because the Messiah's return is imminent?

Maybe. In Kabbala thought, some will be blessed and others won't have time to repair themselves. People aren't aware of how much weight is on their shoulders, personally and as a nation. The Kabbala says we have a responsibility for the

18. Lag B'Omer is the 33rd day in the seven full weeks between the festivals of Passover and Shavuot. It is a minor holiday that commemorates a break in the plague that blighted Jewish communities in the time of Rabbi Akiva.

world. Rav Berg says that the Arabs are in Ha'rabait[19] because they help us. If we rebuilt the temple now, we'd harm ourselves and the world. If we behaved properly, they'd stop fighting us. I know that I'm not connected enough to my inner self and I think that I missed many connections to other people in my life.

If you found that connection would you still go to the Kabbala Centre?

Yes, because no feeling compares to what I reach in prayer. Something is definitely missing in Israel. I've tried other things, I've been in therapy for a few years but Kabbala helps me get this other connection.

Is devotion the goal or is it just a means to something else?

It leads to something else. It's the feeling, the clarity, the state of mind that I get. I don't know what the end is. This is how I am. I work by instincts. The goal is me.

MOSHE, YISROEL AND CHAIA HIRSCH

The roots of faith

After 1948, the bulk of the world's religious Jews made their peace with Zionism. However one group, Neteurei Karta, continues to believe that the founding fathers of the country committed sacrilege when they appropriated the role of Moshiach for themselves. Rabbi Moshe Hirsch is the organisation's 'foreign minister', who served in Yasser Arafat's cabinet as minister for Jewish affairs. In 2002, he was accused of accepting money from the Palestinian Authority. His son, Yisroel Hirsch, denied the accusation. Yisroel's wife is Chaia.

Moshe: I was born into an orthodox family in the Lower East Side of New York City and brought up in a yeshiva. I became a rabbi as soon as time permitted. I just wanted to cater to the Jewish public. I came here in 1956 but I don't see Israel as the Jewish homeland. It's just where Jews found themselves, and where I happened to choose my home. I'm not identified with this state. I haven't even been to the Wailing Wall. I'm an individual in the Holy Land and that's it.

One doesn't join Neteurei Karta. It's an idealistic group of Jews who experience the Torah values which G–d wants to teach all Jews. We dress in the clothes of

19. Messianic Jews believe that a 'rebuilding' of the Second Temple in Jerusalem on the site where the Al Aqsa Mosque currently stands will occur when the Messiah returns. Some wish to begin immediately. The Al Aqsa Mosque is the third holiest site in Islam.

Moshe and Yisroel Hirsch. Chaia Hirsch asked not to be photographed. *Photo by Arthur Neslen*

the seventeenth century Polish aristocracy so as not to appear like non-Jews. Neteurei Karta literally means 'the watchmen of the city'. It refers to the 'holy city' where Jewish people reside. We're in exile and return will not be practised until we receive a divine approach.

If you met a Jew who was thinking of making aliyah, what would you tell them?

Moshe: Don't dare do it. If you make *aliyah*, you'll be swallowed by the foreign mentalities of Jews in their exile. The state of Israel has no ties to the Jewish nation. They're basically goyim who speak Hebrew. We can only stay true to our principles here by living in a Jewish ghetto and following our way of life. If someone gives us money in shekels, we change it into money we can use, like American dollars.

But we have no sympathy for secular anti-Zionists like the Bund either. They're outside the Jewish circle. They may have had Jewish parents but it doesn't make them Jewish in practice. A secular Jewish identity is impossible because Judaism is so closely associated with G–d's will. The central contradiction of Zionism is that it wished to establish a state against Jewish axioms.

Why do you speak Yiddish?

Moshe: We use Hebrew only for holy study. For thousands of years, it was said that if Hebrew were spoken as an everyday language, it would be desecrated.

Can you give any examples?

Yisroel: They changed the word *bitachon* – which over the years meant that if you put your faith in *Hashem*, He would protect you – to mean putting your faith in the security of the state and it would protect you.

Chaia: Right. So what they were really doing was not just changing the meaning of a word, they were...

Moshe: ... changing a concept!

Chaia: They wanted to remove the roots...

Moshe: ... the roots of faith.

Yisroel: From the beginning, the state used words which had very strong symbolic meanings for faith to change concepts in Judaism and weaken religious Jews. *Betuach Le'umi* now means 'social security'. You trust the state and in return it supports you with money. They just symbolically roll these words to move people's trust away from Hashem towards the state. All the phrases they chose were...

Moshe: ... associated with sacrilege.

Chaia: ... and they took many of the words from *loshn koydesh*.

How can tikkun be affected now?

Yisroel: Only if the state falls apart, and comes under another jurisdiction that allows Jews to serve G–d as they did in the Diaspora.

Do you oppose Zionism for its betrayal of Torah values or its oppression of the Palestinians?

Yisroel: Because they're against the Torah. They're so blinded by Zionism that they can't hear the other side of the coin. If they could, they might think differently.

They might say that you don't listen to them, even when Palestinians bomb your neighbourhood?

Yisroel: The day after the suicide bombing in Mea Sha'arim, Abdel Aziz Rantisi from Hamas[20] said that it was a mistake and there had been no intention of putting the bomber in our neighbourhood. They are aware that Jews living here oppose Zionism.

Rav Hirsch, you've met Yasser Arafat before, what sort of man was he?

Moshe: A national leader, an honest man with faith concerned for his people. Sitting as minister for Jewish affairs in his cabinet was the same as sitting with non-Jewish people anywhere, except that they were fighting for their independence.

Yisroel: They have the right to do that. They're not like Jews who are bound by the Torah which says, 'Don't fight! You're supposed to be in the Diaspora.' They are a nation, like any other nation and this land was taken away from them. That's not to justify killing people, but if you look at it from their point of view, you can see why they're doing it. During the American Civil War when they wanted to free the slaves, there was also bloodshed.

Has Yasser Arafat given Neteurei Karta money in the past?

Moshe: He gives money to all those who can use it.

Including Neteurei Karta?

Moshe: To all Jews who can use the money for religious purposes.

Do women have a role in the struggle against Zionism?

Yisroel: The role of the Jewish woman is to be in the home, not to be political...

20. Abdul Aziz Rantisi was appointed leader of Hamas after the group's spiritual leader Sheikh Ahmed Yassin was assassinated in 2003. Rantisi was himself assassinated shortly afterwards.

Moshe: ... and teach the community about Judaism as it should be!

Doesn't that halve your forces in the struggle against Zionism?

Chaia: (laughs) Yeah, but that's Jewish custom. Like the women never went out to war. The women are the foundation of the Jewish nation but they do everything from within the home.

What's your position on Rabbi Tzvi Kook's messianic vision of Judaism?

Yisroel: This beginning of the Messianic era, as he would like to call it, has brought a lot of misfortune and bloodshed with it. Jews are not supposed to rule anywhere until the Moshiach comes. In the Diaspora, we accepted the sovereignty of whoever was ruling, not because we were a minority, but because we were obligated to do so.

But that sometimes carried a heavy price. How do you explain the Holocaust?

Yisroel: This is a decree from G–d that is hard for us to understand.

YONATAN AND NA'AMA HERWITZ

A big plate of scrambled eggs

The growth of Jewish fundamentalism has energised many young Israelis who reject the secular, western and consolidationist vision of Israeli society. Press attention has focused on the 'hilltop youth', fervent young Zionists who erect outposts atop hills in the West Bank as a prelude to settlement-building. Some are the children of settlers, others are supporters of the far-right Kach party, but the consensus that sustains them stretches far deeper. I met Yonatan Herwitz, 21, in the scenic West Bank settlement of Tekoa where he is a yeshiva student. At the time of the interview, he was trying to persuade his 20-year-old wife Na'ama to start a family with him there.

Na'ama: I'm Na'ama Herwitz. I used to be Na'ama Ziff. My father was from a very strict Masorti[21] background in Minneapolis, but he left the religion behind when he married my mother. I went back to God three years ago.

21. The Masorti movement is a traditional stream of Judaism closely linked to Conservative synagogues.

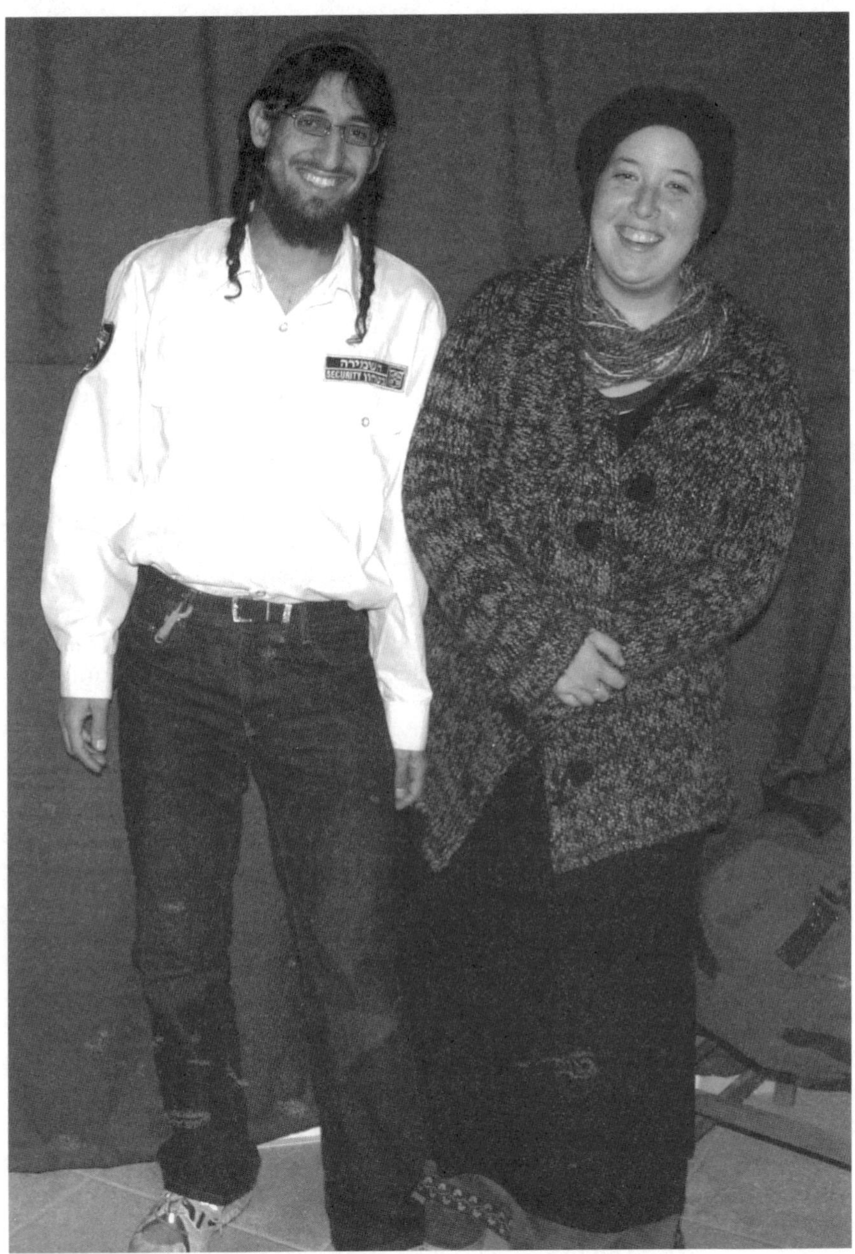

Yonatan and Na'ama Herwitz. *Photo by Arthur Neslen*

Yonatan: I grew up in a modern orthodox family but we weren't like 'black hats'.[22] We kept meat and milk in separate dishes and didn't travel or use lights on Shabbat. But we had a TV and I went to a mixed school in Jerusalem. I got my first sense of real spirituality when I studied in Tsfat.

Na'ama: My background is totally free but the more I got into religion, the more my mother turned away from me. She disagrees with God, with covering your hair when you're married, everything. If we talk, it ends in an argument.

I became religious very suddenly. I was a low point in my life, feeling very depressed and I ran away from home to Tsfat. I didn't understand what triggered it. I was just in a place where I felt like God was everywhere. He was real and I had to change everything from black to white. Ever since, I've been working on how I talk, dress and act.

How did you meet Yonatan?

Na'ama: It was 1999 and we were just hippies hanging out in Kikkar Zion.[23] We kept in touch in Tsfat and then we got engaged. I actually knew we'd get married from the week we met but I wasn't religious then and you weren't *as* religious. Being Jewish is stronger here. You see it everywhere you go, you can feel it. Sometimes it's hidden and secretive but it's a power. Being Jewish in Jerusalem is something primal; like where you're supposed to be. It's the first step. When I say I'm Israeli, I'm very proud. People here can be rude and loud – it's so Israeli to yell and honk on the streets – but I love them because of who they are.

Yonatan: A lot of American Jews who wouldn't actually make *aliyah* send money or have relatives here. They're Israeli at heart. They know they have a home here. Like my parents made *aliyah* from the US 17 years ago. Even my grandparents were born there. It's a shame you have to differentiate Israeliness from being Jewish. It used to mean the same thing.

What do you think you have in common with secular Israelis?

Yonatan: Everything. Maybe not how we actually practise our daily lives but we both went to the army, we both want peace, we both pray for our soldiers' safety and we live here even though it'd be easier to run away.

Na'ama: I'm torn. Sometimes I feel like I have to justify being religious to my secular friends. I could tell a religious friend, 'You know what? Secular people can be just as amazing as us.' But they look at me differently now. They don't understand why I won't touch men – even to shake hands – unless it's a relative. They understand lighting candles before Shabbat but when you magnify it like

22. 'Black hats' is a Hebrew slang term for Hasidic Jews.
23. Kikkar Zion is a central square in Jerusalem.

I do, after you've lit the candles, you enter a totally different time zone, a totally different dimension, and for them it stays the same.

Yonatan: Unfortunately, so many people like Neteurei Karta dress in the same *peyot, tzitzit, kippa*[24] but it's like: Where *are* you? What are you *doing*? *Look* at yourself! Because that's not what you're supposed to be.

How has the economic situation affected your family life?

Yonatan: It's difficult. Unless it's Tuesday or Thursday, I only see her if she wakes me up before she goes to school or I wake her up when I come home at midnight. I work nights as a security guard and every day I go to the yeshiva in Tekoa for three hours, where I meet my closest friends to study, drink coffee and play guitar together. I want to move there. We both want to live in a more natural environment and the Judean desert is amazingly beautiful. The fact that it's a settlement and we need to be there is just a bonus.

Na'ama: I think there's nothing worse than raising a child in a place where there's a high risk that, God forbid, something should happen. It's different for ideological young couples who want to preserve our country. I agree with them and it's fine they're there but it's too big of a statement for me. I read about a woman near Tekoa whose son was murdered. Her mother asked her: 'Why are you still there? You have more children!' To me, that's horrible. If you put yourself at risk, fine. But a child shouldn't be walked to school by soldiers.

Yonatan: Occupation has become a filthy word. It has such negative connotations, but when Joshua led the people of Israel through Jordan, he was supposed to conquer, occupy and even destroy the people if he needed to. That was the commandment, you know? A Palestinian people whose capital is Jerusalem is the most made-up thing I ever heard. These aren't ancient tribes. They're just people who fought us. They lost – badly – so they thought, 'Ok, we'll make the best of a bad situation and stay.'

We let them stay which was wrong, but we gave them water and electricity and all the utilities they need, so its crap to say we occupied their land. They occupied ours! I wouldn't vote for Sharon again because he's giving away things so precious to us for a fake, non-existent peace. This generation has a responsibility to take a stand. It's hard to tell a family, 'We're kicking you out of your home' and why? Because we need to give it to them!

Na'ama: I'd rather not talk about politics. I try not to take sides.

Yonatan: I used to believe that Arab-Israelis were loyal to the state and there were good, peaceful people, even in the territories. Then the Second Intifada

24. A *kippa* is a head covering for males also known as a yarmulke or skullcap. *Peyot* are long sideburns worn by Hasidic Jews. *Tzitzit* is a white garment with strings attached to each of its four corners worn under the shirt.

hit. Sharon didn't start it.[25] They were waiting for something to happen. Maybe they're not all blood-sucking terrorists, but left-wing Arabs aren't making a sound because they worship Islam, which is the law of the sword and the power of the fist. When I heard that soldiers injured a passer-by in a missile attack on a car, I actually used to care about the civilian. I don't any more because they're doing nothing to improve things.

So why should they care when innocent Israelis are killed in suicide bombings?

Na'ama: We're both victims and instigators but I feel that we're more victims, because I'm here and I've had friends killed in explosions.

Yonatan: They think we're just animals who want to occupy their land and kill their children.

Na'ama: Oh, and we don't feel the same thing?

Yonatan: That's why I started with '48. Now everything's mixed up like a big plate of scrambled eggs. You don't know who the instigators and victims are any more. The problem is that we as a democratic, enlightened, western civilisation shake hands with these people, we go to the US (laughs), we get their approval, we make more deals. They don't live like that and wouldn't want to. The only way out is to stop calling it a *matsav* and call it what it really is, which is a war.

Once you do that, the Palestinians will say 'ah-ha! But for a war you need an army.' *That*'s your army right there. 'For a war you need two armies', then so be it and that's your army and we'll go in there and get the job done. At the moment, when we want to take someone out, if there's a kid nearby, we won't fire the missile. Now that is a damn shame, 'cause they get away and go out, planting more bombs. So call it a war, let the UN go 'nu, nu, nu'. That's all they'll do. My grandfather says the UN was only made for one thing: to approve the state of Israel. After that it has no use. We shouldn't care what the world says about pictures of children on CNN (mock sympathy). Aahhh. It's a war! There are casualties.

Why didn't you serve in the army, Na'ama?

Na'ama: Unlike Yonatan, I was never expected to. My family were disappointed because every parent wants their child to serve, but I was a hippy and just the thought of being in uniform horrified me. I told the army, 'Look, you don't want me here, trust me.' Their psychologist said, 'We don't want women in the army anyway', so I was like, 'ok' and then I left. I have a problem with armies. I'm not stupid, I realise we need one to survive, but it makes me sad that it's

25. The first riots of the Intifada are commonly known to have been triggered by a visit Ariel Sharon made to the Al Aqsa Mosque/Temple Mount. Rabbi Froman of Tekoa himself points out that the uprising is frequently called the Al Aqsa Intifada in Palestinian circles.

part of growing up here. Israelis who serve are like a brotherhood apart, with their own slang and jokes.

When Yonatan enlisted, I felt proud but also scared and very alone. People go in one way and come out totally different. They tear you down to rebuild you but some people break down under the pressure. It was weird to see my husband in a uniform becoming something I'd always seen from afar. He changed a lot. He became more anxious and rough, mentally. I felt proud that he risked his life as a medic but it was also a betrayal because we'd just got married. It was like the closest person to me going to the thing I most disagreed with in this country.

Yonatan: I'm still a soldier-medic until I finish the Hesder programme in 2006. You postpone the army with it, study until they need you, go in for a while, and then you're discharged. We'll see what happens in Gaza (laughs).

What would you do if you were asked to evacuate a settlement?

Yonatan: I think that would be the one time I'd disobey a direct order and say, 'Look, I can't do it, throw me in the brig.' If I thought it would bring peace to pull my brother-friend-Israeli-Jew from the house he's clinging to, I'd do it. But evacuating settlements won't make any difference, they'll always want more. I hope it won't come to bloodshed. We have enough Arabs who want to kill us to start beating each other up. But I have this switch in my head now. They want us all dead. I'm willing to say it. I've worked with Arabs and felt that if I turned round, they'd stab me in the back.

You'd think that after so many years, they'd finally leave us alone now we're finally back in our country, but they won't ever. I don't feel threatened. If we really wanted to, we have a fine enough army that we could kill them all or expel them. Before we returned here, it was natural for the Jew – who has been different since time began – to feel scared and hide. Even after the Holocaust it goes on but now we're fighting for our country not our lives. I visited New York once and a friend said, 'You may want to put your *tzitzit* in and hide your *kippa*'. I feel free here because this is a Jewish country.

Do you believe that we're living in the Messianic age?

Yonatan: Yeah, definitely. We have to continue living as if it wasn't happening for now but it began with secular Zionism, and the First Zionist Congress. That was the bang on the door; We need to be back in *Eretz Yisroel*. The seculars would have gone for Uganda[26] but the religious Zionists I belong to said 'No, it needs to be Israel!'

26. At the Sixth Zionist Congress at Basel on 26 August 1903, Herzl proposed Uganda as a temporary refuge for Jews in Russia in immediate danger. By a vote of 295–178 it was decided to send an expedition to examine the territory proposed. The proposal was hugely controversial and nearly led to a split in the Zionist movement.

The Holocaust was a big part of it. The older world of the exile had to be broken down. You can't make an omelette without breaking eggs. Something had to break for something new to be born and it was like a labour that brought the state of Israel. 1967 proved that it was time. We had everything back. What happened later is a different thing but that was Hashem saying, you keep doing that and we'll be just fine. Things are going to be better.

5
Believers and Apostates

Israel, like other nations, is built on national myths. Some, like the Masada legend, are historically questionable but offer crucial counter-myths to Diaspora survival strategies. The story of how 960 Jewish fighters (allegedly) put themselves and their families to the sword rather than live under Roman domination is an implicit rejection of integrationist tactics. The rabbinic scholars who dominated Jewish communal life in the years after the Bar Kochba rebellion believed such episodes proved the recklessness of physical resistance to oppression without wider support.[1] Ironically or not, the mainstream of the European Zionist movement was one of the least associated currents with physical resistance to pogroms and the Nazis.

Many Israelis today still venerate Masada and many more swear by other myths such as there being no such thing as Palestinians, or that Palestine itself was empty before it was settled by Jews.[2] Yet Israel has had a deep tradition of heretics, from Ahad Ha'am through Matzpen to Anarchists Against the Wall. The sometimes violently adversarial nature of the debate between believers and apostates in Israel reflects the stakes in the argument as well as the auxiliary nature of Israeli civil society. For instance, when Tali Fahima, a Mizrahi-Israeli, was arrested and accused of aiding the young Fatah leader Zakariya Zubeidi, a reader in a *Jerusalem Post* talkback forum railed: 'The Brits usually hanged them (female collaborators) and the practical Russians shot them in the back of the head. The Palestinians dragged them along dirty streets, torturing before killing them... Tali Fahima seems to be in fair company.'

1. Cantor, *Jewish Women*, pp. 81–2.
2. Morris, *Righteous Victims*, p. 42. Morris quotes Ahad Ha'am from 1891: 'We abroad are used to believing that Eretz Yisroel is now almost totally desolate, a desert that is not sowed... But in truth, this is not the case. Throughout the country it is difficult to find fields that are not sowed. Only sand dunes and stony mountains... are not cultivated.' Morris also quotes Ben Yehuda (p. 48), the architect of modern Hebrew, from 1882: 'The goal is to revive our nation on its land... if only we succeed in increasing our numbers here until we are the majority... There are now only five hundred [thousand] Arabs, who are not very strong, and from whom we shall easily take away the country if we only do it through stratagems [and] without drawing upon us their hostility before we become the strong and populous ones...'

For newly arrived Diaspora Jews, the tolerance of hate speech against outsiders can be jarring but it seems to reflect a deeply ingrained zero-sum approach to civil discourse. In a reply to Rabbi Shach's injunction to his followers not to join a Labour coalition government because the party violated the *mitzvoth*, a columnist in the Israeli daily newspaper *Hadashot* argued:

> We heard you, senile one. You may return to your historical sewer from which you crawled... For years you have presided here as an arch louse, first and foremost of the gang of parasites which increases and fattens on our backs, sucks our sap and blood, and refuses to join our circulation of blood and pain... The day will come when we shall settle scores with you and the other parasites...[3]

Right-wing protagonists in the debate over 'giving away' occupied territories invoke Nazi comparisons with abandon, occasionally brandishing death threats for good measure. The traditional correspondent's genuflection to 'age-old passions' and 'Holocaust trauma' does not explain why the religious great-grandchildren of Sabras are often the first to throw such slurs at other Jews. Nor why attempts at putting the Messianic genie back in the bottle automatically constitute a threat to so many Israelis who today hold faith-based Jewish identities. Nor indeed why secular Israelis seem unable to decisively refute them. The unifying totems of Israeli identity – the state, army, religion, anti-Semitism and the Hebrew language – are hardly adaptive enough to contain all the contradictory notions of Israeli national belief. In 'the Middle East's only secular democracy', believers and apostates continue to set the terms of public debate, albeit from unequal positions of power.

UDI ADIV

Suddenly I found myself alone

Many Israeli activists have challenged their government's policies over the years but very few have gone as far as the Matzpen collective, which faced off against the concept of Zionism itself. Udi Adiv sent shudders through Israeli society when he split from Matzpen, and tried to translate their ideas of solidarity with the Palestinians into concrete acts of resistance. Udi is a tall man with the slowly affable gait of the kibbutz-born. He is an impressive speaker, determined, thoughtful and candid, but he nonetheless appears incongruously vigilant in public spaces.

3. Amnon Dankner, *Hadashot*, 28 March 1990, p. 5.

Udi Adiv. *Photo by Arthur Neslen*

I was born in '46 in Kibbutz Gan Shmuel, one of the oldest and most left-wing kibbutzim in the country. My father was born there and so was his father. Both of them were Mapamniks.[4] There were no 'Palestinians' in those days, only Arabs, but we believed in good relations with them. I had Arab friends from our neighbouring village. Sometimes I'd visit them and stay a few days.

We didn't talk much about Judaism. Personally, I was a bit of a philosopher, very influenced by Ahad Ha'am[5] and the Prophet Amos – because of his social content and universalistic ideas. We used to campaign for the North Vietnamese and we were always on the side of the Soviet Union. The idea that we should treat Arabs as equals was part of my life. I wasn't aware then of the colonialist war in '48. Such questions were not raised.

But the kibbutzim were completely open – no fences, nothing. It wasn't the luxurious and pompous life you see today. The kibbutzniks were quite the idealists, living in small flats, having debates around issues like whether to allow private ownership of refrigerators. You can't imagine the extent to which they transformed overnight in 1967.

I was serving in the parachute regiment that 'liberated' Jerusalem at the time and becoming critical of the war. It wasn't how it was presented to the people. Israel initiated it because they wanted Jerusalem. I was arguing all the time with my unit – except when we were fighting because then you had to survive – and suddenly I found myself alone. Nobody on the kibbutz wanted to listen. They had suddenly become nationalist, anti-Arab and paranoid. I began to see Israel's history, ideology and existence as the problem and so I joined Matzpen.[6]

4. Mapam or the United Workers party was founded as a 'Marxist–Zionist' alternative to the Labour party in 1948. Hashomer Ha'tzair, its youth wing, had historically been an advocate of a 'binational state' solution to the Israel–Palestine conflict. Its social base in the kibbutzim helped to make it the second largest Israeli political party (after Labour) until the mid-1950s. Mapam was loyal to the Soviet Union until 1953, when it began remoulding itself as a social democratic party following the show trials of Jewish leaders in Prague. It subsequently electorally aligned itself with the Labour party between 1969 and 1984, reformulating itself as Meretz in the 1990s and Yahad today.
5. Morris, *Righteous Victims*, pp. 42–9. Ahad Ha'am was born Asher Ginsberg in 1856 but took a pen name ('one of the people') to argue for a secular cultural Zionism centred on the revival of the Hebrew language. Philosophically, he stood for an ethical and humanistic reinterpretation of Judaism. Ha'am played a significant role in obtaining the Balfour Declaration but was a fierce advocate of Arab rights and against what he called 'a tendency to despotism as always happens when a slave turns into a master'.
6. Orr, *Israel*, pp. 139–42. Matzpen ('Compass') was an anti-Zionist Marxist collective founded by Akiva Orr in 1961. Most of the group split from the Israeli Communist party, arguing that Zionism rather than capitalism was the key motivating force of the Israeli state. Matzpen supported – and continues to support – the PLO's 1970 demand for a non-discriminatory 'secular democratic state' as a resolution to the conflict.

Were you looking to replace the collective group identity you'd lost from the kibbutz?

Certainly. After '67, there was a contradiction between the kibbutz idea and its reality. I couldn't live in dissonance, in an essentially schizophrenic situation. Before the war, the kibbutz leadership had accepted Nasser as a progressive leader. Now he – and Yasser Arafat – were like Hitler and the Palestinians were the new Nazis. To the extent that the kibbutz adopted the dominant propaganda, I took the other course and eventually became completely identified with the Palestinians.

The Communist party were too old and dogmatic for me. I admired Che Guevara and Danny Cohn-Bendit, and by chance I saw the Matzpen newspaper in a library. So I went to Tel Aviv and met Moshe Machover and Haim Hanegbi and then I started going to their meetings.

We would organise 'Stop the Occupation!' demonstrations and graffiti, or leafleting outside films like *Zed* by Costa Bravas.[7] We were a tiny minority – no more than 40 people – and the reaction to us was always hostile. We didn't dare to go to the territories. If we did, we'd be beaten and kicked out on the spot.

Was it an exciting time?

Yes, a very inspiring situation because all the world was becoming revolutionary – in France, Latin America, then the Red Brigades and Baader-Meinhoff, and Vietnam of course. They were all as more or less the same struggle.

For me, the DFLP[8] was like the Viet Cong. They invited Israeli revolutionaries to fight with them but the Matzpen leadership wasn't interested. They saw the Jewish proletariat as a revolutionary subject and would only make contact with Palestinians in Europe, not here. Why? I thought they [Matzpen] were opportunists. The main thing for me was struggle and action.

Of course, today I see it differently. To think and talk is no less important than to shoot and act. But at the time, allying with the Palestinians was a way to symbolically show that class identity was stronger than nationalist identity. So three or four of us split away. I was the first to go. They didn't want us there any more anyway.

7. *Zed* was an influential political thriller made by Costa Gravas in 1969 about the Greek military junta, which at the time was supported by the US.
8. The Democratic Front for the Liberation of Palestine became the third biggest Palestinian faction when it split from the Popular Front for the Liberation of Palestine (PFLP) in 1969. The party stressed revolutionary mass activity – against reactionary Arab regimes as well as Israel – to achieve liberation for Jews and Arabs in a secular democratic state. In 2002, the DFLP leader Nayef Hawatmeh took a stand against the tactic of suicide bombings. However, the group's most famous action, in May 1974, was an assault on a school in Ma'alot that killed 25 Israeli teenagers.

How did your group develop in the way it did?

I met an 'old guard' ex-Communist called Daoud Turki who owned a leftist bookshop in Haifa and we decided to create a revolutionary Palestinian–Israeli group to fight the occupation from within Israel. We wanted to fight in the battlefield of ideas but also to attack the army and military places. Our main idea was to help the Palestinians, to somehow be part of their people. We thought that if we showed them that there was a difference between the government and the people, we could stop them from attacking Jewish civilians.

So we go to Damascus and I meet a Palestinian guy, Habib Kahawaji, who Daoud Turki knows. I tell him my strategy, he seems to agree with me but at the same time he asks me for information about the army. I give him some general info and then he takes me to a military exercise – you know, shooting – and we decide that in Israel I'll try to mobilise some people and we'll be in touch.

From his side, I can see now that actually he took me where he wanted to go. He didn't follow my idea but rather, I followed his, which was completely different. He only wanted us as agents. He didn't believe in a revolutionary struggle from below, only that the Arab armies would somehow liberate Palestine by conquering Israel.

He was well connected to the Jewish… to the Syrian intelligence. Of course, I didn't know this. I just trusted Daoud and he told me he was a Palestinian, a Marxist and a member of our organisation. Certainly he was a Palestinian, but after '68, he was expelled and moved to Syria and became a Syrian agent.

Back in Israel I met with some friends and we organised a group but all we did was talk. Every couple of months, we'd meet in Tel Aviv and publish a 'Red Front' pamphlet. Then, one night in December 1972, a few months after we returned, around 20 armed Shin Bet officers raided my home in the middle of the night and arrested me. Four Jews and 20 Palestinian Arabs in Israel were taken in all.

I'd been very hedonistic, involved with lots of women and sports but from that moment, everything changed. It really felt like the end of my life. I was put in solitary confinement for three weeks and I had time to reflect. I asked myself a hundred times, Why did I do this? Why didn't I become involved the right way, with the right people? Who betrayed us? And what a mess.

Maybe it was inevitable. There were too many people around and Daoud was talking too much. We had an informer in our group. I hardly knew him. He was quite well off, a playboy from a respected family, and Daoud somehow was happy to spend time with him. He went to Syria and did more or less what I did, but he wasn't arrested.

Years later, a Palestinian member of our group who'd been released from prison went to the restaurant where he worked. But he called people from the Shin Bet and when they arrived, they threatened him and told him not to come back.

What happened during your interrogations?

There was a good cop and a bad cop. The bad cop said I was a traitor, how could I do it? 'We as a people who suffered so much and you helped our enemies? They are murderers, terrorists who want to kill us all. You are a naïve, stupid collaborator.' He used these terms.

The good cop, Yossi Ginosar, was more intelligent. He argued with me about socialism and the right of Jews to self-determination. 'You think they are Marxist but you're wrong, they are nationalist. They want to throw us into the sea'. Later, he became quite a famous Likud member of the Knesset.[9]

When his son was killed in Gaza, I think he concluded that the war was unwinnable. He became a close friend of Arafat, his personal banker, and one of his most reliable advisors. You can imagine how I smiled as I followed his career, remembering our discussions more than 30 years before.

Do you think your discussions played a part in his transformation?

I think so, yes (laughs).

Why did you confess?

Because they took me to Daoud Turki, our leader's cell and I heard him revealing everything he knew – names, details, everything. They'd threatened to harm his daughter somehow. Anyway, that's why I talked. I thought there was no point, if they know all the details, it's useless.

Were the Palestinians interrogated in the same way?

No, they tortured the Palestinians. Two of us, Rami Livney, an Israeli Jew, and Chawqi Khatib, a Palestinian Arab, refused to talk. The officers didn't dare touch Israelis and they didn't have any other pressure to bring to bear so they tortured Chawqi and let Rami hear it. Then they brought them together so that Chawqi could tell Rami what they were doing to him. It was winter, and they'd prevented him from sleeping, beaten him, poured icy water on him, strained his hands, left him in the freezing cold for hours on end… it wasn't torture in American or Gestapo terms but it was enough. Rami confessed.

9. Yossi Ginosar was deputy head of the Shabbak until 1986, when it emerged that he had lied to a government inquiry into the 'Bus 300 affair', which shook Israelis' faith in the Shabbak. The affair involved the extra-judicial execution of two Palestinians who had been captured after hijacking an Egged bus in 1984. In a separate scandal, *Ma'ariv* newspaper alleged that Ginosar had financially benefited from his handling of up to $300 million of funds earmarked for the Palestinian Authority, while he was Israeli Prime Minister Ehud Barak's special envoy to Yasser Arafat. The funds were then moved out of Swiss bank accounts to unknown destinations.

How did your arrest affect the people around you?

It was a real shock for my dad. He took it personally as a crime committed by a son against his father. He couldn't cope because he disagreed so deeply with my ideas. With my mother it was easier. She understood that it was a matter of good intentions gone wrong and that I'd been naïve and misled.

My Matzpen comrades were badly affected. They were collaborators with the enemy and terrorists now. It undermined their message and put them under heavy pressure but I always blamed them for not doing what I did. Half of them wouldn't even come to visit me in prison.

The atmosphere surrounding the trial was very hostile. The *Yediot Ahronot* and *Ma'ariv* newspapers ran front-page headlines calling us a 'Jewish–Arab terrorist and spy net' and saying I was the leader. The [current] Shinnui leader Tommy Lapid likened me to Adolph Eichmann[10] in *Ma'ariv*. Even Golda Meir, the prime minister, was asked about me in one interview. She said, 'He is a sick man.'

Mapam and the Hashomer Ha'tzair were also put under pressure. 'How come one of you became a traitor and collaborated with our enemies?' So their leaders produced this narrative: he left the kibbutz. He wasn't a patriot. He was exceptional. He didn't represent the kibbutz. Golda was right, he's a sick person.

The trial was a joke. They broke every rule of justice. The prosecution had my confession but that was it. I thought I'd been giving information to a member of the PLO, not a Syrian agent. But the lawyers only concentrated on Syrian, Syrian, Syrian. And hostile people were let into the court, including an intelligence agent whose brother was killed by Fatah. He somehow made a connection and even though he had nothing to do with our case, he sat there doing this to us (mimes cutting his throat) all the time.

Outside, you had the demonstrations. Every day, people would run after our van, hitting it, cursing us and threatening to kill us. What made people so crazy was that we were Israelis. It confused them. It forced them to think and, instead of reflecting, they blamed us for doing this to them. It couldn't just be Jews against Arabs any more. We were Israelis sitting with Palestinians. We were no longer completely white. There was never any question in my mind that we'd be convicted. In the end, Daoud and I received the harshest sentence possible, 17 years.

We were sent to Ramle just before the '73 war, which was then under an unbelievably sadistic director. Many of the guards were Holocaust survivors and they'd internalised the Nazi idea. Everyone threatened the Jews and it was us against the world. They could understand the Palestinians to an extent because

10. Adolph Eichmann was the Gestapo officer charged with responsibility for implementing Nazi Germany's extermination policy towards the Jews. He was kidnapped by Mossad agents in Argentina in 1960 and sentenced to death after a war crimes trial in 1961. He was hung the following year.

they were our enemies. But the Jews who collaborated with them were outside their conceptual view of the world.

They put us in cell-like punishment caves where you couldn't stand up and then the prison director refused my request for underpants. He said, 'You don't need them.' Our food was stale bread and hot water with pepper and a vegetable, the same thing day after day, year after year. It was important because just an apple, which outside you wouldn't pay attention to, in prison became like gold. Once a week, they gave us rice and an eighth of chicken so the chicken became like money, you know? Instead of cigarettes, we used chicken.

The Israeli criminals were mostly hostile to us until the 1973 war but after that, they lost their self-confidence. They saw that the world was not as stable as they thought. Then came the peace talks and their ideas changed again. Gradually, the old generation of guards changed to Mizrahim, who were less paranoid, more relaxed and at the end of the 1970s, the Russians started to arrive. For them it was just a job, no ideology. We were best friends with them. In 1985, after 12 years in prison, I was released.

What problems did you have readjusting to life outside?

I married my girlfriend Leah but in general it was difficult. The Palestinians had their families and in their villages, they were heroes. But I'd get threatening phone calls saying, 'Traitors, we will kill you! You should die, terrorist.' In 1989, I moved to London for six years.

The real problems started when I returned. The only way I could get a job was through personal contacts. Luckily, my wife had worked in the Open University and she knew people there. Today I'm lecturing in political sciences in Haifa. The reaction of students has changed over the years. Even people of 40 were nine years old at the time of the trial. They don't have that memory. They're curious if they find out and, sometimes, they ask me to explain what happened. Also society has changed. Oslo may have been a political failure but it destroyed many prejudices.

How did you feel when you saw the recent news reports about Tali Fahima?[11]

I was smiling (laughs). You know I have all the sympathy in the world for her. I really feel for her. I had exactly the same motivations but I now understand that you can't change the Palestinians' nationalist ideas by showing them that

11. Tali Fahima, a 29-year-old anti-occupation activist, was arrested in the summer of 2004, shortly before the first of my interviews with Udi Adiv. She was accused of travelling to Jenin, befriending Zakarias Zubeidi, the leader of the local Al Aqsa Martyrs Brigade, and aiding his group's military activities. She denied that she had been involved in terrorist activity and ridiculed press claims that she had been having a relationship with Zubeidi.

you're a different, better Israeli. It doesn't help because there are always individuals, always exceptions. You don't have to go to Jenin. You have to stay here and try to change this society.

I would like to tell Tali not to be so naïve as to think that by individual gestures you can change the world. I would say to her: ok, you did what you did. You showed your solidarity. But for the future, know that you cannot change the world by yourself. Don't do anything by yourself. Whatever you do, look behind to see if there is someone behind you. Don't go alone because it is useless.

LARISSA TREMBOVLER

We have no counter-experiment

The assassination of the Israeli Prime Minister and former Chief of the IDF, Yitzhak Rabin, in 1995 was a pivotal moment for Israeli society. Rabin had signed the Oslo Accords with Yasser Arafat two years previously and embarked on a course that the religious right feared would end in a Palestinian state. Months of hysteria and vitriol directed at Rabin culminated six months to the day before final status negotiations were due to begin. At a Peace Now rally attended by 150,000 people in Tel Aviv, a 25-year-old yeshiva student, Ygal Amir, fired three bullets into Rabin from point-blank range. A state of mourning followed. More than a million Israelis paid their respects at Rabin's coffin and a left consensus developed that his death had critically set back any hopes of peace. However, Rabin had expanded the settlements dramatically since signing the Oslo Accord and, throughout his life, nurtured the movement that would eventually kill him. During his last administration, the Jewish population of the West Bank and Gaza grew by nearly 50 per cent.[12] Nonetheless, his murder scarred the Israeli body politic. As talk of disengagement from Gaza advanced, so did fears of a repeat of 1995. To this day, Ygal Amir remains a hate figure for much of liberal Israeli society. When Larissa Trembovler, 37, a religious Russian academic and mother of four, announced that she had secretly married him, she was met with disbelief, astonishment and opprobrium.

I'm an only child. I was born in Moscow and I came here in '89 at the beginning of the Great Aliyah with a Masters degree in biology. Later, I got a PhD in Medieval Jewish and Arab Philosophy. My mother worked from morning 'til

12. Israeli government press office release, 'Myths and facts about Jewish settlements', 2 December 1997. The Jewish population of the West Bank and Gaza (excluding Jerusalem) grew from 96,158 in June 1992 to 145,000 in June 1996. The period covers the signing of the September 1993 Oslo accord and the September 1995 Oslo II accords.

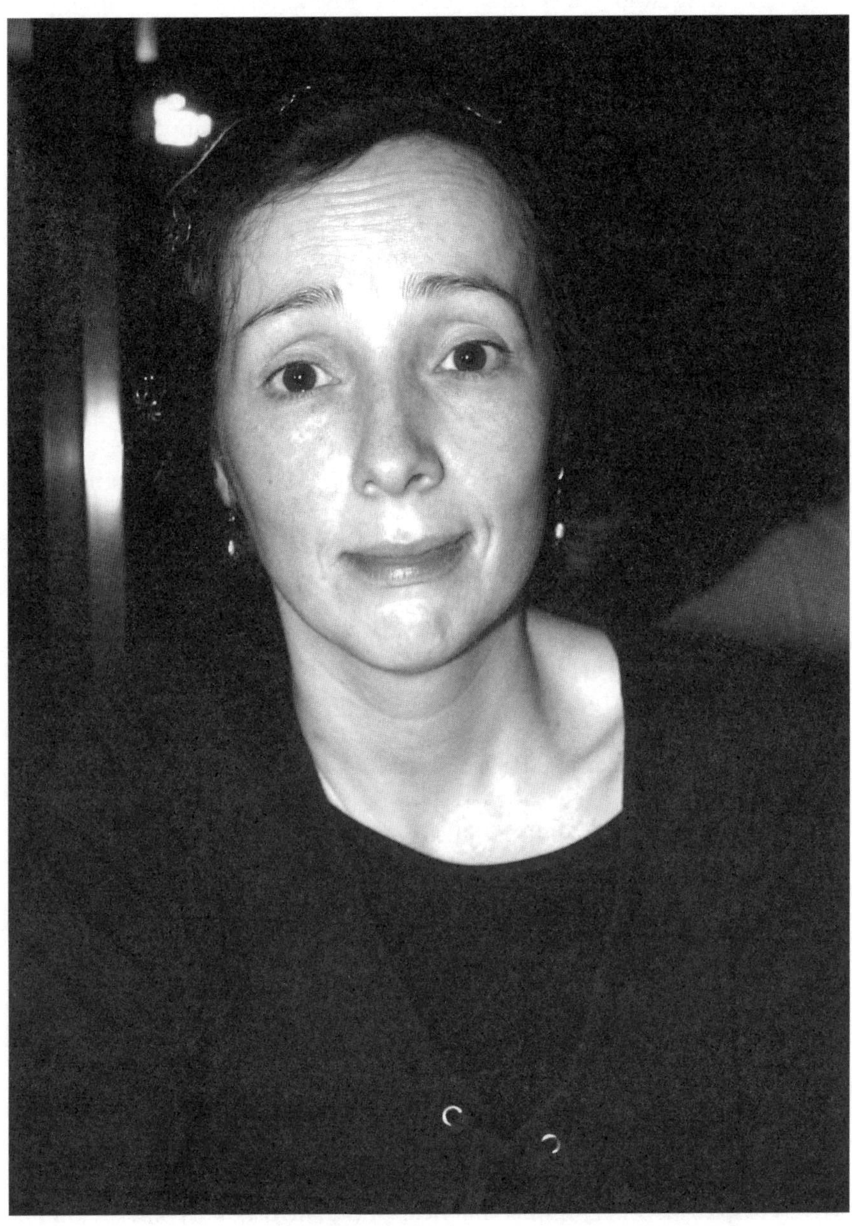

Larissa Trembovler. *Photo by Arthur Neslen*

night as a physicist in a university. I first met my father when I was four years old and I only saw him once after that. He was an engineer in Moscow and he married again, but that's all I know. It was hard growing up without him but divorce was rather common. In some ways I think it's preferable.

Neither of my parents were Communist party members but they weren't dissidents either. When I returned to religion, my mother was secular, like most families in Moscow. I was always made to feel like a stranger in Russia. My mother would explain that it was because I was Jewish, not that she knew much about Jewish identity.

I was the only Jewess at school. When I was six, some older friends told me, 'It's been a pleasure to play with you but we know that you are not like us'. I understood that, it didn't surprise me. I wasn't even hurt by it. I accepted it as something natural. I think that identity begins from hostility in the environment, whether open or hidden. It's the beginning of self-realisation.

At home, books expressed our struggle for identity and values. Jewish children were well-educated, and uneducated Russians treated us with a distant hostility. Maybe it was snobbish but I felt nothing in common with people who hadn't read the authors that I loved – Kafka, Proust, Dostoyevsky and Bulgakov. When I turned 13, I became more religious but it took me years to start keeping *mitzvoth*.

Our orthodox community was a small circle of less than 100 people. Practising Judaism in Russia was risky. I used to have to invent excuses for my absence from university lectures on Shabbat. If I'd said openly why I wasn't there, they might not have arrested me but they would have expelled me. By the time I made *aliyah* in '86, I had already been married under a *chuppa*. I remember feeling a kind of euphoria when we arrived. I was so happy. There were moments of feeling at home.

In those days, they were hospitable to Russians here. I don't know when it changed. My eldest daughter had wonderful Russian but at some stage she and my second daughter stopped speaking it. They didn't want to feel Russian because it's under-valued. But there is a Russian-Jewish mentality. I have it. I think Israelis are kinder and less angry. They live in a tough environment but it doesn't cause as much violence. It's really a very new nation. I mean, they have no historical experience as a society and sometimes they have no perspective. In that sense, we have something they do not.

How did you meet Ygal Amir?

I first heard of Ygal on 4 November 1995.[13] I was finishing my historical novel that night and I didn't think too much about him. You see, in Russia I'd been actively helping political prisoners but here I wasn't involved in politics. Now I'm too connected to analyse it. Israel sometimes sees this assassination [of Rabin] as

13. The day that Yitzhak Rabin was assassinated.

something unique but there are parallels from the end of the nineteenth century. As with all history, we have no counter-experiment.

I never intended to contact Ygal. I got in touch with his family for humanitarian reasons. We were educated on books about dissidents and civic movements so the dehumanisation of Ygal was unacceptable to me. Being a rather passive person, I decided to correspond with his brother, Hagai, in '96. I contacted Ygal the year after. It was a wonderful surprise to find we shared a common language of ideas. I sent him *Crime and Punishment* by Dostoyevsky and Kafka's *The Trial*, and we corresponded about books and our families. We didn't talk about politics or his deed. He impressed me as a profound thinker, intelligent and sensitive, very different from his public image. Media propaganda has spread a false image of Ygal.

Did you agree with his ideas?

I'm opposed to Sharon's Gaza plan. I was also opposed to Oslo. It's forbidden to give away any territory in *Eretz Yisroel*, according to the *Halacha*. But I gave Ygal simple human support because solitary confinement could have been catastrophic for his mental health. Our romance began only after I divorced in 2003 and it developed as a strange, supportive friendship. I certainly wasn't looking for a *shaduch*.

Some Israelis hate Ygal but I've felt little hostility from people in the street. People usually don't say anything, although their thoughts are probably negative. Many people in Jerusalem actually give me words of human support. They say, 'Be strong'.

Has Ygal ever expressed any feelings of remorse for his actions?

Not usually. He constantly analyses the effects of his actions but he has a theory with a deep theological context. We've often talked about the Shabbak agent Avishai Raviv[14] because Ygal has read the so-called conspiracy theories of Barry

14. BBC News Despatches: Middle East, 13 November 1997 and <www.barrychamish.com>. In the wake of Rabin's assassination, Israeli writers such as Barry Chamish and Natan Geffen developed a conspiracy theory, which was lent weight by some bizarre circumstantial evidence. Security for the late prime minister was inexplicably lax on 4 November, there appeared to be major contradictions in the official account of events that night and, most surprisingly, it emerged that a Shabbak informer was working closely with Ygal Amir. Declassified sections of the Shamgar Commission's report into the assassination revealed that Avishai Raviv knew of his friend's intention to murder Rabin and told him that religious law permitted it. However, Raviv did not tell his handlers in the Israeli secret services who were tasked with protecting the prime minister. Indeed, the Shamgar Commission found that Ygal Amir himself had had dealings with the Shabbak. In 1992, Amir went to Riga in Latvia, to work for its notoriously shadowy Russian espionage group, Nativ. Chamish believes that Amir fired blanks on 4 November and the real assassin came from within the ranks of Israel's security establishment.

Chamish and Natan Geffen. He told me he suspected Avishai of being a Shabbak agent before the assassination happened. Their relationship was not intimate or close. It wasn't a real friendship. Ygal was a politically active student and Avishai helped him to organise demonstrations in settlements. When there is a person ready to assist, it helps a lot. I think Ygal pitied him because he was rather despised by the other students. They thought he was simple-minded. Ygal was the leader of the group so he tried to strengthen Avishai's position but no-one had a high opinion of him.

How did Ygal propose to you?

I don't remember his words but it was very natural.

You don't remember his proposal?

It wasn't in the form of solemnity. We both realised what kind of relationship we were in. Ygal even tried to persuade me not to accept his proposal. We initially decided to stay friends but later we realised that it was impossible.

How did you keep the marriage secret from the authorities?

You'll have to ask them because they pretend at least to listen to all our talks and telephone conversations.

Why is it important for the two of you to have children?

I already have children. It's for Ygal's sake and because it's a *mitzva*. Sadly, the security establishment turned our request[15] into a kind of cruel comedy. The state wants to take vengeance. It's coming from the prison authorities not the left establishment. It's pitiful, but for months they tried to separate us any way they could. For populist reasons, the head of the prison service said that he'd oppose our marriage out of reasons of conscience.

There seem to be parallels with your life in Russia where you practised your religion in secret, hiding from the authorities, feeling distant from society…

You're right, but the difference is that, even in this situation, I never feel a stranger. I feel that it's a struggle and we are just estranged from the system, not the people.

Isn't that the same as in Russia? You're even relating to prisoners through books.

No, because in Russia there was a little group of believers or dissidents who were opposed to the whole people. The nation was united behind the establishment. It was educated to support the regime.

15. Larissa Trembovler and Ygal Amir have fought a public, protracted and to date, unsuccessful, legal battle with the authorities for Amir to be allowed conjugal rights.

But the people brought down the regime.

They didn't believe in communism but despite this, they were a part of it. So we had to be a closed community of little groups that struggled together for its existence. This situation is different.

You compared the disengagement plan from Gaza to Oslo. Do you think that a din rodef[16] *would be justified against Ariel Sharon?*

No, and Ygal doesn't think that there is a similarity or analogy between this situation and the past situation either. All the talk about it is propaganda. It's not a coincidence that these fears are increasing now. Political violence may be possible but no normal person would wish it. What happened in '95 was the result of a failure by Rabin's guards. They lowered the shield for Ygal Amir to enter the parking lot. It's possible to guard this prime minister. I don't think that he is the main person at risk in Israel.

But if Halacha forbade Rabin from implicitly giving away land in Oslo, why does it allow Sharon to explicitly give away all of Gaza?

I suppose it's different because then people, including Ygal, thought that it would help prevent the Oslo process. The *din rodef* must help, otherwise it's forbidden. Today I know of no-one who thinks that assassinating Arik Sharon would help. So it's out of the question.

What are your feelings towards the Palestinians?

As two peoples, we are at war, but I speak Arabic and don't feel any personal hostility to them. Medieval Arabic culture was very rich, and I wrote a novel about it because I was fascinated by the Jewish–Arab symbiosis. I think Jews are a very stubborn people who rarely learn from their history. Maybe we are not original in being condemned to repeat it.

16. *Ha'aretz*, 29 June 2004. The rabbi of the Old City in Jerusalem, Avigdor Nevental, 'said that anyone who gives away part of the land of Israel to gentiles is open to a *din rodef* – a religious licence to kill a fellow Jew'.

NATIVA BEN YEHUDA

On the tombs of very old people, evil will be sad

Nativa Ben Yehuda's on-air persona is that of the cantankerous and spiky radio talk show host, reluctantly famed across Israel, indifferent to those she offends. I wanted to talk to her because I had heard claims that she was the grand-daughter of the founder of modern Hebrew, Eliezer Ben Yehuda, and that she had committed a terrible crime during the War of Independence. After a combative interview, Nativa apologised for having been, in her view, a poor interviewee. 'I'm doing it for Zionism, not myself,' she explained. 'It is still part of the war'.

I was born in Tel Aviv in 1928, the youngest of three girls. Maybe I was the rebel. My grandfather was born in Pinsk. You've heard about Pinsk? It was in Russia. He belonged to the Karlins,[17] a sect between Hasidim and Misnagdim[18] who were not as stupid as the usual Hasidim. After he made *aliyah* in 1903, he founded Mapai here while my father finished school in Gymnasia Herzliya in Tel Aviv. It was the first Hebrew high school in the world. You haven't heard about it? You don't know nothing.

I was always ugly. Even as a child, I was already ugly with the glasses. With this eye I don't see at all. Back then, this kind of hair was thought to be very ugly. My father didn't like me so much. He loved my sisters and lived with them until he died a few years ago. My grandfather was like a father to me. I stayed with him on one floor of a two-storey house. I loved him very much.

17. Karlin was a suburb of Pinsk – then in Lithuania, now in Belarus – which became the scene for the revival of Hasidic Judaism in the eighteenth century, after a century of catastrophes in Poland. The Chmielnitzki massacres in 1648 killed about one half of the Jewish population in Poland and the Ukraine. The survivors were desperately impoverished, onerously taxed, and targeted for further massacres and pogroms in the years that followed. While mysticism flourished in Poland, the intellectual centre of the community moved to Lithuania.
18. Rabbi Israel Baal Shem Tov (aka 'the master of the good name' or the beshT) founded the Hasidic movement in the 1700s. A scholar and Kabbalist, his teachings focused on growing closer to God through devotion, spiritual consciousness and joyful worship, perhaps a necessary balm for a demoralised community. The singing, dancing, drinking and storytelling of the movement was exploited by Jacob Frank (1726–91), who converted to Christianity after his orgiastic cult was condemned by the rabbinic leadership. The Misnagdim (lit. 'opponents') were a faction within eighteenth century Polish Jewry who confronted the Hasidim around issues of prayer times, and the Hasidic movement's general exuberance. In the face of external persecution, their differences were eventually put aside. But in Israel they continue to rumble on.

Nativa Ben Yehuda. *Photo by Arthur Neslen*

He was a chess player and an astronomer, a very wise and clever man. He was friends with Bialik.[19]

I was 11 when the war broke. In '43, my grandfather got a letter in Yiddish about the beginning of the Shoah from some Polish Jews who were later killed by Hitler. He sat three months with it, he didn't eat or go out, and then he died. I didn't feel safe. They bombed here also, you know. We had many people killed in Tel Aviv, including friends of mine. I was so frightened that my mother took us to Kfar Saba. You know Kfar Saba? It's near Ra'anana. Probably it didn't ruin my life.

What did you think of your grandfather's politics?

I don't know nothing. I am stupid and people who go into politics are wise. I love Arik Sharon and I loved Gandhi.[20] You know who Gandhi was? He was my best friend. We studied together in the Palmach. I wasn't on the left or right but I have friends on the right. When I finished high school in '46, I had friends in Lehi and Etzel but I was told that they were not learning to fight so I joined the Palmach.

I'd studied agriculture at school and I wanted to be a farmer in a kibbutz. They'd planned to send me to the London Olympic Games in '48 to compete in the shot put and javelin. I was very strong. To this day, no Israeli woman has beaten my shot put record. In the London Games, the woman who won threw less than me. But I didn't go because the war started and Israel didn't participate and, by then, I was a fighting officer in the Palmach.

It must have been hard for you.

So many of our people were killed. In Europe we lost our families. Three million were killed in Poland and Lithuania. Six million died overall, so who was sad that I didn't go to the Olympic Games? I went to the Palmach!

It must have been hard that you couldn't feel your own sadness because it was dwarfed by a horror that dwarfed everything.

Could be, could be. I was friends with Ygal Allon and Itzhak Sadeh.[21] After '46, I trained to fight every month in camouflage so as to (hollow laugh) go on the

19. Haim Nahman Bialik was the most significant poet to emerge from the Zionist movement. Often described as the 'national poet' or 'poet of the Hebrew renaissance', he forged a new poetic idiom, moving away from biblical diction and cadence.
20. 'Gandhi' was an affectionate nickname for Rehavam Ze'evi, the late Israeli tourism minister and founder of the far-right Moledet party, who was assassinated by PFLP gunmen in 2002. Ze'evi was an architect of the idea of 'transfer', or ethnic cleansing of Palestinians from the West Bank, to be conducted 'in the same way that you get rid of lice'. He is one of the famous men that Nativa is rumoured to have had affairs with.
21. Two of the most eminent leaders of the Palmach.

field, army against army. I was in Gimmel unit. By 1947, I was already fighting and doing demolitions, field spying and topography.

Did you ever do anything in the army that you weren't proud of?

Everything I did, I am not proud of. We left the dead bodies of our friends in the fields. I am not proud of killing people. When you're in the army and you see the man you kill, face to face, you can't be proud of it.

In war, terrible things happen... Did you ever kill innocent people?

You've heard about the Davidka? It was a gun that we invented. It fires explosives, like a heavy gun. In the air, the bomb goes like this (moves hands wildly) and it doesn't fall exactly where you want it to. Not all the people you kill are those you mean to.

Did you ever shoot people?

Face to face? Of course.

But innocent people not in uniform, women and children?

I don't know. In those days, there were no uniforms. Probably I did. I can't tell you. When you are in a war, you kill innocent people all the time, especially if you fight at night in towns among civilians.

What went through your mind when you killed innocent civilians?

I can't tell you but it's terrible. If the friends you fight with are killed, then you kill the enemy opposite you. You want to be proud of it, but how? I don't know, especially when so many were killed.

Which is worse, the guilt of killing or surviving?

I think to survive is very difficult, especially when so many friends were killed. It went on and on. In '49, I left the army and I haven't fought or touched a mine since. But I still suffer. You never get rid of it. War taught me the importance of friendship, love, and the readiness to suffer hardship. This you have to know when you are young, especially if you want to build a country and you don't have a choice after six million of you were killed. Every day we were hearing stories. A partisan in my father's family came to Israel and my grandfather's sisters went to America. All the rest were killed.

What was the feeling towards Arabs?

Guess.

Tell me.

Terrible! Not towards all of them. There were a few friendly Arab leaders but we came to Talpiot when I was one-year-old and in Bethlehem they killed 40 Jews on the spot. I heard the stories so many times that I think I remember the real thing, not the stories.

Did you have any Arab friends when you were growing up?

I never had Arab enemies as a friend. I didn't have real friends. I am lonely still. People say hello, but it's not real friendship. It's a kind of knowledge, knowing each other. People know me because of my dictionaries. I was the first person to write an everyday Hebrew language dictionary. Eliezer Ben Yehuda,[22] a man I have no family connection with, wrote the first dictionary of biblical Hebrew. It was good but not the Hebrew we talk, which is always changing. But I told you I don't know nothing. No-one better educated than me had dared write a people's dictionary of Hebrew before, so mine was the first.

When you look around Israel today, do you feel proud?

I'm very happy that my daughter and grandsons are here. Young people, they build more and more all the time.

Even in the West Bank.

You mean with the Arabs? I'm not interested. Let those who are fighting fight for it. I was wounded terribly in the war and I still have shellshock. I don't even leave my house except to appear on the radio. I have a phone-in show once a week. People talk only about good things in a break between the news. You don't have good things? Don't come. The news is always terrible and hard; hot news, which means bad news. So every Wednesday, between 12–3am, we talk about good things, nice people, festivals, barmitzvas... And I play songs from the first *aliyah* until '48.

What are the words of the songs?

(sings) 'On the tombs of very old people, evil will be sad...'

If someone called up for advice and said 'Nativa, I did something terrible 60 years ago and it's tearing me apart. In 1948, I got on a bus and killed 21 innocent civilians and I don't know how to live with it,' what would you tell them?

I don't know. It's very difficult. I believe I'd ask him if he, his family and friends also suffered. So he would know that we fought here, two nations, one against the other, the way we had to.

22. Eliezer Ben Yehuda was the father of the modern Hebrew language.

MORDECHAI TSANIN

The Pope may speak Hebrew, but he will not be a Jew

In the early days of the Israeli state, the hegemony of Hebrew as lingua franca of the infant state was by no means assured. The overwhelming majority of Diaspora Jews spoke Yiddish, a proud ghetto language. Its idiom was proletarian and non-assimilationist. Worse, from the point of view of state bureaucrats, Yiddish had been championed by the socialist – and fiercely anti-Zionist – Bund and was associated with a philosophy of '*doikayt*' or fighting anti-Semitism in the places where Jews lived. When Ruzhka Korchak, a heroine of the Vilna partisans, spoke of her experiences in Yiddish to a Histadrut convention in January 1945, David Ben Gurion followed her with the words, 'Despite the fact that the previous speaker spoke in a foreign, grating language...' He was prevented from finishing his speech by outrage in the auditorium.[23] A conventional wisdom began to evolve in which 'Yiddish was a perverted language reflecting the perversion of the soul of the Diaspora Jew. The revulsion from it [was] a recoil from Diaspora existence.'[24] By the early 1950s, the 'Jewish state' was using police officers and thugs to enforce a ban on Yiddish theatre and daily newspapers.[25] In the years that followed, Zionist enthusiasts and ambassadors would do everything in their power to make Hebrew and not Yiddish the second language of the Diaspora. Mordechai Tsanin, a boyish 98-year-old when interviewed, was the editor of Israel's first Yiddish newspaper.[26]

I am a Polish Jew, not a polished Jew. I am a writer and a novelist. I was born in Poland in 1906. I came to Palestine because of the World War, so I was a refugee not a Zionist. In those days, refugees who spoke Yiddish were treated very badly. I took it as it was.

Newspapers were allowed in English and French, even German, but Yiddish was forbidden. I didn't care, I ignored the rules. Between '52 and '66, I printed a

23. Benjamin Harshav, *Language and Revolution* (Berkeley, 1993), p. 157.
24. Ruzhka Korchak to Shabtai Tevet, 1980 (no exact date), in *Ruzhka, Lekhimata, Haguta, Dmuta* (Tel-Aviv, 1988), pp. 213–14.
25. TZ. R-n, 'Yidishe aktyorn un politseyishe protokoln', *Letste Nayes*, 6 April 1951. Abraham Brumberg also wrote in 'Yiddish and Hebrew: End of a feud', *Mendele Review*, vol. 09.024, 29 August 1999, 'For several decades Yiddish was not only hounded by "legal means," but Yiddish speakers were often insulted on the streets, Yiddish concerts and lectures were harassed by youths wielding stones.'
26. Rachel Rojanski, 'The Status of Yiddish in Israel, 1948–1951: An Overview', *Mendele Review*, vol. 09.02, 14 February 2005. Mordechai Tsanin began publishing the *Ilustrirter Vokhenblat* weekly paper in January 1949 after receiving an Interior Ministry licence. Ten months later, Tsanin launched *Letste Nayes*. However, the authorities prevented him from obtaining a licence to publish every day.

Mordechai Tsanin in conversation. *Photo by Arthur Neslen*

daily Yiddish newspaper, *Letste Nayes*. It wasn't easy. There were no real Yiddish writers here. It was even forbidden to speak Yiddish on the streets – it was that bad. If you tried, officials would come up to you and say 'Please don't speak Yiddish.' So people obeyed.

During the *Tsenna*, newspapers were supposed to receive paper from the government but we didn't. There was a war and it was hard to find paper so I had to buy it on the black market. You could get anything there because the Jew is a smart person, he knows how to handle. There was corruption in the Jewish Agency. They were thieves. So we used green paper, red paper – a strange thing to have a daily news-sheet with red paper.

But many people bought it because we published the truth. There was a struggle between Zionists and Yiddish and we printed the debate. The Hebrew papers lied. We were printing 30,000 newspapers but many of our readers were immigrants who had no money. So one person would buy the paper and take it to the *Mobarot* and read it to people aloud. One issue could reach 50,000 people that way.

At the time, it was forbidden to say how many Jews were living in the camps because they wanted to attract more Jews to Israel. Fifty thousand were in the *Mobarot*! But Zionist journalists wrote that there were only a few thousand. It was painful for me to see lies becoming currency. They didn't tell their readers what happened to the Polish Jews or how many were killed in the Holocaust. They didn't want to count?

My personal line was close to the Bund, but I was not in any party. It was more like a cultural thing. There was news but no line. Everybody spoke Yiddish. It's a beautiful language. In the same way that French or English is beautiful, like Shakespeare is beautiful, Yiddish is beautiful. Yiddish reminded people of their homes because here, they were lonely. In Yiddish, the heart opens.

One man did everything to destroy Yiddish: David Ben Gurion. This is the person. In Zionism, there is a will to be a goy. Herzl was not a Jew. He didn't circumcise his son.[27] Ben Gurion wanted to be a goy with a Jewish name. The Pope may speak Hebrew, but he will not be a Jew. With all his strength, the 'strong' Jew is not strong. There are so many goyim, but such a scant amount of Zionists. They wanted to forget, to run as far as possible from their religion and Jewishness as it existed for thousands of years. If I thought that by being a goy, I would become strong, I would go to *shmud* because I'm not religious at all. I'm Jewish by culture only.

In the *shtetls*, nobody forbade speaking Hebrew. It was only spoken in prayer because people used the instrument that they knew for daily conversations, which

27. Harvey Sicherman, 'Theodor Herzl: An Appreciation', *Foreign Policy Research Institute*, 28 August 1997. In fact, Herzl's only son, Hans, converted to Christianity in later life (as had Herzl's great uncles) and subsequently committed suicide.

was Yiddish. Agudat Yisroel was pro-Yiddish and pro-Hebrew. The Mizrahim today belong to the state and they're almost goyim. They're like Mapainiks but they want to be in the government so they will do anything to be ministers.

Do you see similarities in the way that Mizrahi culture was suppressed?

None at all. Yiddish was an exception. It was hated, it was nothing. English was the big thing, it was looked up to. Everyone was tolerant about German. People sat in coffee houses, reading *Zeitung*. But Yiddish? It was feared to read it in public because it opposed the Zionist state.

But how could a nation have been built if everyone spoke different languages?

German is not a language? French is not a language? Why Yiddish?

Some Zionists said it was a bastard hybrid of many European and Mideast languages, whereas Hebrew was the pure language of the Jews.

It's not true. Every language is raised from nothing. Is English not a hybrid? The word 'Sauerkraut' comes from culture, not scripture. In Yiddish there are many diminutives, in Hebrew there are none. Actually there are, they took them from Yiddish. It hurts. Where is the beauty of the mother? '*Imma*' is a hard, heavy thing. It should be sweet.

If Yiddish dies, what will die with it?

All the beauty of Judaism. A Jew who speaks beautiful Yiddish, speaks Hebrew. There are dozens of popular songs in Yiddish but in Hebrew they haven't created ten. Our songs will not let Yiddish die. It's too strong. Yiddish will survive like Hebrew did for those who spoke Hebrew in the Diaspora.

MATAN COHEN

Beside the honey, you have the sting

Whether the Intifada caused – or coincided with – the collapse of the radical Israeli left, by the time of Yasser Arafat's death, no more than a few thousand Israelis were active in protesting against the occupation. The most vibrant faction was 'Anarchists Against the Wall', a group of around a hundred teenagers and twentysomethings who caught a second wind from the globalisation movement abroad. With an orientation on Queer politics and a baggage-free 'no state' solution to the conflict, they found sympathisers among a much wider milieu. Yonatan Pollack, the group's muscular and tattooed public face, was voted the 17th coolest Israeli in a poll by the right-wing daily newspaper *Ma'ariv*. The group's activities

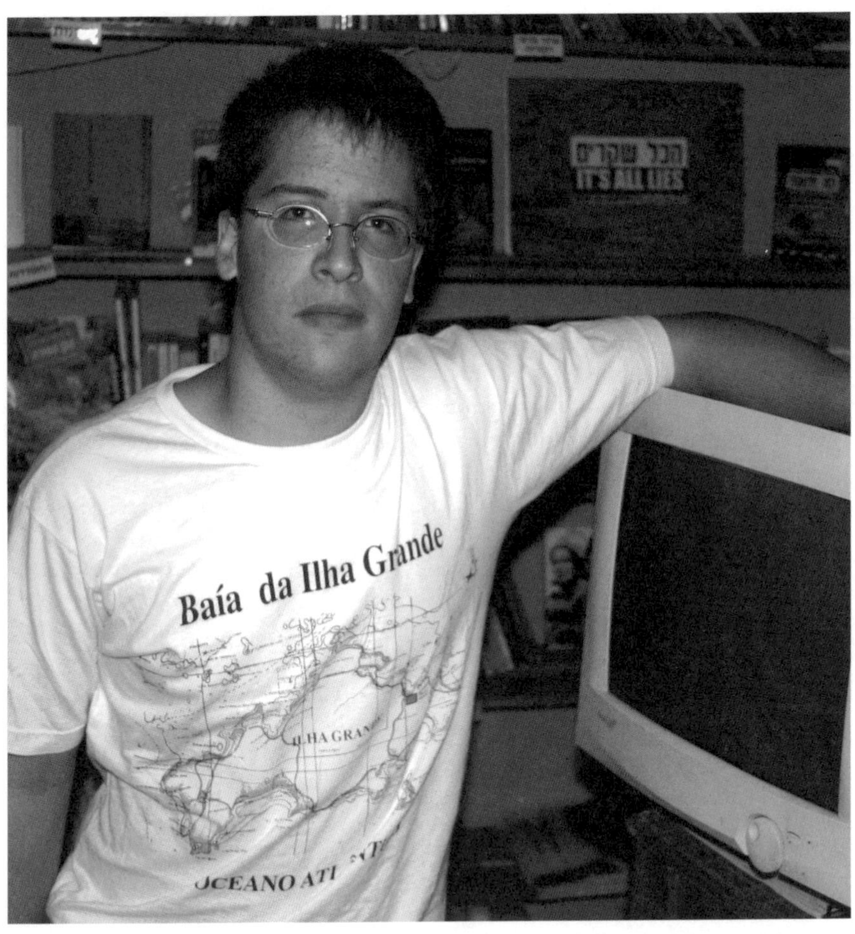

Matan Cohen in the 'Salon Mazal' anarchist social centre. *Photo by Arthur Neslen*

in protesting against the wall encircling Palestinian communities, however, were less popular with an Israeli public overwhelmingly behind the move. Matan Cohen joined Anarchists Against the Wall in 2002 and by the age of 16, was already talking with the world-weariness of an adolescent war correspondent.

I'm from Kfar Valim, the 'village of roses' built by Jews who wanted to live a luxurious life among the poor Palestinian villages of the Galilee.[28] We used Arab workers to build our first house and we went to their restaurants in the neighbouring villages – because they were cheaper – but we had no real connection with the Arabs. When the October 2000 clashes happened in Sakhnin,[29] the typical shocked reaction was: 'But we were their friends! We ate humus together!'

I was only 12 and I didn't really understand what was happening. Sakhnin was 20 minutes away by car and suddenly, everyone was like 'don't talk to them, don't go to their villages'. Our friends higher up Mount Carmel were afraid even to sleep round at our place. The liberal middle classes imagined we had good relations when it wasn't true. The clashes came out of the blue for them and they were very frightened.

My parents had some Arab friends but it was like, 'they're nice people but you can't trust them'. They split up two years ago and I moved to Tel Aviv with my mum. She's still radical but my dad's a social democrat. He hates Arafat because he's a symbol of Palestinian manhood. I think women are naturally more anarchistic.

My parents were typical liberal Israelis: proud of being Jewish but with no connection to Judaism. It's like 'We need a Jewish state' but you never go to synagogue, you never pray, you don't believe in God! In my bourgeois school in central Tel Aviv, maybe five per cent of kids went to synagogue but 90 per cent of them were barmitzva'd. This is the hypocritical mainstream position. I never went to synagogue and I wasn't barmitzva'd. We had a non-religious party and it was accepted nicely.

28. Howard M. Sachar, *A History of Israel* (Knopf, 1996), p. 842, cited in *Challenge*, May–June 2001. '[Ariel] Sharon regarded the Galilee as his initial proving ground. To "Judaize" this strategic northern region, he promptly launched into construction of thirty miniature Jewish settlements on hills overlooking key Arab villages. The project was completed within three years. Although by 1981 only small numbers of Jews inhabited these Galilee outposts, they sufficed to block the growth of adjacent Arab communities. Simultaneously, to obstruct all Arab efforts to relieve their mounting congestion, Sharon denied their villages permits to construct new homes outside local boundaries.'
29. A month after the Intifada started, 13 Israeli Arabs were shot dead by soldiers in Sakhnin during a solidarity demonstration with Palestinians which turned into a riot.

I don't consider myself Jewish. Of course that's how I'm defined by others, and more than half my family was murdered in Auschwitz, but I don't believe in the Jewish ethnic group. I don't believe in any ethnic group.

Do you see anything positive about Israeli culture?

What culture? (laughs) Sorry, I think it's something made up. I can't think of anything good about it.

Israeli music?

What music? Really! All they do is imitate American music and culture. We don't have a distinct, independent Jewish culture. They claim a sense of moral superiority by being Jews but it's like trying to bring life to something that doesn't really exist. There's no solidarity here. Israeli politics are like, I scratch your back and you scratch mine. No-one cares when Israeli workers don't get paid for a year. If they go on strike, half the nation says they're traitors.

You don't see this as your country?

I don't feel loyal to any country because I'm an anarchist. I want to decide for myself what I am. Some Spanish guys told me they felt attached to their culture because it accepts them as radical leftists. Even a radical American will say his culture gave him something. But Israel contributes nothing to its citizens, not even a connection to politics. That's why we want to destroy 'politics' and create a political environment for all the people. Refusing to serve in the army is an important step.

Will you refuse?

Yeah, well I don't know if they'd let me serve, with five arrests and the meetings I've had with Hamas people. Like no way. I met armed men from Fatah. I met leaders of Hamas and Islamic Jihad, mostly by accident. It wasn't nice but I understand why they hate Israelis and find it hard to separate between soldiers and peaceniks. When I was in Ramallah or Nablus, I told people I was American. Some of the Islamic Jihad men knew I was Israeli and welcomed me but I still had all the layers of 'don't trust the Arabs', so it was hard. I think suicide bombs are horrifying but the Palestinians have the right to use violence. It might not be the best or most humane tactic but I understand it after seeing how they live.

I saw shooting. People fell in my hands. I was in a demonstration when they shot live ammunition and people were seriously wounded beside me. I saw someone hit in the head by a bullet, really nasty things. I must've been on fifty demonstrations where rubber bullets were fired. I was hit by one on a demo in Qallandia. Israelis talk about Palestinian propaganda but the occupation is the worst propaganda imaginable. I can't blame a child in that environment for wanting to shoot soldiers. On the other hand, the soldier could be my neighbour

– in one case he was. For four years, we played soccer together and I saw him at a protest firing rubber bullets and tear gas at us! He came over and was like, 'Hey, what's up? What are you doing here?' I said 'What are YOU doing here?' He said, 'Oh yeah, everything's ok' and continued shooting. If you're being objective, you can say that Israel deserves the suicide bombings in Tel Aviv. But of course it could be me or my family and no-one deserves it really. Like the Germans in Dresden, 1945. They didn't deserve to die.

I'm not a 'traitor', I don't want to kill Jews but it's ridiculous that Israelis feel like victims when you see tanks – and I have seen this – shooting at children throwing stones. I'd like to help the oppressed Israeli who joined the army to fuck the Palestinians more than he got fucked by the system. But I also want to fight him because I recognise the injustice of it. I can't explain this feeling of 'we're victims so it doesn't matter what we do' from people who're third generation and have no connection to the Holocaust.

How did you become an activist?

During the first days of the Intifada, they were showing 24-hour live news on every channel and I just started feeling it was wrong and we had to stop it. I got involved with Peace Now and then I went from group to group, just listening, until I arrived at the most radical place. I started taking food shipments to starving areas with Gush Shalom and Ta'ayush[30] and then I went to the Mas'ha camp. Mas'ha was the first time Israelis and Palestinians cooperated in actions against the wall.[31]

Were you rich, white, guilty students...?

Unfortunately, yes. Politicised Israelis often come from the most disgusting, bourgeois places. We have a small leftist ghetto but that's it. We want to open up and expand our group because acting like a secret society is getting too risky. Our phones are tapped and we're watched all the time. It's disturbing because they can put you in jail for nothing.

30. Gush Shalom ('The Peace Bloc') and Ta'ayush (Arab–Israeli partnership) are the two most active left-wing movements in Israel today. To date, neither has mobilised more than a few thousand people to oppose the occupation. Gush Shalom, led by the veteran activist Uri Avnery, supports a two-state solution to the conflict based on 1967 borders. Ta'ayush takes no position on a final settlement, but attempts to build practical solidarity on the ground.
31. The Mas'ha camp's experiment in direct democracy and free organisation eventually proved too much for conservative forces on both sides of the Green Line. According to Uri Ayalon, another activist with Anarchists Against the Wall, 'Mas'ha was an amazing contribution to the struggle against the Wall. It led to information-sharing between Palestinians and Israelis, relationships between the people and discussions around the fire about new ways of non-violent struggle.'

You've been arrested five times, what for?

Blocking roads, entering closed military zones, the normal stuff. I'm facing two trials for assaulting a policeman and resisting arrest. The worst I'll get is community service. I've had horrible experiences though. After a demo in Tel Aviv last year, I was beaten with a truncheon and choked. I almost lost consciousness. In the ambulance the officer handcuffed me and started punching me in the face. He said, 'I'm going to send you to jail to teach you not to demonstrate again.' He continued punching me in the hospital. We were sent to Abu Khibir prison, photographed, fingerprinted and put in cells with murderers who threatened us. I was afraid to go to sleep. They were like, 'Don't look at me', but if you didn't look at them they'd be, like, 'You're not giving me enough respect'. All the psychotic things, you know? I was robbed of four shekels I had in my pocket. I said, 'Ok, take it I don't want to fight, fuck you.' It was really frightening. We tried to sue the police department over that case.

Have you ever had any dealings with the Shabbak?

I met them many times but I think they're afraid to investigate me because I've only just turned 16. I'm at the top of their list though. I'm expecting it. I've already been harassed at the airport. I know people who've been asked to be informers. They say things like, 'You want to be harassed?' or 'You want to face trial?' And if you become an informer, they'll pay you. They're really violent and scary. It's like the KGB.

Israeli society is falling apart. At one demo after ten soldiers were killed in Gaza, a former army chief said, 'Beside the honey you have the sting.' Like beside the honey of the occupation, the sting is our soldiers getting hit. This country is becoming fascist, like Germany was in the '30s, blaming a small group for all its ills so they won't have to look inwards. I want to study Arabic in the territories. I want to visit my 38-year-old brother in Berlin and go on to Chiapas or Cuba. My future plans are extravagant. I don't want to come back.

6
The Home Front

Around a thousand Israelis, the majority of them civilians, were killed during the first four years of the Second Intifada. With perhaps half of Israel's population,[1] the Palestinians suffered four times as many casualties, along with the additional detritus of occupation such as curfews, road blocks, mass arrests, land seizures, house demolitions, crop destructions etc. The IDF fired a million bullets in the first few days of the Intifada, before the Palestinians resorted to suicide bombings. Nonetheless, the loss of life in Israel is roughly the same as that in New Orleans after Hurricane Katrina, and while man-made the psychological effects have been equally dramatic.

By 2003, almost one in ten Israelis were found to be suffering from post traumatic stress disorder, tourism had fallen by nearly 80 per cent, one in five Israelis were living below the poverty line, the economy had plunged into recession and anti-social behaviour was rife. Most significantly, for perhaps the first time, Israel had become a net exporter of Jews to the Diaspora. According to the Israeli Bureau of Statistics, in 2003, some 9,000 more Jews left the country than arrived. In 2004, the figure rose to 11,000.[2] The long-term continuance of such demographics would constitute a threat to Israel's survival as a 'Jewish state'.

Hilla Kernel-Soliman, the director of the Association of Rape Crisis Centres in Jerusalem, told me that evidence linking an increase in domestic violence to the Intifada was strong. She said:

> Women in their 20s are telling us how their boyfriends joined the army and then became extremely tense and quick to anger. Every little thing makes them jump and they have sex with their girlfriends when they don't want it, which I'd call rape. They wouldn't call it that

1. Bennett Zimmerman, Roberta Seid, Michael L. Wise, 'The Million and a half person gap', *Haaretz*, Sep 10, 2005. Estimates of the Palestinian population vary from 2.47 million to 3.8 million. Israeli Central Bureau of Statistics figures put Israel's population at 6.6 million.
2. See migration and tourism figures from the Israeli Bureau of Statistics: <http://www.cbs.gov.il/yarhon/e1_e.htm>.

> because they love the guys. I know a 19-year-old whose boyfriend became angry and nervous when he was in the territories. When he returned at the weekend, he'd anally rape her but it was complicated because she felt sorry for him. It's very hard to admit that someone you love can cause you terrible pain.
>
> There's an atmosphere to humiliate women in the army, that's for sure. It's an unbearable environment for a woman to live in with all kinds of insulting remarks and inappropriate touching. We receive calls about it constantly. The treatment of Arab women is also terrible. Arab callers to the hotline say that when they pass through checkpoints, they're harassed by soldiers who laugh at them, ask them for blow jobs or sexually harass them.

Feminist organisations such as New Profile argue that Israeli civil life has been disfigured by military dominion; weaponry, militant self-righteousness, paranoia and patriarchal hyper-vigilance have all spilt back into a society with few resources to cope with them. They say that the occupation has come home. If it has, sadly, few Israelis appear to have noticed.

ALONA ABT

A fish can't live out of water

If children's TV programmes reflect the societies that produce them, the story of *Rehov Sumsum* (*Sesame Street*) depicts a tragic image of Israel. In the warm afterglow of the Oslo Accords, an attempt was made to launch a joint Israeli-Palestinian *Sesame Street*, set on a junction between two parallel streets where characters from the two communities could meet. In the Israel of the late 1990s, the idea came to be viewed as dangerously unrealistic. In 2002, Alona Abt's production company Hop won the contract to produce a third series, now called *Sesame Stories*. Their formula removed Palestinian characters and the notion of a physical street from the show and switched the action to the basement of a mad professor. Separate Palestinian and Jordanian co-production companies also under the aegis of the Sesame Workshop in New York produced their own versions of '*Sharaa Simsim*', without any Jewish characters. Only in the Mideast, cynics said, could *Sesame Street* be ethnically cleansed. Yet plans for a fourth Israeli series may involve an even more radical departure. Alona Abt is friendly, pushed for time and she presents as a liberal teacher. In front of a camera, she suddenly comes alive, like a goofy character in the opening sequence of a kids' TV programme.

I'm a Sabra, born in Kiryat Gan, which is a small immigrant town in southern Israel. My parents were new immigrants and spoke more English than Hebrew. My father came from South Africa. He was an enthusiastic Zionist and, according

Alona Abt. *Photo by Arthur Neslen*

to his humanistic outlook, Israel was the place for Jews to build their future. I'm sure he wanted to escape from the apartheid regime. Living in Kiryat Gan was part of his vision.

Growing up, my parents were quite opposed to television so we were one of the last families in the neighbourhood to get one. I didn't see *Sesame Street* until I was in university studying television making. I was 22 then. Now I'm 45 and the co-executive director of Hop channel.

Did you grow up in a multi-cultural area?

Not among Arabs, but very multi-cultural in terms of Jews. With less than 25,000 residents and more than 40 different synagogues, the town's community was splintered. But I had a warm and sheltered childhood. I'm sure it's part of what makes me, me.

In the army, I was a social worker, assigned to a unit of Bedouin trackers in the south. Afterwards I studied film and television. When I set up Argofilms, we decided to specialise in children's film, and four years go, we were approached by *Rehov Sumsum* just as we were setting up Hop. We were where their audience was at. They bravely decided to switch to us before we were proven.

A whole generation grew up on the first *Rehov Sumsum* series in the '80s. A second season was broadcast as an international collaboration when the Oslo process started. They stuck to the original concept of a physical street where Arabs and Jews lived together harmoniously. But the reality caught up with them quicker than the vision of their scriptwriters. At the end of the second phase, they turned to us to crack a format for a regional project. The result was a co-production with Jordanian and Palestinian programme-makers for the Sesame Workshop in New York. They had their own muppets and characters[3] but we shared the same bank of materials. We invested some of the money ourselves, and the workshop fund-raised lots of money from the European Union. The Ford Foundation is another supporter – but no characters are sponsored by them.[4]

3. Lee Hockstader, 'A bumpy ride on *Sesame Street*', *Washington Post*, 9 November 1999. The separation of Muppets was not an easy affair. 'The Palestinian producers were determined to match the Israeli show's equivalent of Big Bird [with] Kippi, a lumbering purple porcupine whose prickly personality conceals a heart of gold. When they settled on Kareem, a proud but amiable rooster, some Palestinians complained that Kareem, a hand-held puppet, was a fraction of the size of Kippi, who is played by a human in a costume. After much hand-wringing, the Palestinians decided to keep Kareem as he was, for the simple reason that he was easier to deal with.'
4. Julia Day, '*Sesame Street* airs peace propaganda', *Guardian*, 21 October 2003; *Muppet Central News*, '*Sesame Street* under attack from airing McDonald's commercials', 14 October 2003. The European Commission gave a £1.75m grant to the programme's producers as part of £5m fund Sesame Workshop used to develop 26 programmes promoting 'cooperation, respect for others and self-esteem' in Israel, Jordan and the Palestinian territories. The

How was this different from Rehov Sumsum's second phase?

The Intifada was raging and we didn't want to create something so lacking in credibility that parents would transmit feelings of cynicism to their kids. Children are sensitive to their parents' feelings towards TV. Everybody's emotions were inflamed because busses were being blown up and we were marching into Ramallah. Just mentioning the core issues about Arabs, Israelis, beliefs and rights was touchy. We tried though by creating a new format [*Sesame Stories*], which took place in a house rather than a particular street. Two new Muppets lived there with a human called 'Zaki', or Yitzhak. Our puppets are not ethnically represented but going by their names, they're more Jewish. Zaki's neighbour was Ibtisam.

Ibtisam was an Israeli Arab?

Yes, but he's human. We thought this was the best bridge to break stereotypes about Arab children as most of our viewers are Jewish. We broadcast by cable and satellite to 90 per cent of TV-owning Israeli households. The households not covered are mostly Arabs. Early on, we decided to try to sensitively expose Jewish children to Arab-Israelis rather than aim for a joint Arab–Jewish audience. We taught Israelis to count in Arabic and say hello. It was a brave season really because the last thing any broadcaster with money wanted to deal with was Arabs and Israelis. Israelis have different levels of tolerance and political awareness and we sometimes had to walk on eggshells. Parents trusted us to broadcast to their children so we had to be careful not to expose them to different beliefs and nationalities in an intimidating way.

Now we're fund-raising and format-cracking for the fourth phase. We would like to continue from more of an 'identity' perspective in Israeli society. To create an understanding of the 'other', we have to strengthen children's knowledge of their own identity and self-respect. For example, we might use more traditional stories as the basis for animation, blending day-to-day events with information about the child's background and cultural heritage.

Isn't that a retreat from multi-culturalism and celebrating diversity?

You're looking at Israeli society as a culture that's polarised between Jews and Arabs. It's one of the strongest rifts, but I think Israel is polarised in many more ways. I don't think it will be less explosive in Israel to deal with religious and secular Jews. When you say to me 'multi-culturalism', I'm thinking about secular and religious Jews, Russians and non-Russians.

Ford Foundation and other contributors provided the rest of the money. There was much controversy after *Sesame Street* accepted corporate sponsorship from McDonald's in 2003 to broadcast messages before and after each US programme.

Would you consider Mizrahi and Haredi Muppets?

It's a good question. We've had lots of discussion about that. Should the Muppets have a human identity? We're also dealing with issues of gender as presently, the two Muppets are male. We presume that our target age group are in a secluded environment where they don't meet the 'other', so how do we represent difference to them without reinforcing stereotypes? In the last [third] season, the Palestinian and Jordanian series didn't have Jewish characters.[5] I think it would have made it impossible for them to broadcast in the current political situation.

How true is this to the original concept of a geographical street where children from different cultures and backgrounds lived together and mixed freely?

The street is not some great idea that you have to worship. The idea is people have to get along together and get what they can from their fellow man. In terms of grown-up's symbolism, it's a catchy phrase to say that the street can't exist any more but children are naïve and the way they experience reality, there is such a place, even if it's blue and purple. If we show them a reality in which different people can meet and enjoy each other, then we're creating that possibility for them.

But even your animated sequences – with calves, fish and butterflies communicating only from their own space – imply that friendship is impossible outside one's own turf.

No, they each have to live in their surroundings – a fish can't live out of water and a calf can't jump into the sea – but they find ways to communicate, play with and enjoy each other. It's positive.

It's bittersweet, though, because they'll never be able to find a place…

But that's reality. A fish can't live out of water. That's reality.

5. Julie Salomon, 'Israeli–Palestinian battles intrude on *Sesame Street*', *New York Times*, 30 July 2002; Jon E. Dougherty and David Kupelian, 'Palestinian kids raised for war', Worldnet.daily. With the intensification of settlement and checkpoint building that followed the signing of Oslo, the Palestinian mood hardened. On *Rehov Sumsum*, 'the Israeli puppets could not simply appear in Palestinian territory, they had to be invited.' Alona Abt's Palestinian counterpart Daoud Kuttab actually called for broadcasting to be postponed until a peace agreement was reached. 'Children in Palestine will not appreciate, understand, absorb and react in a positive way to the goals we want to accomplish,' he said. 'You're telling them to be tolerant when Israeli tanks are outside their home!' But even this was an improvement on the pre-*Sumsum* situation. An Israeli documentary in 1998 alleged that a Palestinian version of *Sesame Street*, 'The Children's Club', featured 'children aged 4–10. One young boy sings "When I wander into Jerusalem I will become a suicide bomber." Afterwards, other children stand to call for "Jihad! Holy war to the end against the Zionist enemy."'

Is it reality that Palestinians and Israeli children will never live on the same street?

I hope not. It's not a future that I can conceive but I have to present it in a non-intimidating way. I'm not censored by anyone but my internal censor tells me when I'm gaining or losing my audience. If I show them something so remote from their lives at the moment, with all the existing fears and hatreds of their parents' generation, it won't help. If an Israeli and Palestinian child relate to Ernie and Bert today, it will give them a building block for human communication tomorrow. Just knowing and demystifying the enemy is a valuable thing. It allows people to see that 'Jew' does not just mean 'soldier' and 'Arab' doesn't just mean 'terrorist'.

Some might say that Sesame Street has been co-opted into supporting US foreign policy goals. Its characters are now sponsored by multinationals, the Bush administration is funding it to spread American values and the theme tune was even played at prisoners in Abu Ghraib at deafening levels…[6]

I'm a pragmatist. I don't think any grown-up would say this series was Americanised. It has a strong local flavour. Americans have a strong politically correct code which doesn't exactly accord with Israel's. To make a show realistic for an Israeli child, the parents would have to immediately begin shouting at each other because that's how people fight here, on a good day. Their attitude was that it provides negative role-modelling. Everything reflects something. We create these shows for the reality we live in. If it was different, our format might be too.

6. Ryan Dilley, 'Is Elmo Bush's secret weapon?' BBC News Online, 3 September 2003. 'Is *Sesame Street* really brought to you by the letters U, S and A? The US Army – which partly sponsors the show's makers – certainly loves *Sesame Street*… Iraqi prisoners were treated to repeated playing of the ditty at ear-splitting volume by US psychological operations officers intent on encouraging their captives to submit to questioning. The programme… has been praised by the US State Department officials who have been set the task of turning the tide of anti-Americanism. Charlotte Beers, the former ad executive made undersecretary of State for public diplomacy… said she was "dazzled" by a co-production of *Sesame Street* broadcast in Egypt since 2000. "The children are glued to the set. They are learning English, they are learning about American values." The government's Agency for International Development (USAID) is now giving $6.26m for *Sesame Street* to produce a show for viewers in Bangladesh – a nation with a considerable Muslim population. One unnamed official told the *Daily Telegraph* newspaper that the project is "aiming to promote greater understanding of American morality and culture…" Certainly, the show seems not to have shied away from promoting values which typify the US, such as capitalism. The cute, squeaky-voiced puppet Elmo has just been sponsored by Wall Street firm Merrill Lynch to explain business to American pre-schoolers.'

What did you hope for when you went into programme making?

I always thought that children were the most vulnerable and receptive audience in society and that any change would start with them. I don't remember one moment when I made a decision. You know, sometimes you find you've taken a path without knowing the precise moment that the path was carved out? The values I want to promote are still the same. How can I be true to them? Let's put it this way, I don't think there's been a weakening of the will.

LIAD KANTOROWICZ

The person who doesn't really exist

Liad, a Tel Aviv sex worker, arrives at the Meshugges café in a cloud of glitter and mascara that conceal her face well. She's spent much of her 26 years growing up in the USA, where her father emigrated when she was a child. Her second name, Kantorowicz, suggests that her forebears were rabbis. When I point this out, she plays with her nose stud distractedly. 'See, I can't escape from my Jewish roots even in my name,' she says.

If there's such a thing as an archetypal Israeli, it's not me. I was born in Kfar Saba, a small town next to Qalqilya, on the border of the West Bank. The Green Line actually runs through the towns and now, of course, there's a big wall between them. During the First Intifada, it seemed like there was a bomb scare outside my school almost every week. Qalqilya was a mile away from my house and it was considered the war zone. The war was always 'over there' and it's awful that now you go to that point and boom! There's a wall. It's hidden from you. I don't go back much. I went to a punk show a while ago but I felt like I was on drugs the whole time. I could be clichéd and say, 'you can never go home' because for a long time, Israel only existed in the realm of my imagination, a bit like a fetish.

We moved to the US when I was eleven but I never felt American. Strangely, I'd had a happy childhood here. I think my dad decided we should emigrate because he'd been called up to fight against a civilian population during the First Intifada. I think it seemed wrong to him that there was a gun lying around the house and there were soldiers everywhere. To us it was normal.

We moved to California and after that, Seattle. I really wanted to be part of the Jewish community there but we never were. Anything 'Jewish' felt weird for me because I never went to temple in Israel, so why would I do that now? It

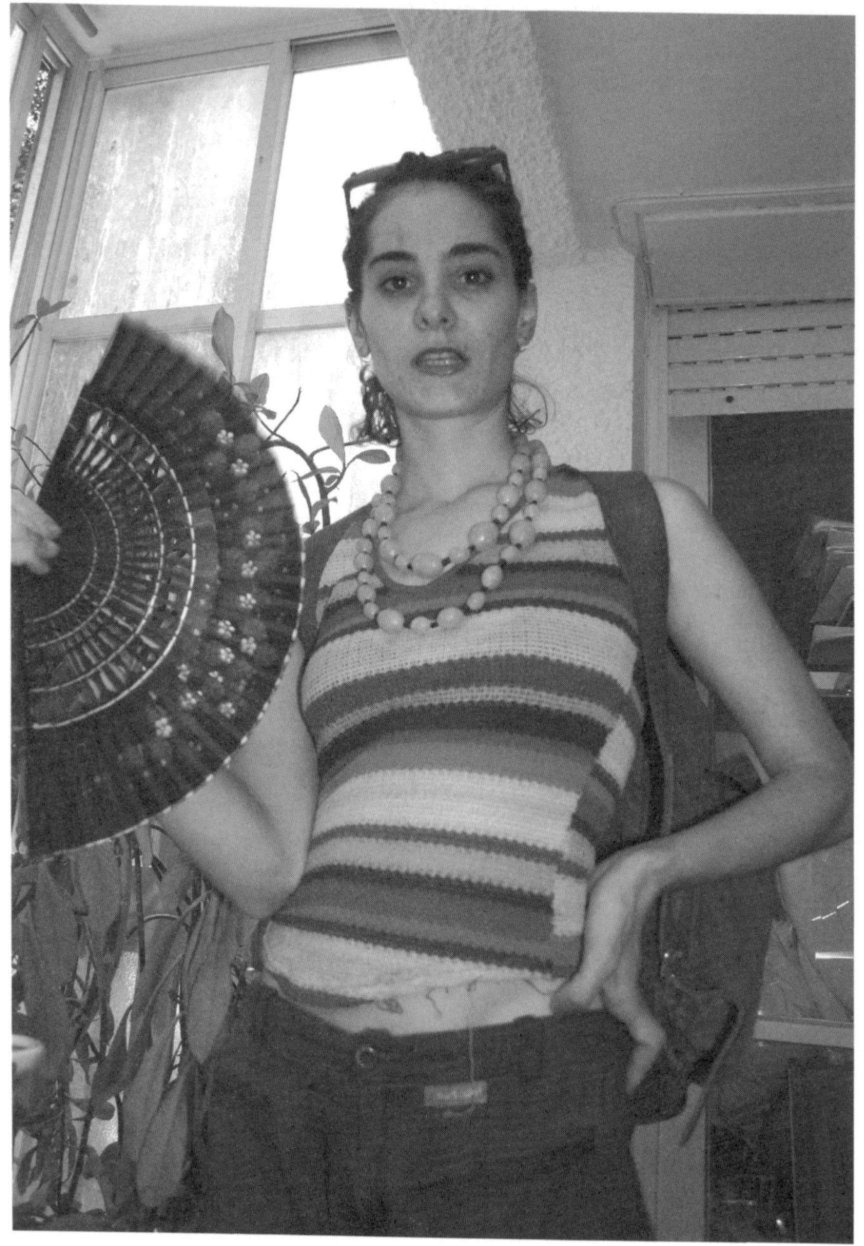

Liad Kantorowicz. *Photo by Arthur Neslen*

wasn't really a part of me. I never went to Jewish anything. I didn't get a Jewish education. Maybe when I'm 40, I'll re-examine my Jewishness.

I feel a very strong sense of being Israeli but not Jewish. I relate to the Israeli sense of community and caring for each other and holding together. Once, in the States, I left my purse on a bus. I was crying and it was raining and I just needed to call the bus depot or *someone*, and people just ignored me as if I wasn't there. In Israel that would never have happened. The first person who saw me would have intervened and asked if I needed anything.

Is that because a sense of external threat forces everyone together?

You know, I don't understand that whole concept of Jewish persecution or being in a minority. It's basic to Jewishness and I lack it. In Israel, if you're Jewish, particularly if you're white, you're not a minority. You're the supreme elite. A lot of racist things are embedded in me.

I came back to study when I was 22. My parents and best friends are still in America but I always wanted to return. The American sense of individualism is not a value at all here. In fact, people oppress you out of having any personality at all for the greater good of the community. But I feel like there are things holding me to the ground here. In the States, you could just get lost. You could die and nobody would know.

I got into sex work for the same reason most people do: money. I had a lot of misconceptions at first. I thought it was demeaning to women. But my boyfriend worked as a cashier in a peep show and he broke down a lot of the stereotypes for me. For a few hours' work, I got paid more than a full-time worker on minimum wage and it was fascinating. I discovered a collective unconscious that's tightly connected to sexuality, I learned a lot about myself and it enabled me to go to school.

When I was working as a concièrge in various American whorehouses, I was like the person who doesn't really exist. People would call and you'd answer the door and try to push customers onto the women. I worked in a peep show for three years, and with professional webcam. I worked as a stripper and in what's called 'lingerie modelling' or fantasy – like peep show but without the glass inbetween.

I still work as a professional dominatrix. It's by far the highest-paying form of sex work – up to 20 times more than prostitution. I do have rules, but they're not morally set. I won't work in high-speed lap dances, because I don't get anything from it. The interaction with customers is on a very physical basis. I don't get to know them and when you're just touching, touching, touching, it's like a body with nothing there. It's unfulfilling for me and it's demoralising for the men too.

Do you think you're mainly looking for a sense of connection to other people?

I feel I can give them a lot with professional dom. It's a place where fantasies are thoroughly explored. My shrink once told me that because my life is so erratic, crazy and it sometimes feels like I have no control over what happens to me, the only time I really have control is in the dom situation. Security for me comes from being part of a community who know me, relate to me, support me and who I can support in return. Sex work is more taboo here than in the States. Israeli men are very emasculated and their identity is based on proving how masculine they are, being on top and squashing everyone below them. They need a release from that, which is why professional dominatrixes are in such high demand here.

Israeli men would probably be better off if they knew where their sexual hang ups and fetishes came from. When they seek to be humiliated, belittled, made irresponsible and, ultimately, punished, it shows that they carry a lot of guilt. As an outsider, I can see that a lot of it comes from having been in positions of power in the military over a civilian population. They want to act out being in the position of a Palestinian. It might mean recreating the exact position that a Palestinian was tied up in. A lot of them have urine fetishes, much more so than in the States. I think it's because it's an ultimate symbol of humiliation and it's also something that's done to Palestinians. Getting slapped in the face, being blindfolded, getting yelled at and being penetrated in the ass – that's a really big one because it's a potent symbol of humiliation. Also, having any sort of sharp items pointed against them. You have the connotation of the gun as a phallic object but it can be anything serving as that object whether it's a dildo, their own gun that they brought with them from military service, or the heel of a shoe or a riding crop.

I rarely see Israeli Arabs for the same reason that pro-doms in the States rarely see black men. If they're constantly on the bottom, why should they pay for someone to recreate that? I've seen it a few times but it was to do with breaking taboos of humiliation or feelings of inferiority, which are worse than among Israeli Jews. Pride and trying to regain pride are more common themes, whether it's on top of women or in their community. I've heard from several sources in the Galilee area, where there's a very high Israeli Arab population, that they're asking the high-class prostitutes there to wear Israeli military uniforms. It's common knowledge. That clues you into some things.

Has the situation changed in the last few years?

The Russian migration has made Israelis more racist and extreme. Like, all sex workers are assumed to be Russian and every Russian woman is a prostitute. In the Russian community, sex work is less stigmatised because a lot of migrants have come from places where it's more prevalent.

There's a very high rate of women-trafficking here. Many migrants are beaten, raped, smuggled across borders, and forced to have sex with up to 12 men a day. Israeli-born prostitutes can work at fancy hotels or their own house. They have their own security and can run their own brothel. Migrants are paid less, have fewer rights and are subject to exploitation and deportation. This is an incredibly disempowered community, if you can even call it a community. Many of them come from Eastern Europe and are very afraid of outsiders. There is a government-owned sex workers' union but it's full of crooks and everyone hates it.

Herzl believed that Jewish prostitutes and thieves would indicate a successful Jewish State. Are you fulfilling his dream?

Ok, I'll accept prostitute-whore-sex worker as one. Look, I don't like Herzl. He's like such a gimmick-guy. But no, because most sex workers are not on *aliyah*. They're migrants from Ukraine and Moldova. Israeli men don't like them because they're too common. Pure native Israeli blood is highly esteemed and Russians are considered cheap goyim. When they were first introduced to the Israeli 'market', they were considered rare and exotic because they were blonde but now they're just a dime a dozen.

SAAR UZIELI

A society needs this kind of valve

The Intifada has been credited with traumatising Israel society, and this in turn has reinforced a view that the occupation will end only when Israel feels secure enough to end it. One of the few trauma surveys, in 2002, found that nearly one in ten Israelis were suffering from post-traumatic stress disorder.[7] Given that more than half of those questioned in the telephone survey claimed to have either been directly exposed to a terrorist attack, or had a family member who had been, the report's authors found the rate of PTSD surprisingly 'moderate'. Nonetheless, the numbers were much higher than in most other western societies and commentators attributed phenomena as diverse as bad driving and domestic violence to PTSD. Natal is the only Israeli organisation that provides one-to-one personal and phone counselling to trauma victims. Saar Uzieli is the organisation's clinical supervising psychologist. Sigal Haimov, whose interview follows, is the director of its hotline.

7. A. Bleich, M. Gelkopf and Z. Solomon, 'Exposure to terrorism, stress-related mental health symptoms, and coping behaviors among a nationally representative sample in Israel', *Journal for the American Medical Association*, 6 August 2003, 290 (5): 612–20. This telephone survey of 742 Israeli residents between April and May 2002 was conducted from the Lev Hasharon Mental Health Center in Tel Aviv University's Sackler School

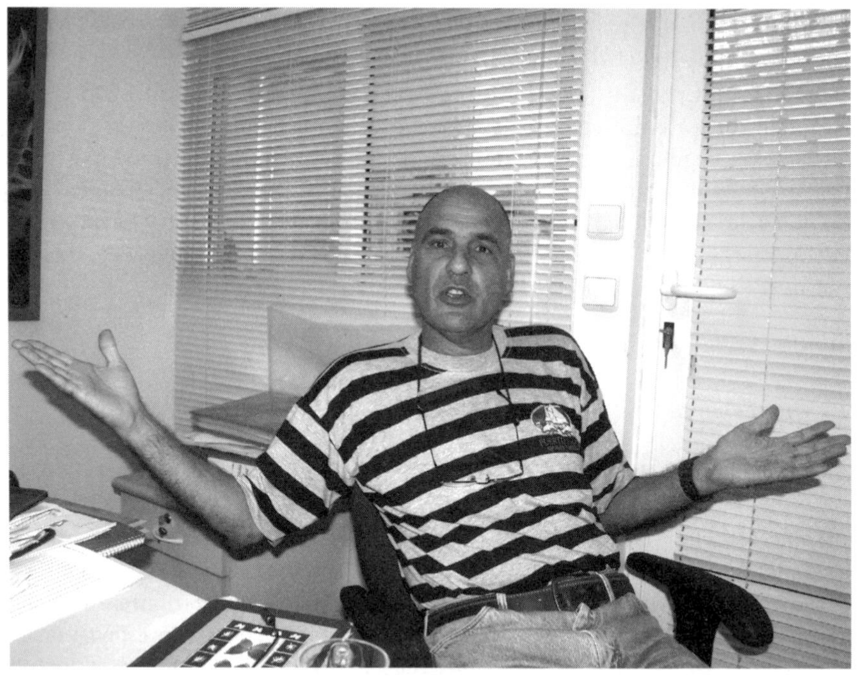

Saar Uzieli. *Photo by Arthur Neslen*

Natal was set up in 1998 to help war veterans who were suffering from post-traumatic stress disorder, but in October 2000 we started getting calls from people who'd been caught up in terror attacks. Some of them were already suffering from PTSD but many also had acute stress reaction.[8] We started getting more media publicity, so more PTSD sufferers realised what their symptoms meant, and that they had a place to come.

In 2002, when terror attacks spiked, there were days when our four phone lines were permanently ringing. We dealt with it. Now we're more flexible with psychotherapists in Jerusalem, Haifa, Hadera and Nahariya. We're giving Israeli society the ability to heal and the feeling that somebody is taking care of them, that they are not alone.

I don't like to think about Israel as a society in trauma. If you diagnose it that way, people may not want to work here. But terror attacks are not stopping people from functioning. Maybe they'll be more careful but they still meet friends and go to the movies. I've just returned from a holiday in the Sinai myself. Many of us are suffering from PTSD but Israeli society as a whole isn't.

A sex worker told me that soldiers from the territories she saw often wanted to be blindfolded and tied up because they'd done that to Palestinians...

I think she is fantasising. I don't believe her. I don't have anything against working girls, a society needs this kind of valve but this is fantasy, I'm sure. I talk to a lot of Israeli soldiers, they're my friends, and we never use working girls.

---

of Medicine. Of the 512 who finally participated, 16.4% had been directly exposed to a terrorist attack, 37.3% had a family member who had been. A large majority of the sample, 76.7% had at least one trauma stress-related symptom but only 9.4% met the criteria for post-traumatic stress disorder. The rate for depression among the sample group was 58.6%, and most expressed low senses of safety for themselves (60.4%) and their families (67.9%).

8. An acute stress reaction is considered a transient condition that develops in response to a traumatic event. The symptoms begin within minutes of the incident and disappear in days or hours. They can include disorientation, daze, depression, amnesia and physiological anxiety symptoms. By definition, it takes place within a shorter time frame than post-traumatic stress disorder, which is a long-lasting anxiety response to a traumatic event. An individual suffering from PTSD might experience feelings of helplessness and intense fear or horror connected to thoughts, dreams and flashbacks of the traumatic incident. This in turn may give rise to intense anxiety and avoidance of cues that act as reminders of the traumatic event. Depression, insomnia, hyper-vigilance, social withdrawal, concentration and memory lapses, and alcohol and substance abuse have all been associated with the condition, even though some experts have questioned whether objectively it can even be said to exist.

Have you ever treated a traumatised Palestinian militant?

Our mandate is to help Israeli citizens, but we also talk to Christians, Arabs and even foreign workers. We don't have a problem with any of these. We will not treat a Palestinian who lives in Gaza though, whether he puts a bomb in Israel or not, because we need to draw a line somewhere.[9] The hotline did help Palestinians but not with psychotherapy.

Do you think factors like ethnicity and class influence how people deal with trauma?

We're getting Ashkenazim and Sephardim and I don't see any difference. Maybe years ago, class would have had an effect but Israel today is melting in a way. You can find rich families that are educated and very articulate but don't speak a word about terror or PTSD. You can also go to very poor families who'll be willing and able to talk.

What kind of family did you come from?

My mother and father fought in the Independence war. My brothers and I also fought in wars and hoped that our children wouldn't have to do the same. Sadly, they did. After I finished my psychology degree, the army asked me to re-enlist as a psychologist. I agreed to go to Sinai for 12 months and stayed for 20 years, treating PTSD sufferers from the Lebanon War. Two weeks before this Intifada started, I was invited to become the clinical director here. As an ex-combat officer, I knew I could help people.

During the Suez War of Attrition[10] and Yom Kippur War, many of my friends were killed. I was lucky to survive but I think I'm still suffering from some kind of PTSD. It's not full-blown but I get very anxious and I'm susceptible to noise. If somebody closed a door on the third floor, you wouldn't notice it but I'd feel it in my body. Sometimes I can be angrier. I think that part of why I became a psychologist was because of what I saw in Suez. In a sense I came to Natal 30 years ago during that war.

9. While Israeli Arabs – Christians and Muslims – have Israeli citizenship (if not nationality), their brethren in the West Bank and Gaza do not.
10. Morris, *Righteous Victims*, pp. 347–63. Following Israel's occupation of the Sinai peninsula in the 'Six-Day War' in 1967, a protracted and corrosive confrontation continued for three years. In the 'War of Attrition', the Egyptian President Gamer Al-Nasser hoped to wear down the Israeli army's capabilities without triggering a full-scale conflict. Israel says that 1,424 of its soldiers and more than 100 civilians were killed in skirmishes, guerrilla actions and mortar shelling during the war, although Egyptian estimates of Israeli casualties are higher. There are no figures for the numbers of Egyptian dead in the conflict but Morris concludes that 'a reasonable estimate would probably be about 10,000 civilians and military killed'.

SIGAL HAIMOV

Amputees of the soul

I don't think there's one person here who considers this just a job. We have so many difficult calls every day from people at the first stage of their grieving process suffering overwhelming emotional pain. They tell us what we call 'plastic details' of horrible things they saw in terrorist attacks. It's very hard because it puts us in the scene, even though we weren't there.

Most people here are volunteers. They come for four hours a week – but stay longer. When you treat people over the phone for long periods of time, you develop a therapeutic relationship. You become attached to your patients and experience their emotional moods. When they're happy, you feel happy.

Do you go through the same mood, or distance yourself so you can deal with your callers' unique problems?

If you can distance yourself, you're doing something wrong. But you must learn to realise where your boundaries finish and you're talking about their experience, not yours. Personally, I find survivor guilt one of the most difficult things to overcome because it's not rational. You survived and others didn't and you can't forget it. It's something you carry. It takes a lot of time, and the survivors have to decide at some point to go on living. We have people who we call the living dead. They're alive but they don't feel or act like it. One post-traumatic from the Lebanon War called up and said, 'We are the amputees of the soul. You can't see the limb that's missing.' That's what we are carrying. Many of them have insomnia, nightmares, flashbacks and avoidant behaviours – like not going on busses – or else they're over-involved with pictures of the dead, talking about them or doing memorial rituals for them.

Do you support traumatised soldiers who refuse to serve?

We don't take positions on any issue. We really don't care what you think the government should do or what we as a people should do and whether we are right or wrong. We're human beings caring for other human beings. We put aside our own beliefs and identify with suffering people.

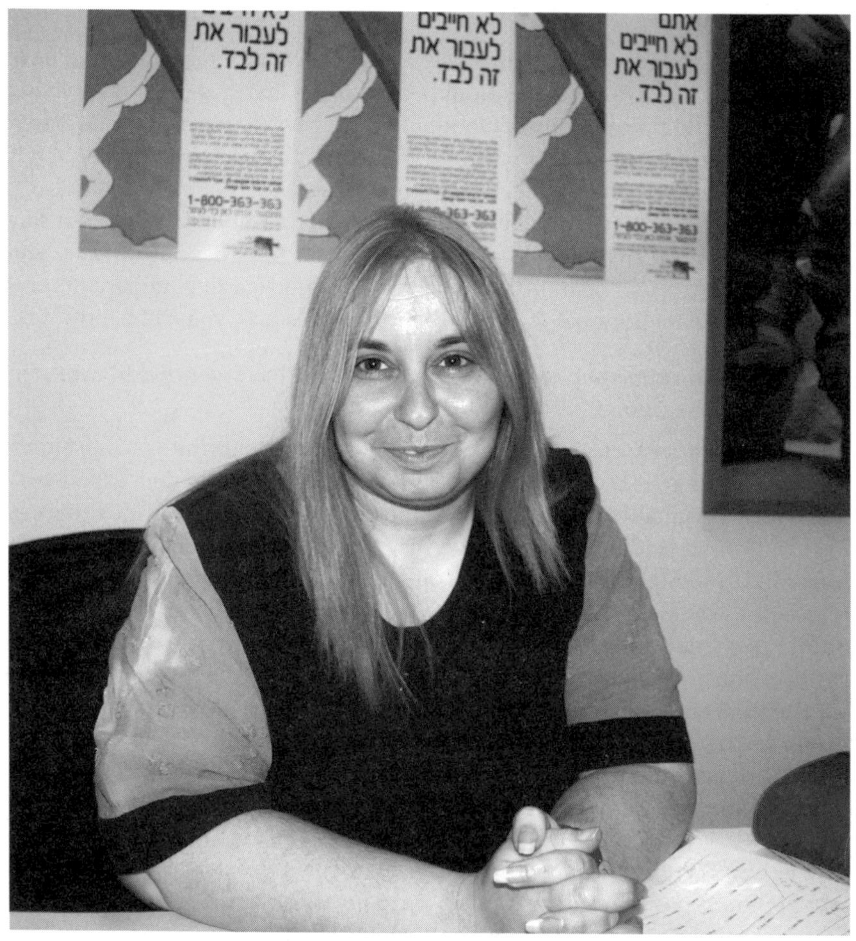

Sigal Haimov. *Photo by Arthur Neslen*

We don't talk to many Palestinians but there is someone who calls us every week. In October 2000, we talked to Arabs who lost their relatives in Sakhnin. That was a very frightening time for us as Jews. We felt that our neighbours were going to do something bad to us. Yet here, wearing the professional hat, you have to just care about what you can do for others.

Do you think that suffering and trauma might ultimately be the one thing that unites Jews and Arabs?

Yeah, if they can recognise it. What's happened is that the amount of pain has got so high that you can only concentrate on your own suffering. But I have faith in our resilience. I think that as a nation and as a people we've been through a lot in Israel and in the Holocaust and we've survived. We lead quite a normal life – not very normal – but an un-normal normal life, ok?

I lost someone close to me but I don't want to talk about it. There were no hotlines on this subject then. I think Israelis and Palestinians are both traumatised, but the issue we're dealing with is who's right and who's wrong. Who's to blame? Who started it? Who should stop it first? Like two children in kindergarten. Who should be punished? And then everything will be ok. We're not talking about suffering.

CLINT FINKELSTEIN

Where is your guard?

The cost of putting down the Intifada was uncomfortably high for the Israeli economy. Tourism collapsed and a booming economy tipped over into recession. During the first two years of fighting, the price was estimated at NIS 35 billion [£4.5 billion] or between 2.7 and 5 per cent of Israeli gross domestic product.[11] It was paid overwhelmingly by the Israeli poor. 'Clint Finkelstein' has an economic life that is part of the infrastructure of conflict. By night he works in Israel's flourishing security industry, guarding an establishment that has already been bombed. By day, he supervises the demolition of Arab properties in Jaffa that have been deemed to transgress municipal regulations. In common with London's East End or Manhattan's Lower East Side, Jaffa, a beautiful and historic port town, is being gentrified and sold off to the metropolitan middle classes. Jaffa residents claim that this 'cleansing'

11. Mossi Batok, 'Intifada has so far cost economy NIS 35 billion', *Ha'aretz*, 29 September 2002.

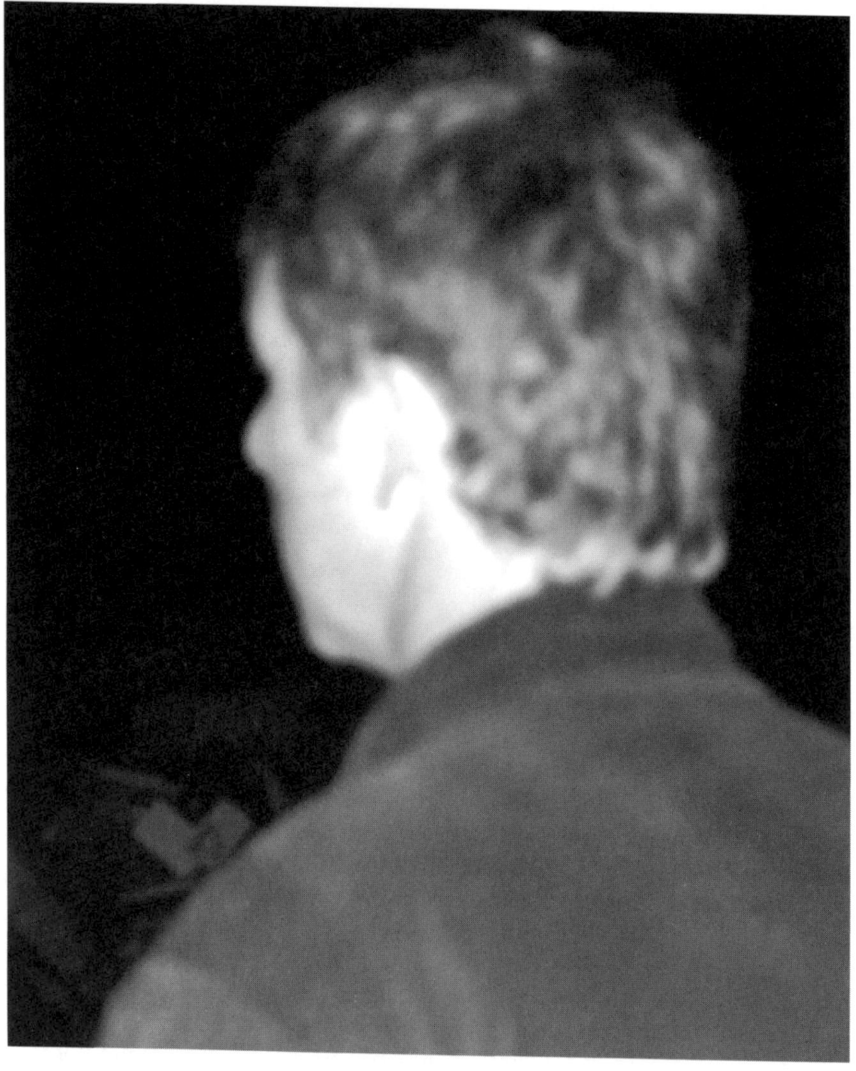

'Clint Finkelstein' wished to remain anonymous. *Photo by Arthur Neslen*

has an ethnic dimension.[12] Clint tries to steer clear of such controversies as he navigates his way through some of Israel's grittiest workplaces.

I don't look like a Jew but I'm proud to be Jewish. I think my ancestors were probably Vikings. I was born in Riga, the capital of Latvia in 1965 and we came to Israel three years later. My only memories of Riga are of one moment of snow and another in a summer resort. They're from pictures. My father was a photographer. He was a big Zionist and a strong man, a figure to worship. All his family were killed by the Nazis. He survived by joining the Russian army's Latvian division at the age of 17. He was wounded five times but he always went back to the front.

I'm a bit sensitive to issues about the Holocaust. There's a story in the Bible, where Eliyahu has a contest on Mount Carmel with the prophets of Baal.[13] He's laughing at them as they dance for three days, trying to make Baal burn their sacrifice. He says: 'Where is your guard? Maybe he's taking a nap.'

12. For centuries under Ottoman rule, Jaffa was a home for Muslims, Jews and Christians. As a merchant trading post, it was of far greater importance than neighbouring Tel Aviv. An outbreak of cholera in Jaffa and Zionist emigration began to alter the balance between the two towns. In the chaotic fighting of 1948, most Jaffan Jews upped sticks for Tel Aviv while the majority of wealthy Palestinians fled to Gaza or Beirut. Only the poorest of both communities stayed behind. After 1948, many new Mizrahi immigrants were settled in Jaffa but Arab refugees who came back were not allowed to return to their old homes. The most commonly held attitude in the new Israeli state was that Arab culture was inferior, primitive and in need of uprooting. The municipal committee extended this analysis to the architecture of Arab homes and began demolishing historic properties to build 'western' housing blocks in the 1950s and 1960s. Only homes in disrepair could be demolished but numerous bureaucratic obstacles were placed in the way of Arabs – or the Public Housing Corporation that owned much of their housing stock – from repairing the properties. When, out of desperation, residents built illegal extensions, developers were accused of paying contractors to damage their properties while knocking down the extensions so that the houses themselves could be demolished or sold off. Rubble from years of such demolitions was dumped into an Arab fishing spot/beach to create 'Jaffa slope'. In the 1990s a new generation of politicised and educated Israeli Arabs allied with progressive Jews from Tel Aviv to launch a campaign against what they perceived as a slow ethnic cleansing. With the beginning of the Intifada, the pace of gentrification slowed. Nonetheless, of 70,000 Jaffa residents today, fewer than 20,000 are Arabs. In 1948, 120,000 Arabs lived there.
13. Kings 18: 17–40. Elijah challenged 450 prophets of Baal and 400 prophets of Asherah to a contest on Mount Carmel to see which deity could ignite a sacrifice and provide rain to end a three-year drought. Each side made sacrifices to their God without building a fire. Elijah mocked Baal's inaction, saying, 'Either he is meditating, or he is busy, or he is on a journey, or perhaps he is sleeping and needs to be awakened?' Then he poured water over his sacrifice and it was consumed in flames. The prophets of Baal were executed by Elijah at Brook Rishon, God sent rain and the drought was ended.

Their guard?

Sorry, their God. Well, I am a small individual but I have to ask, where was God when all those people went to the gas chambers? Was he taking a nap? If He's that almighty, then I'm not religious.

I grew up in a mainly Mizrahi housing project in Bat Yam.[14] It was the sort of area where people trafficked drugs by daylight. Being a blond guy there, I had to fight to get respect. One time three guys cornered me and I had to take my belt off. When my father came home and saw how cut up my lip was, he said 'Enough is enough.' I started to learn karate after that.

Israeli men sometimes put out vibrations; they won't give you any space. They even hit women and it's getting worse. People aren't afraid of violence any more. When I was a teenager, the army was the place that turned boys into men. It was an amazing and shocking experience. In the West Bank, I tracked terrorists or people going to work. We'd go up the hill at night, and even with no moon you could see them for miles around, walking like small ants, one after the other, every night the same. I didn't blame them. They had to feed and clothe their children but I was hunting them down and they knew that if I caught them, they would be detained and probably lose their jobs.

Afterwards, I worked as a swimming instructor and lifeguard. It was great for a while. Every day was another girl and another conquest. I got into security 15 years ago when the manager of my pool asked me to work in the toughest club in Israel. The drugs problem has got a lot worse since then.[15] The biggest Ecstasy producers and dealers in the world are now Israeli.

Are there more gangs in clubs now?

Let's just say the Arabs are more bold. They're getting into clubs and after-parties that ten years ago they'd never even have thought about coming to. The selection now is heavier with all kinds of excuses (laughs) like: 'This is a

14. Bat Yam was established in 1926 as an orthodox Jewish neighbourhood in southern Tel Aviv. After Israel was established, mass migration swelled the population to 134,000 and it was awarded city status in 1958. Since the fall of the Soviet Union, it has become a mainly Russian-speaking suburb.
15. Chris Summers and Jennifer Quinn, 'Israel struggles to keep lid on crime', BBC News Online, 7 June 2004. Organised crime in Israel exploded during the Intifada. According to Gil Kleiman, the Israeli national police spokesman, 'There is no question that when (the Intifada) began in September 2000, a lot of police manpower and resources was diverted to saving lives from terrorism.' A former police chief, Asaf Heretz, claimed that $2.5 billion in 'dirty money' had been invested in Israel in recent years. The drugs industry was among the biggest beneficiaries. In the summer of 2004, a craze for 'hagikhat', a chemically synthesised version of the Somalian natural stimulant Khat ('hagi' means festive) swept Tel Aviv. Following a series of well-reported hagikhat casualties, including one death, the pill was outlawed.

closed party' or, 'It's not because you're an Arab, you just need an invitation.' He'll say, 'Well, the other girls don't have invitations.' So you go, 'Ok, I'm sorry but you have to come with a girl.' There are so many excuses. Even if someone looks Mizrahi, they're saying, 'You're too young, too old, too something' because there is a selector. I know it's illegal but it helps the business because people would be afraid to go to a place with cha-cha-cha'ing criminals, intimidating men or Arabs. You know, drinks, girls and our 'uncles',[16] as I call them, don't mix. I've worked in a few places and it's always the same. You see the problem every weekend with Arabs trying to grab girls' asses.

I started in this place just after it was bombed. One security guy told me how he didn't have time to draw his gun that night. He'd become suspicious when this guy refused to be searched. He walked off, came back and still wouldn't let him search him. So the guard pushed him forwards – but found himself flying backwards from the shock of the blast. Unfortunately, he'd pushed the bomber into the waitresses who were on a break outside, standing around smoking cigarettes. I don't know how he sleeps thinking, 'What if I'd pushed him to the right, not the left?' In my eyes he's a hero. But the bomb brought out the worst in the wounded people who came here afterwards demanding compensation.

How do you assess a crowd outside a club?

Mostly I'm scanning, and the second I see something wrong, I focus on it. If you've got a bomb strapped to your back, you'll be very focused, maybe with tunnel vision. You'll touch your clothing a lot because you think the whole world can see the bomb. Once, I stopped a Mizrahi who was walking suspiciously with his head turned to the right. He shouted in a good voice, 'Why do you think I'm a terrorist? I'm an Israelian!' I can hear if it's our uncles, because it's hard for them to speak good Hebrew.

Is your work supervising house demolitions in Jaffa more difficult?

It's more politically, nationally and religiously loaded. If someone hasn't invaded municipal property there are problems. I know someone who owns his land. It was registered under his ancestors' names by the Turks 300 years ago but we're denying him the ability to even build a shed for his goats on it (laughs). So he's getting pissed off. We are going to have to tear down a whole house he's built. Sometimes it looks illogical and stupid but it has deep roots because they're Arabs and you have to deal with that. There's violence. They're not going to attack the policeman who comes with me. They see me as the guy in charge.

16. 'bneidodaynu', lit. 'sons of uncles', is an oft-used Israeli slang reference to Arabs. While intended to be irreverent, many Arabs find it offensive and college-educated Israelis see it as primitive.

There's so much pressure when you tear down a whole building. You have social workers, family evacuations, you almost never feel good about it. Two hours in the field are like ten hours in the office. They've tried to stab me, run me over with a jeep, one guy even attacked me with a five-kilo hammer. Meanwhile, the cops just want to go for lunch.

Is it only Arab homes that get demolished in Jaffa?

Of course, they build illegally without permits. They could build legally if they gave the plans to the municipal committee for approval.

They say the committee never gives approval because it wants them out of Jaffa.

Maybe there's a policy like that but I'm just a small screw trying to do my job. Maybe the judges and courts are not fair to everyone (laughs). They are not.

When you know a family has nowhere to go to or their possessions will be locked up, it's tough. I saw a young guy and his pregnant wife crying. They'd added another room to his mother's place because it only had two rooms. Your heart sometimes tells you.... But all I can do is call the engineers. I didn't issue the warrant. I'm just the acrobat on a rope. It doesn't matter if you fall to the left or the right, you are going to fall and it will hurt you.

Do you see the developers as honourable, civic-minded people?

In Jaffa? No! But the land they're developing now was never settled. Near the harbour, it was all sand, dirt and garbage mountains that the Arabs made. Around Kedem and in Old Jaffa, you see more developers but it looks great. The Israelis developed it, not the Arabs. They throw their piss and sewage on to the street. They just don't care.

Jaffa residents believe that contractors are paid by developers to needlessly damage properties so that they can be knocked down as safety hazards. Have you seen that?

It happens everywhere. In Jaffa it's a little bit harder.

They also say that criminals and drug addicts are moved into the houses next door to them to make their lives so unbearable that they'll move out.

This is the private policy of companies, not the municipality. It can happen if they don't find another way. I've heard about it. The managers have to get things done. They want to get a road built so they extort as much money as they can for their shake (laughs). Maybe they know bad elements that can make this happen. People go there and tell them – I imagine – 'You're going to sign the contract, settle for this amount of money and leave.' Then they'll get their commission. If they're not strong, it's done. Even if they don't have the legal rights to the land, they'll come with the police. There is corruption everywhere.

How do you cope with it?

It's draining me and grinding me down mentally. Every day is a grey routine. I started off in the garbage department and I'm hoping to be transferred back there. It's unbelievably hard to hold down two jobs like this and get by with just four hours' sleep a night. My family is my one comfort in life and if you agonise every day about demolitions, you're going to come home pissed off and inflict your misery on your kids. I've had to fight all my life. A future without fighting would be amazing.

DINA PELEG

My little Holocaust

Perhaps no single event had a more profound effect on the psyche of Israeli Jews than the Holocaust. It became the stone on which the post-Independence Zionist narrative was carved, namely of an Israeli phoenix rising from the ashes of six million dead. The survivors of the Shoah were a shadow self of this vision, a shameful example of craven submission to many Israelis, and a haunting reminder of the potential consequences of military defeat. For decades, survivors, Diaspora Ashkenazim and 'weak' Israeli Jews were routinely dismissed as 'savonettes' or 'soap', an allusion to the bars the Nazis made from the melted fat of Jews in Auschwitz and Treblinka.[17] It was incumbent on Israeli citizens not to talk to their children, or anyone else, about the Holocaust. Many of the 1.25 million survivors who immigrated to the country thus lived with a black hole in their memories, even as they were rehoused in the homes of ethnically cleansed Palestinians who themselves formed a black hole in the country's collective memory. After America and France instituted Holocaust memorialisation, Yom Ha Shoah (Holocaust Memorial Day) began to be commemorated in Israel. The injunction 'Thou Shalt Not Remember' began to morph into 'Thou Shalt Not Forget'.[18] Today, Israeli children are routinely taken on school trips to concentration camps, the subject is endlessly discussed in the nation's media, and used as both shield and battering ram in international diplomacy. Zionism has belatedly discovered that victimhood can be

17. Warschawski, *On the Border*, pp. 154–5. Warschawski's description of hearing the 'savonette' slur is apropos. '"Blasphemous" was the word that stuck in my mind the first time I heard the expression. I remember my whole body trembling as if my mother had been called a whore or someone had urinated in front of the tabernacle of the synagogue. It was absolutely terrible yet commonplace in the Israel of the 1960s, where weakness was considered a flaw… I was dealing with Jews like myself who seemed to have suddenly donned the cassocks of inquisition priests, Cossak tunics or SS uniforms.'
18. Idith Zertal, 'Memory without Rememberers, Israeli collective memory of the Holocaust', Hebrew University of Jerusalem. From a talk given at 'Crossing Borders:

Dina Peleg. *Photo by Arthur Neslen*

a weapon as well as a weakness. For survivors like Dina Peleg, however, it remains an arena of loss, denigration and stigma.

I was born into a rich Parisian family of non-believing Jews in 1933. They were more French than the French. My father was a close friend of Leon Blum[19] and they worked together as lawyers. When the community asked him to give legal help to the German refugees who were arriving during the 1930s, he said 'of course – but send the musicians'. Everything was about music with my father. Of course, the refugees came to him every week.

Nobody knew what was going to happen with the Germans. We got out of Paris before they arrived but my father decided to go back. I learned later that he was arrested on 12 December 1941. The Gestapo made a list of the most important and wealthy Parisian Jews and they disappeared. As a girl, no-one told me. With my brother and my grandparents, we travelled to Perpignon, near the Pyrenees, but Spain wouldn't let us in, even though my grandparents had Spanish passports. We were hungry all the time.

Jews had been ordered to register with the authorities and my mother – who thought the French would never give us up to the Germans – gave them all our names. But many French people admired Pétain because of his history in World War I and we were put on a list for deportation. By the time the big arrests began in July '42, we'd moved to a farm near Chateau Rouge. We pretended we were Protestants and went to the church every Sunday. It was horrible.

One day, my mother received word that we were about to be arrested. I was at school so she left a message with the guard outside saying 'don't come back to the house. Go to the farm.' She took my brother there. A French policeman lied to the Germans that they were his wife and child. When I got out at six o' clock, I cycled eight kilometres to the town's checkpoint. I didn't have papers but I didn't look Jewish so they let me through. I wasn't afraid. For me it was like a game. We were always running away whenever something happened.

Walter Benjamin conference' in Barcelona, 25–27 September 2000, reported by Esther Leslie.

19. Leon Blum was the first socialist – and Jewish – premier of France, between May 1936 and June 1937. A brilliant law student, he was politicised by the Dreyfus Affair and became a Socialist MP in 1919. Blum united Socialists, radicals and Communists in an electoral alliance called the Popular Front, which won power in 1936. Blum's government introduced collective bargaining, a 40-hour working week, paid vacations, nationalisation, and other reforms. But he refused to support anti-fascist forces in Spain and French business leaders campaigned against him under the slogan 'Better Hitler than Blum'. He was forced from office in 1937 and deported to a concentration camp by the Vichy government in 1942. He survived and went on to become an international statesman.

My grandfather was blind and he knew he was making it difficult for us to be mobile, so one night in December '42, he got out of his bed and just lay on the floor for three days until he died. It was suicide.

The war was hard on my mother. When it finished, she was in a difficult spiritual situation so she went back to the farm and sent us to boarding school in Versailles. My father's money had been stolen from the apartment. Whenever I asked about my father, she'd say, 'Wait 'til the war is over. You'll find out then.' I was so sure that he'd be waiting for me at the boarding school station that when I arrived, I jumped out of the train and ran along the platform looking for him. The people I was with ran after me, shouting 'don't be foolish, he died a long time ago'. I passed out. When I awoke, I had amnesia. My migraine and insomnia problems started then. I used to run away from the boarding school to the town because it was the only thing I knew how to do. I felt free there. I had nowhere else to go. The next year, they threw me out of school and my mother took me back in.

For me, the Holocaust – my little Holocaust – began after the war. My brother and I weren't as close as before. He seemed Jewish, he was older and as a boy, it was more difficult for him. I felt lonelier than I can say. We became prisoners of the sleeping pills we took and my brother never escaped them. We were still getting anti-Semitism from the French but I didn't even know what Pesach or Yom Kippur was.

I went to the Communist party but I also wanted to feel Jewish. I wanted to begin a new life and forget about what happened before. A classmate in my school introduced me to Hashomer Ha'tzair and I decided to come to Israel when I was 16. Nobody in the group was talking about what happened to us in those days. It was a complete taboo until we were in our 50s and 60s. We all came from orphan homes and most of us had no parents at all. By the time we arrived at a kibbutz in '53, I was the group's leader and most of us were in a bad way. The worst thing was that no-one thought that we'd suffered. We weren't survivors. We hadn't been in the camps. We were the lucky ones, nothing happened to us.

Around this time, Ben Gurion said that Europe's Jews 'went to their deaths like sheep'. It was the way of thinking in Israel. People who were in any way connected with the Holocaust were embarrassed to talk about it. You were like a person with a cold. Ben Gurion would say, 'With half a million Jews we fight 200 million Arabs but these people did nothing!' The only people they liked here were the partisans or the ones who got bashed standing up to the Germans. They didn't understand. When a father has children, he has to take care of them. He can't join the partisans. And the partisans of the Warsaw ghetto were people who knew they were going to die. Israel made survivors feel they had to prove they were not weak or cowardly all the time.

What happened to us was so terrible that we tried not to think about it. When I thought about my father, I felt like an opium taker who'd had her supply cut off forever. It was very human. Two people in my group committed suicide and a lot of others tried. We'd missed out on our childhoods, and we had horrible stories which followed us all our lives. Most of the kibbutzniks were born in Israel or the USA and didn't understand. We thought that there was something wrong with us and we felt it was shameful to speak out. We already felt guilty for the deaths of our parents and now we were told that only weak people were talking.

Ben Gurion said 'the better part of our people was the first to be exterminated'.[20] *Was there a sense that only the dead were real, worthy victims?*

When Ben Gurion was asked to give money to a French Jewish orphanage for blankets, he replied, 'They will receive blankets when they come to Israel.' That was the atmosphere. If we had at least been aware of our suffering maybe we could have fought it. But our ignorance made us weak. I never spoke to my children about the Holocaust. In 1980, I left the kibbutz and went to the Negev after someone very close to me committed suicide.

The first Israeli generation were afraid to approach the Holocaust. Everyone had lost someone and they needed distance. But time passed and the next generation began to talk and write about it. Then you had the Yom Kippur War and although we won, Israel's psychology changed again. People realised that we could lose a war and it would be the end. Still, I heard a woman on the radio a few years ago saying, 'All the people who were in the Holocaust, I hate them!' The journalist should have told her to shut up. There were people of the Holocaust listening to that show. Why did they have to hear that?

How do you think the Holocaust affects the Israeli psyche today?

I think you have two types of Holocaust survivor: those who say it must not happen again and those who are afraid to lose their human face. During the Holocaust, people lost their human faces. Terrible things were done to them. Afterwards they were not the same.

How did you feel about the Israeli soldiers who made a Palestinian violinist play for them at a checkpoint?

Horrible, horrible, horrible. It's exactly what I'm saying. This war began from the day we came to a country that was not ours. We became soldiers against people weaker than us. They lost their human faces because now we were the strong ones. I feel terrible about it. A journalist recently said that 20 per cent of soldiers

20. Zertal, 'Memory without Rememberers?'

have been brought up to hate Arabs. I don't try to defend them when they shoot children in Gaza but don't ever forget that soldiers are going to jail here because they refuse to do it. I don't know if Palestinians can say the same.

In '67, a lot of people went to Gaza but I knew we had to get out. I am afraid to be among people who hate me because I am Jewish. But it's not the same as the Holocaust. Begin always equated the two but I think the Holocaust is the Holocaust and now is now. Some Israelis confuse the situation and try to confuse other people. You can understand why Jewish people feel a little paranoid.

Can you tell me more about the people who committed suicide?

One of the more important boys in our group shot himself in the head. Everyone admired him and he was always helpful and responsible. He would do anything for others but he lost both his parents. Ultimately, he lost himself. Another girl left the kibbutz and committed suicide afterwards. Her story was unimaginable, really. You couldn't understand how someone could go on living with that. Another two of my best friends – who were sisters – also committed suicide. We always felt there was something wrong with us. Why were we weak? Why didn't we have the energy to do things? I have so much admiration for people who are happy.

You know my brother also committed suicide? He was a captain on a boat in the French army. He was one of the most intelligent people I ever knew but you couldn't speak to him about our father or the Holocaust. When something like that happens to you, you are left without skin. Everyday problems take on the proportions of what happened to you then. I remember how when my grandfather died, I wanted to die. I felt so alone and I didn't understand why nobody loved me or wanted me. My father left me and my mother left me and I was angry with them all. Even today, many people think that it's weak to talk about this. I don't think it is a weakness.

7
The Forgiven and the Forgotten

The Hebrew language is unique in having the same word for both blame and guilt, 'ashm*a*'. To blame a person is to push guilt upon them. Equally, to question a feeling of guilt is to deny responsibility. Possibly the only group in Israeli society who are officially exempted from this blame game are the families of the Holocaust, war and Intifada dead. Yet for this they too pay a price. In a society where the highest moral value is imbued on those who have suffered most for the nation, the families of the dead, like the dead themselves, are idealised representatives of the national narrative. But they still must deal with issues from 'survivor guilt' to understanding the meaning of their loss in an unbearably loaded context.

One legacy of a permanent war society is a discomfort with losses that cannot easily be transformed into a redoubled determination to soldier on. Traumatic disorders do not generally become evident until a crisis has passed. Israel's paradigm was perhaps set in its eventual acceptance of the Holocaust as a dual signifier of both eternal persecution and national resurrection. The dead, either way, were claimed for off-stage parts in a grand epic while survivors often suffered in silence.

Today, the families who lost loved ones during the Intifada can similarly be revered as martyrs and overlooked as morale-sapping casualties of war, depending on the expediencies of the day. The private wounds they nurse, like their losses, belong also to the national story. They can be forever forgiven for the sacrifices they have made, and at the same time utterly forgotten in the dust of an Israel racing to face its next national crisis.

DANIELLA KITAIN

You can't weigh pain

In the early 1970s a group of idealistic Israeli Jews and Arabs decided to establish a communal village as an experiment in co-existence. Today 40 families, 20 Jewish, 20 Arab, live in Neve Shalom – Wahat al-Salaam ('Oasis of Peace') on a scenic hilltop between Jerusalem and Tel Aviv. Three hundred children from nearby Jewish and Arab villages attend what is the only mixed and bilingual Jewish–Arab school in Israel. By most reckonings, the village has been an all too rare Middle East success story. In 1985, Daniella Kitain moved to the commune with her family. In 1997, her 21-year-old son Tom died along with 73 other Israeli soldiers in a helicopter crash as his unit travelled to Lebanon. Tom had been one of the commune's first children, and the Kitain family wanted to build a memorial for him. However, many of the village's Arab residents opposed the move, arguing that honouring Tom would also mean honouring his participation in the brutal occupation of a fellow Arab country. The community divided on the issue and the final compromise – a plaque affixed high on a wire mesh basketball court – left a bitter aftertaste for the Kitains. The mottled blue plaque reads: 'In memory of our Tom Kitain, a child of peace who was killed at war.'

So I live in Neve Shalom. My parents came here from Poland in '36 and I was born in Jerusalem eleven years later. It was a stormy time. There was a siege around the city and water was cut off. I remember growing up in a divided town, the capital of Israel in a spiritual sense but still a very small place. People used to say the best thing about Jerusalem was the road to Tel Aviv, but I liked it then. As a youngster, I never came into contact with Arabs. My parents were left-wing but they didn't know any Palestinians. They'd tell us about good Arabs but also about the ones who wanted to throw us into the sea.

After I graduated from high school, I joined Hashomer Ha'tzair and went to live on a kibbutz near Be'ersheva. Between '65 and '67, I served in the army. After that, I was a kibbutznik until '85, when we moved to Neve Shalom. My husband had heard about it through the kibbutz high school where he worked as a principal, and it sounded interesting. We were at a stage in our lives where we thought we'd try something new. It was a chance to put our theories about co-existence into practice.

We were Neve Shalom's twelfth or thirteenth family and we were welcomed instantly. I brought up four children here. Tom was the eldest. In the beginning, the kids didn't like it so much as there weren't many other children but they

Daniella Kitain under the plaque commemorating her dead son at Neve Shalom's basketball court. *Photo by Arthur Neslen*

found ways to be happy over the years. It was a very ordinary life filled with the feeling that we were doing something unique.

After many years, I think the situation between Arabs and Jews here is not good. There hasn't been enough dialogue and, looking back, I can say there wasn't enough dialogue in the beginning either. I know that I'm part of this situation because I haven't been interested in dialogue about these things. It's too difficult for me. It's too painful. I think in the past when I was more involved, we had the illusion that we agreed about things that we didn't really discuss deeply enough.

Did you hear the reports last year that shouts of 'death to the Arabs' and 'death to the Jews' were heard in the village school's playground?[1]

About 85 per cent of pupils at our school aren't from the village. There's been a successful attempt to get them to talk about the situation's complexities. But of course we're naturally influenced by the outside society. I think if a phenomenon like that happened, it would be taken care of. But I'm not sure.

Are there more inspiring success stories you would point to?

Let's skip that question. I'm not the best person to talk to about it.

Ok, Edward Alexander recently wrote that Jews wanting to commemorate Independence Day here had to leave the village or else celebrate quietly so that Arab kibbutzniks wouldn't hear them. He said, 'It recalls the stereotypical, trembling ghetto Jew that Zionism was to supplant'.[2] *Is that how you see yourself?*

I've never been to a ghetto so I don't know. I think that sometimes we are over-sensitive to the Palestinians and under-sensitive to ourselves. It's because the Jewish population tends to be from the radical left, which blames Israel for the situation. They say that because we are the majority, what happens to Palestinians is always our fault. Many people here think like that. I agree that it's putting ourselves down.

1. 'Jewish–Arab co-existence groups tested during unrest', Jewish Telegraphic Agency, 11 April 2004.
2. Edward Alexander, 'No, an exercise in Jewish self-abasement', *Middle East Quarterly*, vol. V, no. 4, December 1998. '"If I organize an evening of song, I am careful not to choose nationalistic songs," explains Jewish resident Etti Edlund. No Israeli flags are displayed in classrooms in the village school. When the Arab residents objected to the celebration of Israeli Independence Day in Neve Shalom, the town's Jews agreed to go "to Jerusalem or Tel Aviv to partake in the nationwide celebration". When they returned to Neve Shalom later that night, Arab resident (now mayor) Rayek Rizek recalls, "they made a campfire – out where they couldn't be heard".' Alexander also quotes Danielle Kitain as saying, '"the symbol of the tragedy of the Palestinian people [is that] people who I like… defend acts of terrorism or express understanding for such acts"'.

We might have more power but saying that Palestinians bear no responsibility reduces them to the level of powerless victims. They, as a people, share responsibility for the fact that peace was somewhere quite close but it slipped away. It's no coincidence that this type of government was elected. We are all victims. Israel has more power but I am still a victim, Tom was a victim. So you can maybe talk about who is more moral, it doesn't matter. You can't weigh pain.

What sort of person was Tom?

He was very young, a nice, lovable, popular boy with lots of potential. He was a good listener, very responsible, a really good kid. Tom was never very involved in Neve Shalom. In fact he was the first to leave the village, when he went to a kibbutz high school. It's interesting that he used to say 'I can't see myself ten years from now.'

Tom felt it was his duty to join the army. The truth is he didn't see much beyond it. Maybe he had plans but he never told us. He didn't want to be in a combat unit but that's where they took him. I think he wanted to influence things, but everything I say about him is already my interpretation. He's not saying it. I think he chose to be in Lebanon rather than the territories because he would face a guerrilla army there, with less danger of killing civilians. But he was already starting to think that it was important for Israel to stay in Lebanon.

The night he died, they were supposed to fly over the border but someone got mixed up and two helicopters crashed.[3] We heard about it on television. I kept saying 'No, it's not his helicopter, they were going somewhere else.' At about 2am, they came to tell us, officially. The military is very organised in this way and they usually tell the families before the media but this time it was shown on the news first.

The weeks that followed are very hard to describe. It was such a difficult process and it lasted years. I've never really been religious but I always had some kind of faith. I am a believer in the sense that I think we're here for a reason and maybe our goal in life is to find it. Maybe it was easier for me because I also believe that Tom is still here, in a way. At least I don't think he's vanished. Somewhere, some essence of his is still here. I don't say it as a thought, it's something that I feel and it supports me.

I'm very aware that memories fade. This is how the human mind works. It becomes hard to remember the voice or the movements and photos don't help really. So I try to remember his essence, and keep it with me. I guess everyone

3. 'Military helicopters collide in Israel, killing scores', CNN.com, 4 February 1997. The crash was caused when two military transport helicopters ferrying elite troops to southern Lebanon collided in fog and heavy rain. Both aircraft were carrying ammunition, and explosions continued at the site of the disaster for several hours afterwards. There were no survivors and the incident was – and remains – the worst military air disaster in Israel's history.

finds their own path. My husband goes to schools and talks about it. The children have different ways.

I don't feel anger at the military for what happened. Afterwards some parents said 'this was wrong, that was wrong', always something. In any system you can find things wrong but on the whole it was the mistake of a pilot and he paid the price like everyone else. He was killed. You can't even be angry with him. I felt angry maybe with the government for starting the war and keeping it going but not the military. For me, Tom was part of the military.

What was the reaction of people in Neve Shalom when he died?

In the beginning, they were very much with us and then it was a very difficult time. Their reaction was very hurtful. Now I'm on the other side, maybe. But I don't get involved too much in the community. That's my way of keeping myself. To talk about it is not good for me, so I don't want to get into the memorial plaque issue. Let's say I learned a lot from the experience.

Why did you decide to stay here?

I didn't so much decide to stay. It's more that I didn't decide to leave. I was here when Tom was in the army. We built a house in the village and the graveyard is wonderful, really a beautiful place. In this sense, I'm luckier than the Jerusalem people whose cemetery looks like a factory for dead people. I don't have any energy to start a new life somewhere and I have many good friends here who helped me a lot. It's true that I feel less connected to the Neve Shalom idea in its simplified form. Living together doesn't mean anything, it's how you live together. I was disappointed but not enough to become active in trying to change it. My reaction was: 'So, the world isn't perfect. It's not my responsibility to make it perfect.' This place is good for me because of the nature, the view and our home.

If you could go back to the 'you' arriving here 20 years ago, what advice would you give yourself?

I don't want to go back in time. I'm in another place now and I've learned a lot from being here. I developed my abilities and it was a good move to get out of the kibbutz. I was stagnating there. It was the same life and work but with few possibilities to grow. It's hard. It's like asking in history 'what if?' but you can't. I don't know.

HAIM WEINGARTEN

The soul is in the blood

At the scene of every Palestinian attack in Israel, the sight of yellow-vested, bearded medics combing the wreckage for survivors and body parts has become commonplace. As well as helping the living, volunteers from Zaka reassemble the missing limbs of the dead for religious burial. The group's first action was in 1989 when a Palestinian commandeered a bus heading from Tel Aviv to Jerusalem and drove it into a ditch, killing 16 people.[4] In 1995, Zaka was launched in its more recognisable form by Rabbi Yehuda Meshi Zahav. Zahav had previously been a minor irritant to secular Israelis because of his role as spokesman for the Eida Haredit, a religious non-Zionist organisation. By Independence Day 2003, he had been brought into the mainstream fold to the extent that he was honoured at an official state ceremony with the lighting of a torch. These days, many Zaka volunteers undergo Foreign Ministry training to prepare them for interviews with the international press.[5] Haim Weingarten is Zaka's co-ordinator, and his body is bedecked in buzzers, bleepers and mobile phones that erupt intermittently throughout the interview in response to traffic accidents. A slight and gravely focused man, he smiled as he pointed them out to me. 'That's why I'm so full,' he said.

I'm 33, I don't look it but it's true. My family is fourth-generation Jerusalemite but after that it starts to get a bit Russian. I was raised in an ultra-orthodox neighbourhood on the stories of righteous men, Hasidic tales of the Karlins, Rabbi Shach and Rev Steipler. I went to a Haredi yeshiva until I was 22, when I got married. I then had three children and worked in my father's supermarket for two years. I had my own supermarket for ten years after that but it closed two months ago because of the economy. Now, I send out the Zaka bike unit's emergency response teams.

Zaka was founded after a terrorist attack on a bus in Tel Aviv. There'd been stabbings before but it was the first incident with many casualties. People went to help but it was total chaos. One guy found a leg and – because you've got to observe the path – he put it in his car boot and went back to help. In all the confusion, he forgot about it and drove home. The next day he went to the market, opened his car boot and there was the leg! At that point, we decided we needed a body to deal with the bodies. Today, we have over a thousand volunteers and more than a hundred bikes.

4. 'Volunteers collect body parts after bombing', AP, 23 May 2002.
5. Nissan Ratzlav-Katz, 'True benevolence', National Review Online, 21 August 2003.

Haim Weingarten. *Photo by Arthur Neslen*

It says in Genesis that man is born in the image of God. The emphasis is on man – not Jew or Arab – so we treat every body, including the terrorist's, with respect, however difficult that may be. It's important to bury every drop of blood respectfully and completely. A man should know that he will have all his parts – his arms, his legs, his blood – when he goes to rest. It says in the Book that when the soul leaves the body it is in the blood. The soul is in the blood. I believe in the Messiah and the resurrection of the dead, and when I'm resurrected I want to have all my parts.

Zaka is made up of religious and secular Jews and Arabs. Our initials stand for 'identification of victims of catastrophe' but we volunteers say they stand for 'ingathering of brothers'. There are women and secular people in the rescue unit but it's a Halachic problem in the true service because a woman is not allowed to treat a man. Ninety per cent of the true service is religious. To see a baby without a head is very difficult. Only a believing Jew has the inner strength to deal with the horror. If someone volunteers, we first bring them to clean the dead bodies and see if they can stand it. Then we put them through police and criminal evidence courses so that they won't destroy evidence.

I myself am a Magen David Adom paramedic[6] but I wear the Zaka yellow strip under my red vest and turn it inside out when I need to. Magen David Adom charges $100 when they arrive at a site and $200 if treatment is needed. Zaka does not charge. We are funded purely by donations from groups like the Jewish Agency. We won't approach the Knesset because we don't want to be a burden on the state of Israel.

Before I got involved in Zaka, I couldn't sleep if I saw a man having an epileptic fit. At my first Zaka incident – a man who'd murdered his wife – I waited until they took the wife out before I mopped up the blood. Even then, I couldn't sleep for a week. Little by little I got into it. The explosion in Sbarro[7] was my first real incident. I arrived and saw a whole family dying. One little boy looked at me like 'Why are you treating me? Treat my father'. He didn't say it, his eyes said it, and it paralysed me. I knew his father was dead but I couldn't do anything. This boy looked into my eyes and, to this day, I can see his face staring at me.

We are constantly exposed to terror. There are often secondary explosives or terrorists at the scene of a crime. In Netanya, one of our volunteers was shot by terrorists. In Jerusalem, another volunteer was killed in a triple explosion. Everyone here knows a victim of terror. I personally volunteered for Zaka six

6. Magen David Adom (Red Star of David) is the Israeli equivalent of the Red Cross.
7. The explosion in the Sbarro pizzeria killed 15 diners, including several children, and injured another 130. It was the first major suicide bombing in Jerusalem of the Second Intifada. Five members of one religious family died in the blast, as did Malki Roth (see p. 205).

years ago, after my uncle was murdered in a terrorist ambush in Pisgat Ze'ev on the border of the Green Line. They shot him because he was a Jew. I saw how the Zaka people treated him afterwards and as I stood by his body, I said, 'I'm going to start doing this work for Zaka'.

Is Zaka's work a way for traumatised people to put themselves back together?

I think the reverse. At the scene of a murder, I see people going through what I went through and it puts me back into it. So I take a lot of holidays, and we receive trauma counselling. The religious Jews didn't accept its importance at first but when we started to talk to the psychologist, unexpected things came up. Many of us had had similar experiences like getting up in the middle of the night to check that our children were alive. If they were sleeping in strange positions, we might rearrange their limbs. We opened up a little and now every month we talk and it lightens us.

Recently, I had a dream that I haven't even told my wife about. I was driving towards a terror explosion and when I got there, I saw a man without a leg. Suddenly there was another explosion and I was without two legs. I woke up and screamed. I was sleepwalking. My wife said 'what's the matter with you?' I said nothing and went back to sleep. It was three or four days after an incident on Rehov Aza where they found a secondary device that hadn't blown up. It really bothered me because I thought, 'What if it had gone off?' There is always this fear but still we go. Why, I don't know.

On the anniversary of the attack on the French Hill, some TV people wanted to reunite our crew with the survivors on a live broadcast. When I saw the people there without hands and legs, it gave me palpitations. It took me back to the event and I had to try very hard to disconnect. I wish I could keep in touch with these crippled people but I can't. The worst incident for us was the bombing of the Number 2 bus in Jerusalem's Prophet Samuel neighbourhood. The bus was filled with religious people who we knew. When we arrived, to my shock, I saw a neighbour crying out 'Haim, Help me!' I got out the respirator and first-aid kit but he just grabbed my hand. I felt it slowly leaving me and then it fell and went limp. I felt a man I knew die in my hands. A doctor arrived and said, 'Leave it, there is nothing to be done.' I didn't continue treating. I went home even though there was lots of Zaka work to do.

Was it more painful than the loss of your uncle?

That was something else. It's much harder but it's just something else. Two kinds of difficulty: heaven and earth, you can't compare them. I am not resigned to the death of my uncle. I see my children and I think of him. Every family event, he's not there. They say that the dead man is forgotten from the heart so at every family event we talk about him. The most important religious value for me is kindness. I have seen so much terror and destruction but if you came and told me you'd seen a terrorist who was a little boy, I couldn't kill him.

I try very hard not to bring my activities home. If I told my wife about my Zaka work she wouldn't sleep at night. After one incident at Mt Scopus, the moment I got home, my daughter complained that her sister had stolen her dolly. I said, 'What do you mean she took your dolly? Say thank you that you're alive!' Then I got a grip of myself. My daughters live with it. They know what their father does and they're proud of me. I worry all the time about what might happen to them. If I know about a terrorist warning in town, I won't let my family go out. It's like, if my child gets on a window, I know what happens after the window. I know what it looks like and it scares me. Similarly, if I had a house with a balcony and every day my children went out on to it and fell, would I not put up a fence, even if it obscured the view for my neighbours? Children are being murdered on their way to school. We have to stop it. I know the security fence divides people from their homes but it's not a political issue. It's a state of emergency. Arafat preferred murdering children to making peace so there is no-one to talk to.

Do you see any parallels between this Intifada and Jewish persecutions of the past?

Definitely! Anti-Semitism today is mostly a Muslim phenomenon but down through the generations, we read about suffering and persecution and this is part of it. I still can't believe that during the Holocaust, Jews stood in line for furnaces. The Jewish people suffer because we are Jewish. It's not a matter of faith or fairy stories. You see it with your own eyes. In France, they desecrate graves not because of Israel but because they are Jewish. I think an Israeli is a Jew, it's the same thing. Religion ties us to this state. If I had no religion, I could live in Argentina, what would it matter? If Zaka asked me to go to Brooklyn, I'd do it but our religion has A, B and Cs and one of them is to settle the land of Israel.

Would you say that since starting this work, you've become more whole as a person?

It's divided in two. Saving lives gives me a feeling of satisfaction I've never experienced before. To revive people and bring them back to their families gives an elation of a very special kind. When the police arrive, I see them running away, they can't handle it. I feel that I'm doing something very holy. I feel wholeheartedly that I'm doing something to raise my uncle's spirit to heaven.

RONI HIRSCHENSON

Two graves

When Roni Hirschenson's son Amir was killed in a suicide bombing in 1995, he joined the newly formed Families Forum, an organisation of bereaved Palestinians and Israelis working towards reconciliation. The group supported Roni when his second son, Elad, subsequently committed suicide. Today the Forum has more than 500 members, split evenly between the two communities.

I'm 62 years old, born in Jerusalem and married here when I was 21. I had five children; three are still with us, two are not. Amir was 19 when he was killed in 1995, and my youngest son, Elad, committed suicide in October 2000. Bereavement didn't change my mind, it sharpened it. I always knew that between the Jordan River and the Mediterranean there were two peoples – Israeli and Palestinian – and that we'd have to compromise on our dreams to live together. I used to own a garage workshop in Jerusalem, but in 1995 I helped found the Families Forum.

Amir volunteered for the paratroops, three months after he joined the army. He was a good, generous person, very close to his brother. He also believed in two states for two peoples but he was proud to be in the army. He wanted to be an architect. I was at my workshop when I heard about the attack that killed him at 10am on Sunday, 21 January 1995.[8] It was on the news that a suicide bomber blew himself up among a group of soldiers at Beit Lid junction. I knew Amir was staying at another base so I thought he was safe. I didn't know that he'd been sent to the junction to guard against terrorists. He wasn't hurt by the first explosion but when he went to help his friends, another suicide bomber blew himself up, and he found his death.

My son Elad called to say that three army officers and a doctor were at the house at 2pm, and I realised then what had happened. People were coming to see us, our friends, people we knew, people we didn't know, they were all coming and the *shiva*[9] was starting. It was a carousel of emotions. You don't really know what is going on in such a situation, you know only one thing:

8. On 22 January 1995, 21 people, mostly soldiers, were killed in a double suicide attack on a bus stop at Beit Lid junction. Islamic Jihad claimed responsibility. Fathi Shiqaqi, the group's leader, was assassinated by Israeli agents in Malta later that year.
9. The *shiva* is the traditional mourning period in orthodox Judaism, in which TVs and radios are turned off and mirrors covered for seven days.

Roni Hirschenson. *Photo by Arthur Neslen*

that something very bad has happened to you and your life will never be the same.

The funeral was very hard. People lead you there but it's not real. It's like living in a nightmare. You don't believe what you see. Some ministers from the government came, the mayor came. I don't remember what they said. You can't mentally prepare yourself for losing a young son or brother. The pain is indescribable and you live with it every day. I know some people feel guilt after these kinds of tragedies, but it leads you nowhere. Looking for a reason why it didn't happen to someone else is a dead-end thought. I try to accept it for what it was, but I can't.

Elad was also a soldier. The last words he wrote were that he couldn't stand the pain of the loss of his brother and that life was useless when you have lost your closest one like this. There were no warning signs that he was depressed and you can never know what is in a 19-year-old's head. He wasn't very open. We asked him many times what he was feeling about Amir's death. He'd say, 'You will never understand our relationship so there's no point in my explaining it to you.' We thought that maybe when he grew up it would be easier for him to talk about it. He was very sensitive.

His best friend David was the first soldier to be killed in this Intifada. He was guiding a convoy of settlers going towards Netzarim in the Gaza Strip when Hamas ambushed and killed him. Three weeks later, Elad killed himself.[10] The two of them were buried side by side. Two graves. I never wanted revenge. I told people: 'I lost my son, I didn't lose my head.' Unfortunately, I didn't lose my head. So what's the use of revenge? He's not going to come back. Of course I'm angry but my anger leads me to work harder for peace. I knew from the first moment I lost Amir that it was because we older people failed to resolve this conflict.

I don't want even my enemy to share this pain. No human being deserves this. I don't want to take another life because I can't avenge all the people. It wouldn't give me any comfort, just more pain. Those who killed my son killed themselves too, so what, their families? Their brothers? But you can skip the forgiveness. I wouldn't meet with the suicide bomber's family. The Families Forum is not about forgiveness. It's not like Christianity. I can reconcile without forgiving. I meet a lot of Palestinians and we share the same pain and ideas about grief. Our idea is that to end this conflict, we have to end the cycle of violence. That means understanding the other side's pain.

Even the suicide bomber and his family are victims of the conflict. Political leaders try to move it to a religious war but it's not. Terrorism is the ugliest way to fight for freedom. There is a non-violent path. But we Israelis also use

10. *Israel Wire*, 20 October 2000. Elad Hirschenson was found shot in the head with a gun at his side, according to IDF officials at his military base. He was 19.

unnecessary force so we are no more moral. People who live in dignity, without desperation or hunger, don't use terror. If their needs were met, the flames of terror would be lowered. And of course Israel will have its security only when both peoples live in peace.

At the Families Forum, we work towards reconciliation. Politicians signing contracts is not enough, we have to get through to each other's hearts and stop being frightened of one another. By showing that the Israelis and Palestinians who have paid the highest price of this conflict can sit together, we show what the leaders and politicians could do. We may not meet but we can still talk. In less than two years, we've facilitated about 800,000 phone calls between Israelis and Palestinians.

People who want to take part give us their numbers and we put them in touch. At first, they usually shout and blame each other for the situation. But later on they ask, 'Where do you live?', 'What do you do?' and 'What's happening in your life?' I've done it. They're normal conversations. We've had some negative reactions, especially on TV talk shows. They put us up against bereaved families who say: there's no point talking to the enemy, this conflict has been going on for a hundred years and it'll go on for another hundred, so we'd better be strong. Some of them think the shock of our loss drove us crazy, but I don't mind. I have my beliefs and I do what I think is right to try to end this conflict.

It's very difficult because you don't feel any progress in the peace process. But the solution is just behind the door. It only seems so far because people are not ready to give up their dreams and symbols. Myself, I say that between the Mediterranean and Jordan River, there are 3.5 million Palestinians. They won't disappear and they won't become Zionists. If we can't find a way to live together, both people can still kill each other for years and this circle won't end.

The Palestinians are more militant than us because we have our state, flags and symbols already and they do not. So we try not to raise any flags, or to compromise at least. The Palestinians suffer more every day from roadblocks and army closures so they want it to be shown everywhere, endlessly. We're trying to say: let's not compete over who is suffering more. It doesn't offer a solution. Everyone is suffering. For a farmer who can't get to his land because of the Wall, this is his biggest loss. For me, the loss of my sons is the biggest pain.

Do you think the Wall would have saved Amir's life?

Well, of course, it makes... But it creates so much desperation and anger that it increases the hate. If it was built along lines both sides agreed on, I'd support it. But even Sharon's disengagement plan won't bring peace without negotiations and agreement. If one settlement is evacuated, it will be good because it'll show that it's possible. But I tell you: I'll believe it when I see it.

The settlers are powerful here for the same reason that Hamas is very strong on the other side. People will rally around those who take the flag and scream, and governments will surrender. The settlers are very patient, they move by religion. They see the Bible as a contract between us and God. This is our land and here we stay. The passions of those people are so high that our universal moralities seem disorganised and weak.

In both societies, though, people want to listen to the bereaved families. I had the same ideas before but now they put a mike in my face and ask, 'What you got to say?' We use it and they hear us. Peace is a kind of embroidery. It's stitches and stitches. You have to prepare the hearts of people. You can't do it in one big go. You have to work very slowly. It doesn't come like justice.

ARNOLD ROTH

Part of the same flow

On 9 August 2001, Izzedine al-Masri, a 23-year-old from the West Bank village of Aqaba, walked into the Sbarro pizzeria in downtown Jerusalem and blew himself up, killing 15 Israelis, seven of them children. Hamas claimed the bombing as an act of revenge for an Israeli helicopter raid on Nablus the week before, which killed eight people, including two Hamas leaders and two children. In the aftermath of the pizzeria bombing, Israel closed down the PLO's Orient House headquarters in East Jerusalem and the Palestinian military and political headquarters in Abu Dis. They also blew up the Al-Masri family's home. The world's media covered the story intensively for two days, and then moved on. No such option was available for family members of the dead, such as Arnold Roth, an Australian-born lawyer. Roth decided to set up a foundation to honour the memory of his late daughter Malki. It offers help to Israeli families of all religions who are struggling to provide home care for disabled family members. The Malki Roth Foundation's website[11] has also campaigned around specific issues such as the Separation Wall or Security Barrier. I first met Arnold at The Hague where he had travelled to speak out against the International Court of Justice (ICJ)'s hearing into the legality of the demarcation. We met again in Jerusalem a few days before the third anniversary of Malki's death.

I was born in 1952, a child of Holocaust survivors who came to Melbourne after World War II. Almost every Jew of my parents' age was a Holocaust survivor with tattoos on their arms. Very few of my peers had parents. None had grandparents.

11. <http://www.kerenmalki.org>.

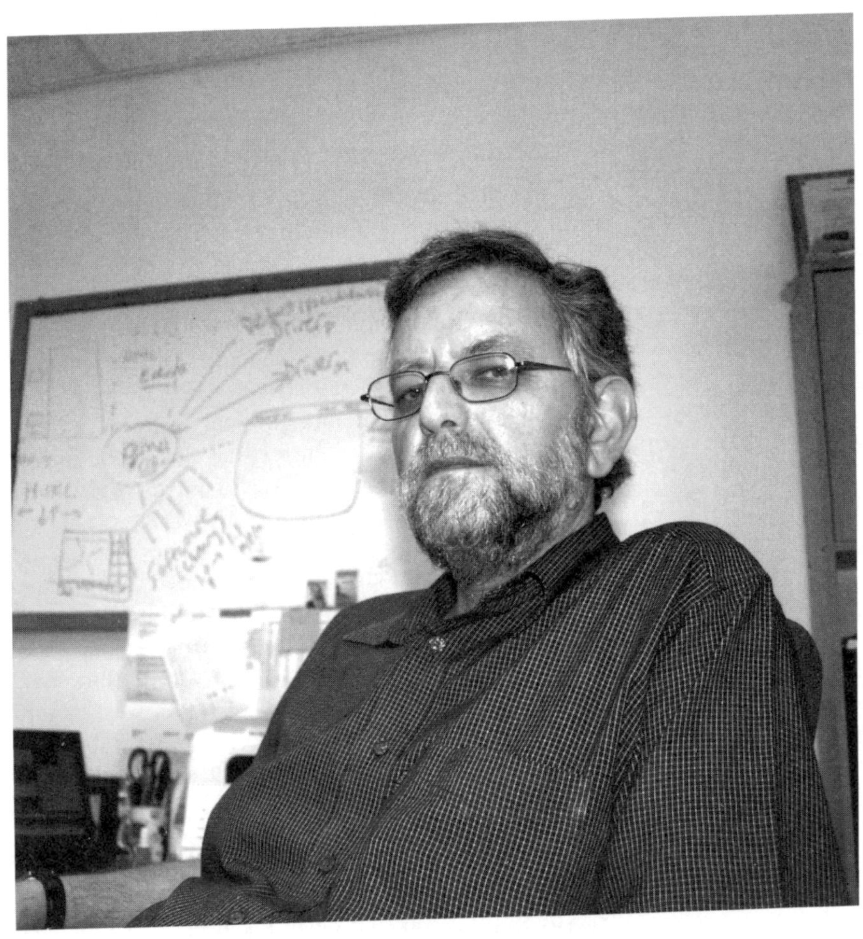

Arnold Roth. *Photo by Arthur Neslen*

As a child I remember my parents telling me not to associate with some anti-Semites from Eastern Europe in our neighbourhood. They looked at large swathes of humanity as anti-Semites and wanted me to do the same.

Israel was always very important in our lives. I remember, in June 1967, my parents and their friends were in a state of great anxiety. There was a real perceived existential threat to the state of Israel and the fear was palpable. But even more than the threat, I remember the euphoria afterwards and the parties to celebrate Israel surviving against all the odds and ending up back in Jerusalem.

I started to read more about Jewish and Zionist history. We were by no means an observant family. My father's family in Poland had been Hasidic but he lost his faith entirely in the war. Halfway through university, I started keeping Sabbath and *kashrut*. Now, I couldn't tell you whether I'm a Jew or an Israeli first. From where I'm sitting, you can't peel them apart like an onion.

In 1976, I married an American woman called Frimet and we made *aliyah* with our children in '88. I was under no illusions that Jerusalem would be safer than Melbourne. The so-called First Intifada was in full swing and we were aware of the dangers. Melbourne was paradise on earth. I had a terrific career, I was making money and we were comfortable. But we wanted to raise our children in Israel because it's the one place in the world where Jewish history has always converged. Frankly, if we'd known about the tragedy that was waiting for us, we would never have come here in a million years. But that's not the way life works.

My daughter Malki was 15 years old when she died but in her short life she did a lot. She was only nine when our youngest child Haya developed catastrophic epilepsy and she spent a lot of time in hospital supporting Frimet. Communicating with Haya is impossible. She's blind and has no control over her body. Every night, Malki would carry her to bed and sleep by her side so that she'd feel the presence of somebody else. In her last summer, she fed, washed and read to a neighbour's son who was terminally ill with Canavan's Syndrome.[12] She also became a Madricha in a camp for disabled children in the Galilee. Two days after she came home from camp, she was murdered.

Why did you both go on a demonstration in January 2001 to protest Dennis Ross coming to Jerusalem to try and salvage a peace deal?

This was the biggest Israeli demonstration that's ever taken place. There were almost 900,000 people there. The atmosphere was buoyant with singing and dancing. It was an expression of love and support for Jerusalem. The city is very central to Judaism. You can't pick up a prayer book without finding it on every

12. Canavan Research Foundation. Canavan's Syndrome is a rare degenerative and fatal brain disease, mostly affecting people from certain Semitic backgrounds such as Ashkenazi Jews and Saudi Arabians. It causes severe neurological dysfunction and the eventual degeneration of the brain into a spongy mass.

page. Jerusalem is only a metaphor in Christianity. For us, it's a physical city with its walls, Old City and remains of the ancient temple. No Israeli wants to see it divided. It's the most important place on earth for us.

I spoke to Malki several times by cellphone on the demonstration but I never actually saw her there. Certainly, she had a sense of history. I remember when we recovered a picture of my grandfather's sister, Feiga, taken in 1945, she was her spitting image and Malki was struck by it. She felt part of the same flow, a connection based on blood. Her ties to the Jewish people, to Israel, were very strong. She loved the land.

How did you hear about her death?

I was working that day when my wife called at 2pm. She was hysterical, screaming and shrieking. She said, 'There's been a *pigua* in the centre of town and I can't reach the kids.' I tried to calm her down. We located all the boys but Malki's cellphone was in answering machine mode, and then the entire cellular phone system collapsed.[13] Ok. About two hours into this nightmare I started to feel really sick. Frimet went to the local hospital because she was going out of her mind.

I was much more worried than I let on. I cancelled all my afternoon conference calls and, on the bus home, my head was filled with dread and horror. Frimet met our second son Shaya in the hospital, where it was like Dante's Inferno, with hundreds of injured people and family members and blood everywhere. There was no sign of Malki. In the end, Frimet came home and we prayed the *Sefer Tehillim*. At 7.30pm, they announced on television that Michal, the friend who Malki had gone out with, was dead. We all broke down crying.

At 11pm, a neighbour told us another girl was being operated on and we raced to the hospital, but it wasn't Malki. While we were standing there, one of the surgeons came out and said, 'Oh, we've just finished with a 15-year-old girl in the next room, she's dead.' I just stepped outside myself. I thought, 'This is so nightmarish, it's beyond description. Here I am in a place that I never wanted to be, listening to people deal with death in ways which are completely mechanical. They're taking limbs off people, removing nails from people's skulls. This is madness, I'm going mad.'

We went home and as we rounded the corner of our street, there must have been a thousand kids from Malki's local youth group spilling out on to the road, holding a prayer vigil. At 2am, Shaya called to say they'd found Malki. It was like the breaking of a dam. My wife ran out into the street, screaming and hysterical. She didn't know where she was. It broke her totally. I just sat there collecting my thoughts.

13. Invariably, the Israeli phone system collapses about half an hour after every suicide bombing, owing to the sheer numbers of people trying to contact loved ones.

There were 15 funerals in Jerusalem the next day. It was intensely hot and there were people for as far as you could see at the cemetery. I was mostly looking at the ground but I had the clarity of mind that when one of the government ministers approached me, I told him, 'Go away. I don't want any representative of the state of Israel to speak here. You've nothing to say and I don't want you to speak. If you want to pay respects to my daughter you're very welcome.' I delivered a simple eulogy in English. I couldn't speak in Hebrew, I can't really tell you why, I mean I'm perfectly capable of speaking in Hebrew but I just wasn't able to.

Being a male and having obligations outside the house during the *shiva* made things easier for me. It was immeasurably more difficult for my wife. Of course, nothing ends when the *shiva* ends. The most shocking thing is when you go out onto the street and see that, my God, the Martians didn't land! Life is still going on and you're the only people who've really been affected. Anyone who says that you've got to get over the loss of a child, or reach closure or move past it, all these other clichés, is talking nonsense. You don't 'recover' because you weren't sick to begin with.

We lost a lot of our friends. People would cross the street when they saw us coming – some still do! I'd hear them whisper, 'I don't know what to say, it's hard for me.' If they ever said it to my face, I'd reply: 'How do you think it is for me? We need you. I need to know that you're there for me as a friend and nothing's changed.' There is an endless need among Israelis to get past it, to fix those broken windows, move on. They transfer that need onto the victim's families and it's highly, highly inappropriate when you've lost a child.

Why did you reject a joint interview with the family of the bomber, Izzedine al-Masri?

I'd consider meeting them in the future but the issue was: am I willing to tell the story of my daughter's murder from the perspective of a shared experience with the family of the murderer? It wasn't hard to say no. I was told that Mr Al-Masri felt terrible about what his son did and believed in peace. But I've since read interviews. He says he's happy and proud of what his son did.[14] I have nothing to say to him. There's nothing in our experiences that is mutual.

14. Kevin Toolis, 'Walls of death', *Observer*, 23 November 2003. 'Suicide bomber dropped hints', AP, 10 August 2001. The Associated Press quoted Shehel al-Masri as saying that Ariel Sharon 'is continuing the policy of killing our people and my son succeeded in carrying out a suitable response'. In a longer *Observer* story, Toolis reported Shehel al-Masri as saying, 'The Jewish children – they are so important to them. But our children are important to us. I hope everyone becomes a martyr because this occupation causes tears in every Palestinian heart.'

I have pictures of a replica of the Sbarro pizzeria they built at An-Najah University[15] in Nablus and I remind myself of it all the time. The grieving process is very difficult and there are books to help you, but no book will help you deal with people taking pleasure from the murder of your child. Being as politically correct as you like, they were literally dancing in the streets and singing for joy after the massacre. It was extremely upsetting and it told me that there is a fundamental difference between our societies, lives and attitudes to difference. We have nothing in common with their society. There is something terribly wrong in the way they live their lives.

Is this part of the reason you went to The Hague to protest the ICJ hearings?

I went because I thought a major con job was being done and it outraged me. Israelis are apparently the only people in the world who understand that the security barrier is the only thing protecting us from Abu Qureia's wet dream of permanent war.[16] We don't have to volunteer to be slaughtered. We can protect ourselves. Twisting the argument by calling it a land grab, ethnic cleansing or an apartheid wall is dishonest and irrelevant. Nobody can make these points more effectively than someone who has lost a child and knows that the security barrier is the last thing we have left.

Isn't there a danger that by aligning Malki's death with such a political campaign, her memory could become a tool in the propaganda war?

Malki's memory is an issue that is entirely independent of any political consideration, and I will preserve it by any means available. It's the only thing I can do as a father. The barrier exists to keep us away from the people who would kill us, including every Palestinian leader. They say it. I don't know why you don't believe them.

You told me in The Hague that you would feel sympathy for Palestinians who had lost children in comparable circumstances but that there were none.

'To an act of hatred' I think was the expression that I used.

15. Reuters, 'Arafat orders closure of Hamas exhibit in Nablus', 26 September 2001. Reuters reported that Yasser Arafat ordered the closure of a Hamas exhibit at Nablus's Al Najah University, which featured a replica of the Sbarro pizzeria. Inside it, a model of a pizza oven had been built. A pizza slice lay on a table marked with fake blood stains. Photographs of suicide bombers and Palestinian children killed by Israeli soldiers hung on exhibit walls. In another part of the museum, a tape recorder reportedly played a message from within a rock in front of a mannequin of an orthodox Jew, saying: 'Oh believer, there is a Jewish man behind me. Come and kill him.'
16. In the summer of 2004, opinion polls showed around two-thirds of Israelis consistently supporting the building of the Separation Wall, regardless of the consequences.

'Hate-filled terror' was the expression but I was thinking of Baruch Goldstein...[17]

Goldstein's murders represent an exception that proves the rule. If Israelis harboured feelings of hatred in their hearts which produced murder all the time – not Israeli soldiers bruising someone with a rifle butt – I'd say ok. But we're not living in parallel situations. We don't raise our children to think of them as nothing but animals. The way they educate their children to hate and despise us is a disgrace.

If there was a desire by Israel to massacre people on the other side, we could kill them all but we don't want to. Were the tables turned, any sane person knows that the Arabs would carry out a massacre the very minute they could. I'm repelled by the idea that we're two sides of the same coin or that we're doing to them what they're doing to us. We're protecting ourselves and they want us destroyed.

You don't see any relation between Israel's behaviour in the West Bank and Gaza and the attacks in Israel?

That position has some logic but as someone whose sons put on the uniform of the IDF, I know that it's bogus. The terror attacks and the hatred that motivates them were here long before there was a state of Israel. I'm not naïve enough to say 'poor desperate people'. They're not poor and they're not desperate.

At the end of Malki's essay on your website, she says, 'You're not allowed to give up hope'. Where do you find hope?

My wife and I believe in the fundamental goodness of people. Through the Foundation, we provide practical support for disabled people of all religions. It's almost three years to the day since Malki's murder and the pain today is just as fresh. But I'm hoping that by being able to say, 'In Malki's name we did this,' we'll get through this and someday it'll be possible to understand why God allowed these barbarians to do what they did.

17. Baruch Goldstein was a settler who massacred 29 worshippers at a Hebron mosque before he was overpowered and beaten to death. He remains a hero to far-right Israelis, who commemorate his death.

MALKI ROTH

The meaning of time

Malki Roth had gone to the Sbarro pizzeria to plan her 16th birthday when she was killed. A conscientious and extraordinarily kind teenager, Malki was also a talented musician who had secured a place with the Israeli Symphony Orchestra. She described herself as the 'sandwich' of the Roth family because she was a middle child, but her father Arnold said she was more like its glue. Her gumption supported many of her friends. The following diary entries, which focus on her school experiences, were written two months before her death.

Wednesday 6 June 2001:

The test got really messed up. I didn't have time for anything and I didn't know the answers. I'll get around 50–60 per cent. Right afterwards, all the girls from Efrat went to the funerals for two children from their town. One of them, Orit, had been a counsellor and a graduate of our youth group's local branch. Everyone at school cried. It was really hard to do the test. In Philosophy, Batsheva started crying and I talked to her. Revital, Rachel and I went down to the library during the lesson and we also talked about the *matsav* (situation). It was really hard but we had to. The thing is that nobody talked to us about it at school. During Geography, we made a song book for Shabbat and afterwards, I went to Camp Leah with my friend Odelia.

Thursday 7 June 2001:

During Home class, I couldn't concentrate at all. It was very difficult for me. Everything that's happening with this *matsav* has really sent me into a depression and I've been very sad. Avigayl didn't come to school because she'd gone to the two funerals yesterday and couldn't get over them. I left English, halfway through with Shira and Miri. Shira spoke in a very scary way about the funerals. She planned her own funeral with us. She said she'd told her mother that she didn't want journalists there, and that she should organise bullet-proof busses so we could come. We tried to quieten her because it was so frightening. In Jewish Thought class, we did what we were supposed to do yesterday. In Literature, I couldn't concentrate at all and the teacher just picked on me through the whole lesson and drove me crazy. I wasn't in the mood for school. In Sport and History I was supposed to hide out with Ela, but then we saw our whole class on the bus. We were let out early because of the test and a Shabbat event that needed organising. After school, I went to Lord Kitsch (a popular

Malki Roth, shortly before her death. *Photo kindly supplied by Arnold Roth*

clothing store) to meet Hadass and Tamar. I bought two shirts for myself and one for Rivki (Malki's sister). I cried at home for the rest of the day. It was a really tough one. At my flute lesson, I was very depressed and it was difficult to play. I called Yael and cried to her. I talked to Shulamit too. I haven't started learning for this test at all.

Friday 8 June 2001:

I didn't do the test. I just wasn't able to revise yesterday, I was so depressed. At first I really wasn't sure whether I should go on the Shabbat trip or not. In the end, I got on the bus and we saw *The Truman Show* on the way. I was still depressed. I was put in a group led by a boring counsellor who didn't have much to say and after the first unit, I sat and talked with Shira. I tried to tell her how I was feeling about everything that's happening with the *matsav*. I told her that I do understand what she's going through even if I'm not feeling it 'on my flesh' and she understood me. Leah and I organised the Kabbalat Shabbat prayer.[18] I played the flute and she played the guitar. We made song-books and they came out beautifully. Our teacher Rivka Genot brought her relatives. What a beautiful family. They were so nice!

Saturday 9 June 2001:

My mood really improved when Shabbat started. We sang a ton during the meal. I really felt the Neshama Yeteira (the 'extra soul' of Shabbat) entering me and it gave me such a good feeling. During the songs I broke down a bit and cried. They had such great power, it was amazing! When the Hadracha [training] units started, Revital Rabin and I started talking with Rachel Gold. I told her about the feelings I've had for some time, how I just can't learn and how it's tough for me. Vardit, Nati and some others joined us and listened to what we were saying. Finally we were really talking. I explained to them that it isn't just tough for girls who live in settlement towns but also for the rest of us. And that someone had better talk to us... Then we joined the Q&A.

The girls attacked the counsellors with tough questions about the *matsav* that were hard for them to answer. At one point, some counsellors were asking questions. It was a bit annoying because Shira is always saying that the *madrichot* [leaders] don't form their own group. When people started to scatter, I joined a group with Meir, Shira, Liora, Batya and someone else. There was one question I couldn't understand. How can we change things if everything, including evil, is decreed and predestined in heaven? It took Meir three hours to explain it to me – until three in the morning! In the end I understood it so well, that I could explain it to my friends. Everything is known beforehand but without the meaning of time, so when you pray you can prevent a terrorist attack. This

18. A communal prayer said in synagogue to welcome the Sabbath.

structure is known. It's just that from our eyes, with our meaning of time, it looks like we're moving things up there.

During the morning prayers, it was announced that there had been a terrorist attack at the Dolphinarium in Tel Aviv last night and many people were killed.[19] That was it, I broke down. Rafi's group sat in our room and everyone just cried. We were broken. When Rafi came in, he said the Kiddush but didn't know what to do or say after that. He gave us the usual slogans like 'We're in a process', 'These are Chevley Moshiach'[20] etcetera. By the time we ate, we had lost most of our energy. I talked to Rivka Genot about how I felt and she really helped me. There were *hadracha* (leadership training) units afterwards but I was very tired so I went to sleep until afternoon prayers. After the Shabbat lunch, we sang and one of the counsellors told us some really amazing stories. There was a circle dance and even though I couldn't take part, I had the most amazing Shabbat. I got so much from it. It was just magnificent.

19. On 1 June 2001 21 young people were killed when a suicide bomber blew himself up outside the Dolphinarium nightclub in Tel Aviv. The attack was the first major suicide bombing of the Second Intifada.
20. The birth pangs of the Messianic age.

8
Business as Usual

A visitor to Israel could be forgiven for not noticing there was a war on. At a glance, daily life has been surreally unaffected by the occupation grinding on just a few miles away. The sight of adolescents with rifles slung over their shoulders at holy sites predates the Intifada. Soldiers, security guards and checkpoints may blossom at every shopping mall, bar and market but this comforts an Israeli public used to bridling every time an Arab boards their bus. In terms of pure surface disruption to ordinary life, the protests against the *hitnatkut* (disengagement) achieved more than the occasional suicide bombing ever did.

In the nineteenth century, Marx meditated on the effect that the occupation of Ireland was having on British workers. He concluded that, 'No nation that oppresses another shall itself be free.' While Israel's Jewish citizens enjoyed one of the most egalitarian societies in the world, some thought it the exception to this rule. Today, those same citizens live in a country where one per cent of the population is estimated to own 50 per cent of the property wealth and inequality of economic income is comparable only to that existent in the US, one of the most unequal societies in the world.[1] In the road map of 2002, continuing US funding was for the first time made conditional on a neo-liberal economic plan that aimed to 'slash public sector jobs and wages and lower taxes'.[2]

Israeli academics now argue that the real objective of Benjamin Netanyahu's privatisation programme may have been 'to lower the salary level in Israel so that it will be possible to compete with the Third World'.[3] As the 2004 general strike demonstrated, business as usual in Israel can no longer be disguised as the hidden disenfranchisement of Palestinians alone. The prospects for joint economic or political endeavour with Palestinians, though, remain slim.

To explain the Israeli public's entrenchment towards the Palestinians, Adam Keller of the Israeli peace group Gush Shalom told me, 'It started when Ehud Barak, the former prime minister, said that the Palestinians had rejected the most

1. Momi Dahan, 'Leading the world in inequality', *Ha'aretz*, 15 January 2002.
2. Sharmila Devi, *Financial Times*, 1 May 2003.
3. Peter Hirschenberg, 'Poverty becomes Israel's new enemy', Inter Press Service, 1 November 2003. Cit. Yuval Elbashan, centre director at Hebrew University.

generous offer they'd ever been made, and so peace was impossible. Ninety-nine per cent of people believed it. The feeling deepened with the suicide bombings. Think of how people reacted to the IRA's bombing campaign in London. At least no-one there thought that the IRA wanted to take over London. Here, people do.'

Wasn't the problem, I asked, that Israelis weren't being asked to confront the way in which their state was founded? 'People are very aware that the state was founded by ethnic cleansing,' Adam replied. 'It's exactly because they're aware of it that they're not prepared for it to be reversed.'

BARRY CHAZAN

Meaning-making

Every year, Birthright Israel funds free holidays to Israel for thousands of Jews between the ages of 18 and 26. The group's name is a reference to the belief that it is every Jewish person's birthright to visit Israel. 'Your great-grandparents prayed for the return to Zion and rebuilding of the temple,' its website says. 'Your own grandparents were probably touched and ignited by the struggle to create the new Jewish state... Israel is a central part of Jewish history, culture and religion. It's part of our family. It's a beacon of Jewish pride and creativity.' Barry Chazan, the group's 63-year-old international director of education, is a thoughtful, liberal American Jew, whose philosophy sometimes seems at odds with such unambiguous eulogies. His first wife was the Meretz MK Naomi Chazan. As we talked on Tisha B'av[4] he was mindful of returning home to see his 4-year-old son from a second marriage.

I moved to Israel in 1968 after I finished a Philosophy of Education doctorate in the States. In '62 I'd led a youth group here and it struck me as a young exciting country carving out its future. The Jewishness of Israel touched me. I loved the Hebrew, the mix of old and new culture and the possibility of bringing up children here. I didn't come because of catastrophic or ideologically Zionist reasons. I wasn't suffering in America and I don't believe all Jews should live here. It was just a personal journey. I met the Israeli woman who became my first wife, we finished our degrees and I made *aliyah* after the war.

4. Tisha B'av is a day of mourning to commemorate the destruction of the First and Second Temples. Religious Jews fast on the day and remember more recent national tragedies.

Barry Chazan. *Photo by Arthur Neslen*

In the late '80s, I began working for the Bronfman family[5] who helped found Birthright. Birthright affects the personal identity of non-affiliated[6] young Jews through 'meaning-making', it brings them closer to the state of Israel and it deepens and enriches their sense of Jewishness. This age group is not a lost tribe, they simply hadn't been touched so we created a wonderful Pandora's Box of ten very significant days for them.

What is meaning-making?

It's what our lives are about, the core of our beings, a sense of purpose. I've been a significant figure in shaping Birthright but we all believe that Judaism can help create meaning for people. Hebrew is a defining factor of Jewish ethnicity because a people need a language of their own. This wasn't a narrowly defined Zionist project.

Was it a response to reports that around half of American Jews were marrying out?

A lot of people would say that, yes. The 1990 National Jewish population study was a wake-up call for some of the people behind Birthright. They felt we had to do something dramatic. The concept of marrying out doesn't exist in Israel. Marrying out here would mean an Ashkenazi marrying a Sephardi. Before Birthright, most Israel travel was teen travel. We appealed to the 18–26-year-old market with a free gift. The Israeli government, Diaspora Jewish communities and a group of 14 philanthropists agreed to each give us $70m over five years to fund the project.

Does he who pays the piper call the tune?

Yeah, it's true with Birthright. We don't want to present Israel as our great-grandfathers, or a CNN war zone, or a Middle Eastern country with camels and people in robes. We look at the arts and link Israel with core Jewish values like social justice, making peace and fighting poverty. Then they travel to Jerusalem, Tel Aviv and the north.

Is it true that you stopped taking people to meet Israeli Arabs because they were critical of the Israeli government?

Birthright did meet with Arabs in the Galilee at one point, but things changed dramatically after the Intifada. Israelis don't meet with Arabs and there's a

5. Jewish Virtual Library. Charles Bronfman, the owner of the Montreal Expos baseball team, is reported to be the fifth richest man in Canada, worth $2.2 billion. He explained his commitment to Birthright thus: 'Israel is a miracle... if you are Jewish and you don't have a real emotional connection with Israel, you're missing something very important to your *neshama* [soul].'
6. Jews not affiliated with synagogues or other community institutions.

complexity in our meeting with them, related to security issues more than politics. We show the overall Israeli concern for peace, but this is a journey into one's Jewish soul, not a political trip.

At first, Birthright took a hit from the Intifada. Now it's back to normal. Most participants are college students, and maybe 60 per cent are women. They come from 40 countries but mostly the US, Argentina, France, the FSU and Canada. We're still the largest Israeli visiting programme taking 11,000 people this summer and 70,000 over the last five years.

Brandeis University did some research into changes in a control group who went on the course.[7] People said things like, 'It changed my life', 'I didn't realise this is what being Jewish was about', and 'I'll go back and marry a Jew'.

How do you feel about participants who go on to the occupied territories with the ISM?[8]

Not good. I think there should be integrity in life. People are entitled to their views but that's not what the programme is for. Fortunately, it's a really minuscule minority. The media never say anything about the 200 Birthright participants who've settled here. Still, we're concerned about the phenomenon and we'll do more to try and stop it. We can Google the name of every applicant to see where they appear, and if they've written any articles. We can change our interviews and ask more direct questions like, 'Have you participated in such and such?' We don't want to do that because this is a no strings attached thing, but I think there are limits.

7. Rachel Pomerance, 'Researchers find that Birthright Israel program helps build Jewish identity', Jewish Telegraph Agency, 21 December 2004. The Brandeis University study found that Birthright Israel had a 'profound impact' on a participant's Jewish self-identification. '"It changes Jewish identity," Leonard Saxe, co-author of the study, said of Birthright... Before going on Birthright, participants typically are less engaged with Judaism and Israel... Several months after the trip, 60 percent of participants said they felt very connected to Israel. Two to four years after their trip, more than half of the participants said they still felt very connected to the Jewish state.'
8. Daphna Berman, 'ISM participants use Birthright program to get to Israel', *Ha'aretz*, 16 July 2004, Gil Hoffman and Hilary Leila Krieger, 'Birthright Israel concerned ISM activists are exploiting trips', *Jerusalem Post*, 21 December 2003. In the summer of 2004, a row broke out in Israel over a number of Jewish International Solidarity Movement (ISM) activists who used the Birthright programme to fly to Israel – before going on to the occupied territories. 'According to the Israeli foreign ministry, the ISM, which was founded in 2001, is "at times... under the auspices of Palestinian terror organisations". The ISM, which describes itself as a non-violent resistance group against Israeli occupation, denies the charge.' In 2003, Laura Gordon, a 21-year-old American university student, became the first Birthright participant to go on to volunteer for the ISM, spending nine months in the Rafah refugee camp. She had previously expressed an interest in immigrating to Israel but abandoned the idea as it might 'ruin her record' with the Palestinians.

Some Birthright–ISM travellers say they had a more sympathetic attitude to Israeli soldiers afterwards because they'd met them. Isn't that positive for you?

It could be... but it ain't gonna fly. The funders did not put up a huge amount of money so that people would afterwards go on a free ticket to Gaza. I think the Israeli government could legitimately complain about it. If people want to do that, they should fly there themselves.

But aren't Jewish values deepened by seeing how one's neighbours live?

That's a legitimate issue. I think Jewish values deeply affect how we treat the Palestinians. The idea of Shabbat, the holiness of time, is also a very important Jewish value. But there are other prophetic values, like how you treat the oppressed. Peace goes two ways, and Israel has to be willing to compromise.

Some Jewish leftists believe you're just training a cadre of Zionist ambassadors to come back and accuse them of anti-Semitism on campus.

Not true. We've actually been mocked by some on campus for not doing more to teach Zionism. Certain lay leaders think the major crisis of life is anti-Semitism. They say, 'You've got to prepare these young people to come back and fight on campus.' But the research indicates that people who return having seen the country and travelled with Israeli soldiers are better equipped to deal with the issues.

So how would you respond if a participant said, 'These Israelis don't even seem Jewish to me. They're humourless, aggressive, they don't talk Yiddish...'

That's why we bring 'em here. Hopefully we can change their minds. As descendants of the Diaspora, we're not only geographically lost, but religiously lost as well. I want to change the notion that being Jewish means going to St John's Synagogue three or four times a year and having bagels at Blooms. I've never bought the line that Israelis were 'Hebrew-speaking gentiles'.[9] I think Israel is very Jewish. Friday is still Shabbat[10] and today is Tisha B'av. It's a weird paradox that restaurants and entertainment places will close down tonight even though

9. Orr, *Israel*, p. 23. 'The Israeli is a Hebrew-speaking gentile [with] a secure (secular) cultural identity and no 'identity complex' (nobody doubts his Israeliness), unless he insists on defining himself as Jewish rather than as Israeli.' Orr quotes Amos Oz's citation of the settler leader Israel Harel: 'The Jews are those who want to live, to one degree or another, in accordance with the Bible. The Israelis pay lip service, maybe, to their heritage but in essence they aspire to be a completely new people here, a satellite of western culture.'
10. Fridays are a de facto public holiday in Israel when it's religiously forbidden to work, shop, drive or turn on lights. In cities such as Tel Aviv, these injunctions are largely ignored.

most Israelis are not religious. In Tel Aviv, they're bitching about it but somehow it happens.

Is that a failure of Zionism to create a secular Jewish identity?

It could be, or it could be a new expression of Jewishness. To me, Judaism is a civilisation with customs, history, heroes, values, lifestyle, behaviours and food. Israel is a laboratory for this civilisation and the Knessett is its debating society. Jews treat each other badly here and it's very disturbing sometimes, but I don't think there'll be a civil war. Israel is wrestling with a unique identity and there are a lot of angry people here.

But Israel is a very dangerous place for Jews, why bring young people here?

Yeah, it's a big issue. Ironically, we're supposed to be safe. I know Americans say statistically it's more dangerous to live in New York but I don't know if that's true. The issue of people being killed is just too sensitive for me. I don't think Birthright is holy at all costs. I'd be very happy if there was no need for it.

We bring young people here because it's the most unique experience a Jew can have and we've got the best guarantee we could that they'd be safe. I mean, God forbid, a loss of life would be a terrible thing. But not bringing kids here would be depriving them of a unique life opportunity.

Could there be a need for a Birthright to take Israelis to the Diaspora?

They're going there anyway.

AMRAM MITZNA

Don't trust anyone

Amram Mitzna led the Israeli Labour party into the 2003 national elections on a Gaza withdrawal platform denounced by Ariel Sharon as a 'surrender to terrorism'.[11] As well as disengagement, Mitzna proposed an immediate resumption of negotiations with the Palestinians from the January 2001 break-off point. He lost handsomely. A former mayor of Haifa and hardline commander of Israeli forces in the West Bank at the time of the First Intifada, Mitzna first developed a public profile when he took charge of the evacuation of the Jewish settlement of Yamit in the Sinai after the peace deal with Egypt. During the Kahane Commission's inquiry into the Sabra and Chatila massacres, he made headlines again. When the then-Defence Minister Ariel Sharon claimed that the massacres were nothing

11. Mark Lavie, 'Cloud of corruption hangs over Sharon's party', Sapa-AP, 26 December 2002. For instance, in a speech given to an election rally at the Likud party's Jerusalem

Amram Mitzna. *Photo by Arthur Neslen*

special, Mitzna asked the chief of staff if he could go on leave until Sharon resigned.[12] Today, Mitzna presents as a complex, committed and obliging figure, intent on moves to peace but uncompromising in his support for a Separation Wall. We met in the Knesset on the day of a budget vote that led to Sharon's administration becoming a minority government.

My youth was deeply influenced by my upbringing in Kibbutz Dovrat. I belonged to Ha'noar Ha'oved.[13] They taught me Israeli songs and dances and on their tours, I discovered Israel and learned to value the land beneath my feet. I never felt part of an elite. I was proud to be a kibbutz product because more sons of the kibbutzim built and defended this country than any other group. Later in life, I lived in a kibbutz for 14 years and raised my children there.

Why do you have a Bible on your bookshelf?

You know the Bible is not just a religious book. It's also our history book. I'm not religious but my mother's father was a *chazan* and I still love Jewish prayers and songs. I appreciate our traditions and history. I value being here in the state of Israel but I am secular.

You've said before that you don't believe in God, but you do believe that no gentile could ever be prime minister of Israel. Why?

Israel will always have a majority of Jews. For as long as it's a democracy, you will need a majority among them to become prime minister. This would be impossible.

You don't think there can there be a Jewish identity without religion at its root?

Religious Jews are defined by the questions 'do you believe?' and 'do you live by religious rules?' My Jewish identity is based on the values of Rabbi Hillel who summarised the Torah with the words 'do unto others what you would have done to yourself'. I'm not praying all day and I drive on Shabbat. But if you recognise your history, roots, and obey some moral principles, you are a Jew. The bottom line is that I'm more Israeli than Jewish.

Zionism was a rejection of living in the Diaspora while we prayed and waited for the Messiah. The idea was to initiate a unilateral decision by force of will. The religious people criticised it. By building settlements, we, our fathers, the founders, took the future into our hands. Zionism is not yet over because we

Convention Centre on Wednesday 25 December 2002, Sharon rejected Mitzna's peace proposals as 'surrender to terrorism… A unilateral withdrawal would broadcast a message of weakness that would bring all our enemies to our doorstep, that would show them that the time has come to deliver the final blow to the Jewish state.'

12. Jonathan Freedland, 'An unlikely dove', *Guardian*, 4 October 2002.
13. The Labour party's 'Working youth movement'.

are still not recognised by our present enemies and future neighbours, and our borders are not accepted by the world.

Your parents were refugees from Hitler's Germany. What stories did they tell you?

My parents fled from Germany just before the war with nothing. They didn't talk about it. They didn't want to ruin our souls. But they did teach us that in order to live safely as the new Jewish people, we needed our own state and military power, to protect ourselves. The idea I was raised on, and which carried me through the wars was: Don't trust anyone. Do it yourself. Initiate. Don't expect the outside world to help you. Understand that the world is full of interests and fight for yours. Don't misjudge the situation. It can be blue skies and birds singing and, within a minute, you can find yourself in a disaster. So never relax and imagine that you're safe, plan for tomorrow. I never told my children stories about the Holocaust. I had enough stories about myself, fighting here in Israel.

The Holocaust is still a great influence on the Israeli psyche. We live with this fear that everything can be destroyed. The '67 war partly cured the fear that we were weak and the world was against us. But it created a triumphalist and problematic atmosphere. The religious community felt that their dreams were coming true. We freed Jerusalem, reunited it. It was a miracle. One day we were sitting in fear, the next it was all over and we were controlling so many places. Three armies were completely destroyed and the religious took it as a sign from the sky. We started a new era and it was a big mistake. We are still in a situation of having to ride the tiger, or hold the bear. You can't throw it off and you can't swallow it.

The Yom Kippur War took us back to the feeling hiding deep in everyone who came from Europe that you can't trust even the generals and political leaders. We have to be always on guard. I think we're frightened of peace – and peace processes. We're less frightened of war. Nobody will take risks, even though we know we're the strongest empire in the Middle East.

Are the attempts at suppressing the Intifada by military might a symptom of that?

Suppressing the Intifada is a must. So is fighting terror. But we've been brainwashed into believing that there's no-one to talk to. The real question is what we'll talk about. Right now, Israelis would rather sacrifice our sons and moral values than make concessions. The occupation is corrupting us. Golda Meir once said, 'I will not forgive the Palestinians for what they have done to our society,'[14] and it's true. We are behaving like the cruellest enemies the Jewish

14. Asmi Bishara, 'Apartheid consciousness and the question of Palestine', *Between the Lines*, March 2001. Golda Meir was actually quoted as saying 'I will never forgive the Arabs for forcing our children to shoot at them'.

people ever had. You know, people accuse us of behaving like Germans and we say, 'No, we have morals, we don't put them in ghettoes.' The reality is that we are occupying three and a half million people against their will.

What for you have been the Labour party's biggest mistakes?

Supporting settlements in highly populated Palestinian areas and believing that, ultimately, we'd be able to annex parts of the West Bank and Gaza. The settlers became the new pioneers by giving the impression that they were continuing the idea of settling Israel. We didn't think beyond the horizon. Our leaders didn't think about the future, only today. We are less secure as a result. If the Labour party doesn't reform itself, it won't lead the country in the near future.

You knew Ariel Sharon well when you fought in Lebanon. What impression did you form of him?

I knew that he was trying to generate wars. He was looking for an excuse to go into Lebanon for a long time. His mind works on zero-sum ideas: we have to fight against the Palestinians. We have to win unconditionally; we have to throw them out of Lebanon and give it back to the Christians. These ideas served Sharon since he was a player in this place.

You mean since '53?[15]

He never really represented a majority of Israelis but people trust strong leaders in traumatic times.

Perhaps his message plays to the 'Don't trust anybody' ethos you mentioned?

Yes, he came in when the collapse of Barak's strategy and leadership opened the door. He was nothing just a short period of time before and he became prime minister when people were saying we had to use our military power. This idea which is so human: let's go for it, let's finish it, let's hit them, let's kill them.

Do you believe he knew about Sabra and Chatila?[16]

Of course, he knew for sure that they were going in. Israel was responsible for the area, the Phalange were our allies and I think that he was well aware, or let's say he should have been aware that it might happen.

15. Shlaim, *The Iron Wall*, pp. 90–3. Following the murder of an Israeli mother and her two children by gunmen who had crossed the Jordanian–Israeli border near Qibya, the Israeli commando Unit 101, under the command of Ariel Sharon, attacked Qibya on the night of 14–15 October. By the next morning, the village had been reduced to a pile of rubble. Forty-five houses had been blown up and 69 civilians, two-thirds of them women and children, killed. Sharon claimed that he had no idea anyone was hiding inside the houses.
16. Ibid., pp. 416–18. 'Sharon ordered the IDF commanders to allow the Phalangists to enter the Palestinian refugee camps Sabra and Chatila on the south side of Beirut

You've said that when you were commander of Israeli forces in the West Bank during the First Intifada, you were always afraid of imposing a curfew on Nablus. Why?

When you impose a curfew, you have to police it. What do you order your soldiers to do if people disobey? Nablus was the only city I imposed a curfew on[17] because once a measure has been used, it loses its power. If I'd put tanks in Hebron or Jenin, people would have been afraid for the first two days but then they'd approach the tanks and we'd hesitate to shoot. The next day they'd throw Molotov cocktails at the tanks. Would we open fire with machine guns? You have to think about the fourth step before you take the first.

Do you see any symmetry in the Palestinian and Jewish experiences?

I don't even want to go into it. They have the basic right to their identity and sovereign state but they never learned our most important lesson: take what you can get and keep your dreams. Imagine if they'd agreed in '48 to the UN resolution! They missed another opportunity after Oslo, when Arafat came to Gaza. But I still believe the Labour party must raise the flag of deep negotiated concessions because we need to separate ourselves from the main problem, the occupation.

What if Jews and Palestinians could live peacefully together in one state as equals, sharing resources, with guarantees on freedom of worship…

It would be the end of Zionism because the majority would be Muslims. With one man one vote, there would be a Palestinian state. Israel was established as the sole homeland and shelter for Jews. It's unique as a democracy that exercises one religion as the majority. But in one state, no-one could live according to Jewish values and traditions.

---

in order to "clean out" the terrorists who, he claimed, were lurking there. Inside the camps the revenge-thirsty Christian militiamen perpetrated a terrible massacre, killing hundreds of men, women and children… the Palestinian Red Crescent put the number at over two thousand.' The Kahan commission report of 7 February found Ariel Sharon 'personally responsible' for the massacre and called for his removal as defence minister. Sharon was reshuffled to become a minister without portfolio.

17. Morris, *Righteous Victims*, p. 573. Mitzna was criticised by the left and the right for the tactics he used in suppressing the Intifada. However, an incident at the Balata refugee camp in the uprising's early days demonstrated his flexibility. 'On May 31, the IDF moved in. A curfew was imposed and units drove into the camp in search of wanted terrorists, political activists and weapons… After several thousand young males were rounded up for questioning, the bulk of the population, led by masses of women and children, rioted... Some of the detainees broke free of their captors and joined in. The troops had to either let loose with live fire or else withdraw without accomplishing their mission. The commanding officer, General Amram Mitzna chose the second course.'

You talked about painful compromises earlier. In the context of the Geneva Initiative, who did you think should control the West Bank's water?

Let me tell you there are so many issues where we could have used our veto to break the negotiations. The best solution would have been to let decisions be taken by a joint committee headed by an outsider who both sides respected, but the Palestinians wanted to exercise every sign of sovereignty. Therefore I think that Israel must find water solutions involving desalination and other artificial ways in the long term. We have to separate ourselves. The disagreement, distrust and hatred between the parties are so high that we must find ways to have as little coordination as needed in the future.

Why are there so many ex-generals in the Knesset?

In Israel, security is so important that the majority will always vote it their first priority above economic or social issues. People are unable to contemplate a head of government who's unfamiliar with the military option. I didn't feel bad when I was derided as 'nice but naïve' in the election. In Israel, you're either a co-opted politician or you're naïve, there's nothing in the middle. Likud simply said 'Mitzna's going to give up our security' and noted that I wasn't fully supported by my own people. Of course, if your own team work against you in an election campaign, then people will say he's a nice guy *but*.

Party members elected me against almost all the second- and third-echelon leaders and they couldn't digest it. I was elected in early November, and by late January there was an election. I couldn't even practise leading the party beforehand. I wasn't familiar with its informal structure, which is a political playground. I wasn't ready. People criticised me for not being vague enough. If you want to reach people from right and left, you have to satisfy everybody. So the one and a half a million people who voted Labour was a big achievement. I spoke clearly and honestly to an electorate driven by fear alone. Even if we didn't succeed, I always said it would help us for years after. Now Sharon is moving to implement my election proposals, we could gain a lot from it.

Doesn't Sharon's appropriation of your platform suggest you weren't radical enough?

I was radical enough but it's not a personal issue. I never felt that I was born with the prime minister's chair in my hand. This was not my dream. If I've succeeded in changing some people's minds – including Sharon's – this is my satisfaction.

You'd never consider running again for the party leadership?

A politician never says never.

Shortly after Amir Peretz's election as Labour Party leader in November 2005, Amram Mitzna left national politics to become mayor of Yeruham.

YAFFA GEVA

Work enables life

Ever since Kibbutz Degania was founded in 1909, the kibbutz movement has been an Israeli icon. The 'Socialist Zionist' movement aspired to create state-subsidised communal villages in which land, labour, profits and duties would be shared equally. Kibbutzniks often fought in the front-line battles of 1948, frequently appropriating Arab land. However, when the state began redirecting money to settlements in the occupied territories after 1967, many kibbutzim were forced to take out loans to survive. They were hit hard by the inflationary spirals of the 1980s. The last twenty years has seen a 'youth flight' from Israel's 270 kibbutzim, which has reduced their population by a quarter to around 11,000.[18] To staunch the haemorrhage many turned to privatisation. In 2005, the first kibbutz industry was floated on the London stock market.[19] Shomrat was the first kibbutz to be established after the Declaration of Independence in 1948 but it is famous in Israel for darker reasons. In August 1988, a 14-year-old girl from the village claimed that she had been gang-raped by six boys from 'good homes' in the kibbutz. A phlegmatic media response by Shomrat's representatives aided perceptions that the kibbutz was protecting the alleged rapists while hounding their victim out of the village. The case was eventually dismissed in controversial circumstances, but it marked the end of the kibbutz movement's age of innocence for many. Today, Shomrat is a quiet place. Most young people have left. The kibbutz has begun a privatisation process, leaving older stalwarts like Itzik Nevo facing financial hardship after a life dedicated to the movement. Nevo, whose interview begins on p. 226, refused to discuss the rape case. Yaffa Geva is one of the pioneers of privatisation.

I'm a 54-year-old teacher and I've lived in Kibbutz Shomrat for 31 years. I was born in a *moshav* called Avigdor and I always knew that one day I'd settle down in the countryside. It's what I was used to. My parents were farmers who came here from Poland and the Ukraine after the Holocaust. On the *moshav*, we had our own farm with cows, chickens and avocados. We sold them with other *moshav* produce and kept what profits we made. Things weren't pooled and

18. Chris McGreal, 'Israel's Kibbutzim swap socialist ideals for personal profit in struggle to survive', *Guardian*, 31 August 2004.
19. Nick Mathiason, 'Bio-tech Kibbutz set for London float', *Observer*, 17 April 2005. 'For the first time, a company spun out of a kibbutz will be floated on the London market, marking a watershed for businesses developed by Israel's co-operative movement. Kibbutz Yad-Mordechai owns 80 per cent of Bio-Oz, an Israeli biotechnology company which inoculates crops against disease.'

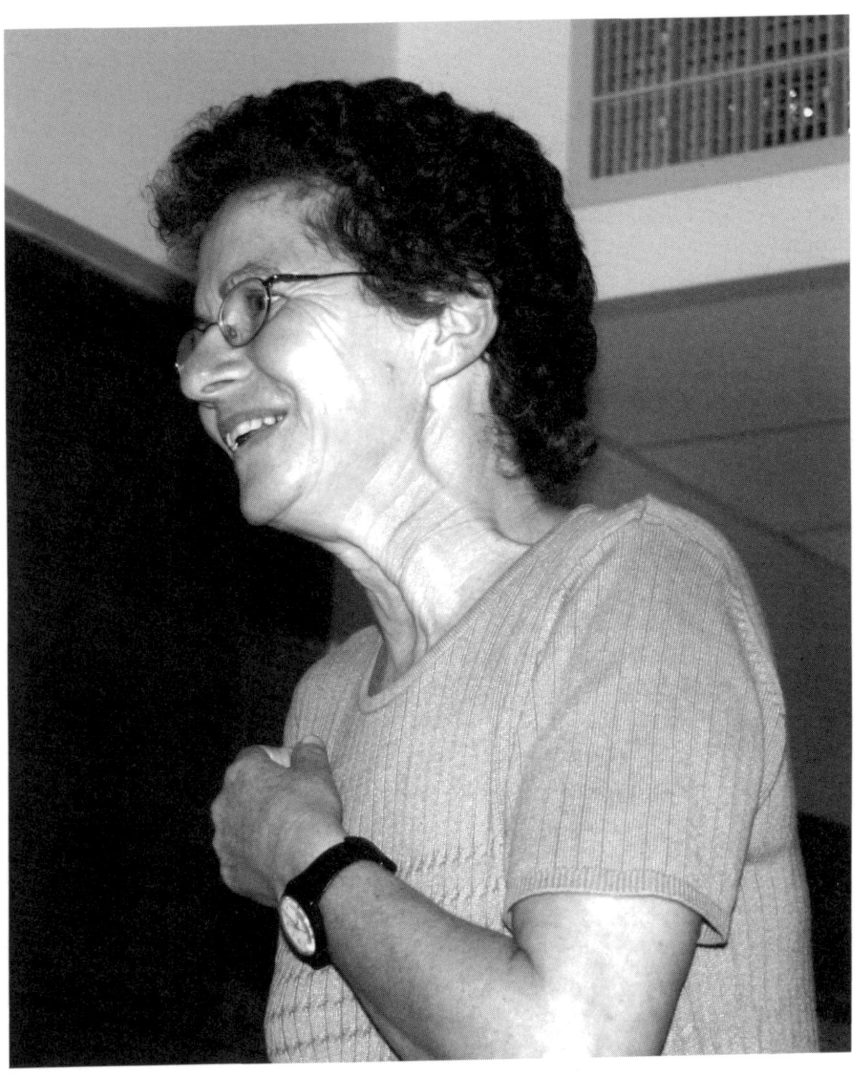

Yaffa Geva. *Photo by Arthur Neslen*

everyone had their own house but we celebrated holidays together. Work was very important. When my father wanted to punish my brother, he wouldn't let him work on the farm... and that was a big punishment!

Avigdor was the size of this kibbutz, with about 500 people. Today, it's twice as big and it has a synagogue. We were raised to help other farmers or soldiers. The kids who didn't were condemned and excluded from social circles. I left the *moshav* when I was 18. People lived simpler lives then. The gap between rich and poor was much smaller and political leaders were less corrupt. Hebrew-language books were written in a completely different language, which kids today wouldn't understand. They make basic mistakes in grammar, particularly around gender nouns. They mix it up with English and Arabic slang and they don't care. Their vocabularies are limited and they use words like 'az' (so) or 'kehilou' (like), two or three times in each sentence. It's shallow. Our language was richer.

In those days, the kibbutzim were seen as the idealistic elite. They were more socialist than the moshavim but they related to Arabs in the same way. I was completely against them and so were my parents. People interfered in each other's lives too much there. They'd see what their neighbours did, what they ate, how much they made or didn't make. I didn't want anything to do with it. The kibbutz kids in my high school were spoiled. They didn't know how to study because their schools didn't even have exams.

I came here because I married Amichai. We fought about it but Amichai was an ideological fanatic and he convinced me. It was hard for me to see him on demonstrations and coming to Shomrat was awful. The kibbutz dream didn't work out so well but I didn't even think it was a good dream. That's the difference between us. I hated this place.

In the beginning, he had these awful baggy work clothes and when he did the laundry, he looked so miserable. They sent me to work in the children's house, and I was really upset when a supervisor got mad at one girl who ate too slowly. It took me years to fit in. I felt comfortable with Amichai's group, the kids from the States and Canada, but I never liked the system. People were assigned duties in the kitchen, children's house or fields and they'd be paid an equal proportion of whatever money was made. You didn't have to worry about money for education, health, food or having kids. Life was very easy. Few kibbutzim are still like that. They used to go to meetings and vote in a committee every Saturday night. They were much more involved then.

About ten years ago, the kibbutz nearly went bankrupt and the dissatisfaction began with people who earned good money outside. At every meeting, they heard that our debts were growing and we had to lower our standard of living. People weren't pulling their weight. Something in our way of life wasn't right.

The crunch came when interest rates went up. We'd taken out loans to build a furniture factory and the cow ran dry. This was the time for change.

We called a professor from Haifa University to research what people wanted and then we divided the kibbutz into a mass meeting to discuss the results. We had about 20 or 30 group meetings and there was a big argument. My view was that if people worked harder and didn't clock off at 4pm, there'd be a closer relationship between what they earned and spent. Work enables life. Other people thought that we could maintain the old system.

The older people were terrified because the kibbutz was like a big sun-house and they were used to being taken care of. They panicked because they didn't know how to use a credit card or write a cheque. In the kibbutz, they didn't have to. Almost all the older people were Holocaust survivors who received compensation from Germany or the Israeli government. At first, they gave it all to the kibbutz. But in time, their kids needed money to study so they started giving it to them instead. They'd tell the committee, 'You can't speak to me because you didn't suffer what I suffered.' Other people said, 'If he doesn't give, why should I?' Finally we agreed that they'd keep the money for themselves.

Now we don't have so many committees. We're not as active and there isn't so much communal life. We celebrate some holidays and people are more responsible for themselves. We don't have workplaces any more. They weren't profitable enough so they closed. We moved the cows to another kibbutz close by. Most people work outside these days, and they like it. The foreign groupies haven't visited for years. It's still an in-between system because salaries go straight to the kibbutz, where they're taxed and charged for goods and services they've used. That will probably change soon.

Like Israeli society, we're less homogeneous, which makes decision-taking harder. It's still too much of a kibbutz for me. I see Shomrat becoming a village with some collective ownership. Everyone will work for themselves and the only taxes will be for gardening and preserving the quality of life. The biggest mistake we ever made was not listening to people at the beginning because everyone had to think the same.

Did the Kibbutz mentality cause particular problems during the crisis in 1988?

That was a big blow to the kibbutz. It's still a cloud hanging over us because of the newspapers. It's not true that the kibbutz defended the six rapists and rubbished the girl. The kibbutz found it difficult because it had to support both sides. The boys and the girl both had parents here who couldn't afford lawyers, so the kibbutz paid for both sides. It was a hard situation. They had to meet each other, which wasn't easy. People were very upset for years afterwards. They felt they'd taken responsibility for something that wasn't their fault.

Even today, if you're going to Shomrat, a bus driver will still give you a funny look. It's hard to say whether the kibbutz could have handled it better. I think they should have gone to the police earlier and they should have taken into account the way the media would report it. But the people that took positions here weren't professionals. For something like this, you need professionals.

ITZIK NEVO

The movement decided for us

I was born in Montevideo in 1934, the year my parents migrated to Uruguay from Stucin in Poland. My father had a furniture factory and he worked long hours to bring home food to eat. I was a *yeshiva boche* but as a student, I saw the problem with religion and became a socialist. Hashomer Ha'tzair was very strong in Montevideo and they taught us about equality and building a new society. I broke with my parents when I dropped out of college to make aliyah, along with 4,000–5,000 South American Jews. We didn't decide to come to places like Shomrat. The movement decided for us. They wanted to strengthen the kibbutzim. The only problem I had was leaving my parents. My mother wanted me to become a doctor and she was very upset when I left. But I made a life here. I'm not completely disappointed.

In those days the kibbutz was small and we lived in wooden houses, three people to a room. The dining room was heated by a big pile of wood and there were no chairs. We had to go outside to brush our teeth or pee. I changed my surname from Osnofsky to Nevo. We felt very united. It was a different time. If we hadn't supported each other, people would have left the kibbutz because there was so much suffering.

The kibbutzim were very important when Israel was created. Without us, Israel would not be what it is today. We defended the borders and each other. Judaism and Zionism for me are almost inseparable.

Did you find a new family here?

Yeah, my father never came to visit. My family is here. I built it myself. Because I left my family, my children could also decide to go. Two of them left because they couldn't envisage becoming what they wanted to be in this society. Maybe I failed in my education. My son is living in Sweden. He has three children by a Swedish woman who's not Jewish. One of my daughters is married and living in the south of Israel. Another runs a real estate company in London, where she

Itzik Nevo. *Photo by Arthur Neslen*

has four children. Maybe she learned from my socialism because she married a Negro and had two children with him.

Did you have contact with any Arabs in this kibbutz?

Many, I worked with them in the fields for 30 years. I went to their villages and they knew me but no Palestinian could live on a kibbutz. That'd be impossible. They wouldn't know how to live here. They'd have to think in another way because they're educated so differently.

Did you see the kibbutzim movement as a 'light unto the nations'?

I did think that once but we're not an example of anything any more. I don't even have a pension because the kibbutz changed its security net. We used to have a community life. Now you have an income and you pay for your washing, movies and electricity. People don't meet so much now and the way they communicate isn't the same. We stopped connecting because we stopped supporting each other. Everyone is only out for himself. Young people from abroad used to come here. They don't any more.

At least 23 sons of the kibbutz have returned although they don't like the old system. We welcomed them because the community is ageing. People left because they didn't accept the ideology of personal sacrifice for the greater good. They'd say, 'I want something before I give.' We made under-the-table deals with them and it led people to stop supporting us. What is the point of living here? I don't know exactly.

I'm actually running to be the next *maskil* myself now so I have to find what the community is prepared to do together. We have to grow so I want to bring the young people back. They're returning because of the privatisation. I don't like it but my wife has accepted it. For me, privatisation means going back to the system of my parents. I will be a slave of money again but I have to support the changes if I want to become the *maskil*.

I don't know if the privatisation was so hard for the Holocaust survivors. They get compensation payments from Germany, so they have money to live on. The privatisation has also given pensions to those who work outside. But I don't, so I'm surviving on 3,400 shekels a month and the 2,000 shekels I get for four hours' work every day. You don't work now, you don't eat. Our naïvety, honesty and idealism have been lost. My mother told me to graduate before I went to Israel. Her vision was clearer than mine. But in 30 years, I've ploughed all these fields more than once and that makes my spirit feel fantastic. I don't feel betrayed. I can't revisit my decisions. I might shoot myself if I could.

TANJA G

She's in parties

The Second Intifada had a double-edged effect on Tel Aviv's hedonistic party scene. It helped fuel a devil-may-care abandon among young Israelis, while contributing to the economic woes and safety fears that unsettled their clubs. While Gaza burned, Tel Avivians took to their roofs, beaches and bars to dance the night away. Tanja G is one of the only female DJs in Israel. A celebrated artist, she has been voted awards in magazines from *Time Out Tel Aviv* to *Iton Ha'ir*.[20] She arrives for our evening interview at Tel Aviv's Banana Beach bar dressed in an 'It's better with Heineken' T-shirt, overflowing with apologies for being late. It is still early for her.

Music was always the most important thing in my life. It affected everything I ever did. When I arrived here from Switzerland, aged 13, my sister took me to an underground punk and new-wave club. It triggered something off in me. I started to buy music by Crass, UK Subs and The Exploited. When I was 17, my entire record collection was stolen. It was terrible but I always kept a song by Conflict in my mind. It went (sings), 'You cannot win a nuclear war...' It reminded me somehow of Israel because of the wars and that you can't win by violence. I loved Joy Division but Ian Curtis was in Warsaw before and they had this song 'They walk in line'. I don't know why I liked it. Another song 'She's in parties' is how I'd describe my life now.

Were you a happy teenager?

I was a very unusual teenager. I had a British mother and a Swiss father, and I went from being a very well-behaved girl in Switzerland to a rebel in Israel. I was kicked out of my first school, Gymnasia Herzliya, and the American International School after that. My father stayed in Switzerland and my mum couldn't control three kids, so I had freedom to do whatever I wanted. I remember when we landed here I was so overwhelmed with happiness that I wanted to kiss the ground. Switzerland was strict. Here, people just went out and met up and you didn't have to talk to their parents. I couldn't be bothered with school so I started going to clubs. It was happy but strange.

At 17, I went to a boarding school in England to do 'A' levels. I would have ended up a bum if I'd stayed. I went on to do a law degree at East London Uni

20. A popular national arts and listings magazine owned by the Ha'aretz group.

Tanja G on the decks in a Tel Aviv nightclub. *Photo by Arthur Neslen*

because a lot of Israelis studied there. I never wanted to be a lawyer. There was just an expectation that I'd get a degree. My father went to Cambridge and I wanted to make him proud of me.

He's a partner in a Swiss bank now and my mother, who's from Leeds, has a translation business. Like a lot of Jews, she wanted to be in Israel. I always felt very Jewish but our upbringing wasn't religious. Like, I fast and go to synagogue on Yom Kippur, I believe in God, and I always felt a strong connection to this country but I wasn't batmitzva'd. I really wanted one but I never asked for it and I was 13 when my parents divorced and we left. I wanted to be here but I was also angry that I'd been taken away from my father.

After Uni, I studied fashion for a year and went back to Israel. I'd started getting into electronic music at English clubs like the Brixton Fridge. By the time I came back, I'd built a record collection and bought turntables. Music was my big escape from my parents' divorce.

Arriving in Israel the second time wasn't the same. But my friends and family were here, it was still free and fun and I felt a connection. My father would say, 'Tania, you can't always be with Israelis. You must meet other people.' The only time I had other friends was when I was at boarding school because I didn't have a choice. I had friends from Oman, Spain, even Lebanon. It's funny, when I go to Switzerland, people think there's a huge war going on here, with bombs flying around, but to me Israel is the one safe place, where I feel I belong. It's home, you know? Like at night, when you go to your bedroom and get into your bed, that's how I feel here: comfortable and happy.

Did you serve in the army?

I was never called up. Being the kind of rebel I was, I might not have gone. I feel a bit of regret because all my friends did their service and there's something missing. My brother was in the army for seven years.

Anyway, some Russian Jewish friends said I could practise in their club, Fetish, during the day. They gave me odd gigs and eventually, a Thursday night residency, playing techno and then house. It was a struggle. People told me that being a woman would make it easier but it didn't. I had to build myself slowly.

There are hardly any female DJs here. Most of the people I work with are men and I'm surrounded by guys all the time. But I feel kind of equal. I'm lucky because other DJs respect me for playing quality music. No-one's had a bad attitude to me because I'm a woman. I was voted second-best Israeli DJ in *Iton Ha'ir* recently but I'm really living in a man's world. Maybe there are more female DJ's abroad because there are more career women there. Women get married and have children earlier in Israel. There's a strong sense of family.

Israel has such a small club scene and it's mostly centred on Tel Aviv. There are fewer options for underground music because the crowds are smaller. It's Americanised and everyone wants money. Trance and hip-hop are the biggest scenes. The best thing about trance is that it's popularised so many Israeli DJs abroad. They're giving something Israeli to the world. An Israeli trance DJ abroad can make $20,000 a night – split with his agent. I'm really proud of these guys. I make much less but what I play is completely different. Even my techno is more groovy, like a happy house party thing.

Goa was the place where every Israeli trance DJ learned their trade, met other DJs and swapped music on DAT. Now in Israel you have open-air parties all the time, and even the big Sundance parties have commercial sponsors like Heineken. I was never really interested in going to Goa.

Why do you think so many Israelis did?

It was probably the biggest escape they could get. People went there after the army until they heard about Thailand. It's still the one place where you can completely chill out and come back a new person. The flight is expensive but living there doesn't cost much. You just pay for your ticket. People coming back are like the calmest people in the world. Actually I don't know where the younger generation go. At 31, I'm the older generation. I never had an 'after that'.

What effect has the conflict had on the dance scene?

It's changed things. There's more stress. Even Jewish people won't come here for holidays any more. It's not the easiest place to live. A lot of my friends have no jobs and no money. Everybody is struggling and it wasn't like that a few years ago. They were better times and it's affected the clubs. The party scene used to be much stronger, the house scene has gone down and the big clubs are in trouble too. They open and shut all the time. Nothing is stable. For two or three months, you can have brilliant parties and then suddenly boom, there's a bomb and things look black.

How do most of your friends view the conflict?

Pass.

How do you view it?

Pass.

Do you feel you have anything in common with young Palestinians?

Yes, survival instinct (laughs).

How would you feel about DJ-ing at a joint Israeli–Palestinian rave?

It's a very beautiful thought.

In the West Bank?

An even more beautiful thought. I'm hopeful for the future and very idealistic. I believe that peace will come and people will be kinder to each other. People should respect each other. I try.

NITZANA DARSHAN-LEITNER

This is a nation that wants a war

One of the first casualties of the Intifada was Israel's tourism industry. After a record year in 2000, it suffered an immediate collapse in volume of some 50 per cent.[21] Partly in response, some specialist operators began advertising 'terror tours' to danger-seeking Zionist travellers. Leading the way, Shurat Hadin aka The Israel Law Centre offered 10-day 'Ultimate Mission' tours for $1,600 per person plus a tax-deductible donation of $500–$5,000. The success of their tours can be measured by the participation of figures such as Azmi Bishara MK.[22] Yet the Ultimate Mission ('to explore the continuing threat to Israel's survival') funds the Israel Law Centre's campaigns. The Centre has fought 'civil rights' cases in defence of the soldier who killed Tom Hurndall, a teacher who refused to teach the Rabin legacy, and four Israelis arrested in a New Jersey car park in the aftermath of the 9/11 attacks.[23] It has also petitioned for the imprisoned Fatah chief Marwan Barghouti to be charged with 'crimes against humanity', won $13m lien against Yasser Arafat's assets and campaigned for legal action against the Palestinian leader Abu Mazen for alleged involvement in the Black September attack at the 1972 Munich Olympics. Nitzana Darshan-Leitner, a 30-year-old lawyer from Petach Tikva, is the group's director. Her offices are decorated with

21. Molly Moore, 'Israel cultivates new breed of tourist', *Washington Post*, 13 December 2003. Ya'acov Fisher, 'The Intifada and the economy', <JewishMinneapolis.org>.
22. BBC News Online, 'Profile: Israel's Arab Voice', 9 January 2003: Azmi Bishara is the leader of the mostly Arab National Democratic Alliance or Balad (Homeland) party. A supporter of equal citizenship rights for all Israeli Jews and Arabs, he became the first Arab to run for prime minister in 1999. In 2002, he was at one point banned from standing in elections after he appeared with Hezbollah and Palestinian radical leaders in Syria.
23. Steve Plaut, 'Putting a "blood libel" to rest', FrontpageMagazine.com, 20 September 2004. The Israel Law Centre filed a lawsuit against the Department of Justice in the US district court in New York alleging unlawful imprisonment and violation of civil rights. 'According to [the plaintiff's counsel], Leitner: "The infamous arrest of these young Israelis on 9/11 has been used by anti-Semites worldwide as 'proof' of Israel's

Nitzana Darshan-Leitner. *Photo supplied by Nitzana Darshan-Leitner*

sketches of lawyers in hysterical grand-guignol poses and an inflatable representation of Edward Munch's 'The Scream'. Nitzana herself is neat, professional, and dresses modestly. As she talks, she plays with a pair of scissors on her desk, gently cutting at the skin of her fingers.

My parents came here from Iran as children just after Israel was created. They weren't suffering any persecution, they were Zionists. Most of their village came with them. By 1979, none of my family was left. They had a wonderful life in Iran (laughs). They lived peacefully with their Arab neighbours, who were very sorry when they left. The Shah was good to the Jews and none of them worried for their survival.

My father was a teacher and my mother was a dressmaker. They raised me religiously. We kept all the *mitzvoth* and I never felt the need to violate Shabbat. I'm still married to an observant Jew and we keep a religious house. Sometimes, people who're aware of my work compare me to heroic Jewish women in the Bible, like Deborah the prophet or Tamar who fought for the life of Israel.[24]

Did you fight in the army?

No, I did my national service in Magen David Adom because I wanted to go to university and you spend fewer years in Magen David. Serving in the army helps build your Jewish identity. If you weren't raised a Zionist, it helps you distinguish yourself from non-Jews. But my schooling and upbringing were based on national and religious identification so I didn't need it.

Being an Israeli means loving this country, the people, government, army and authorities. Unlike in the US, here the government sees itself as above the people. When Yitzhak Rabin said 'the settlers can fly like propellers', he spat on half the people. I voted Likud last time, for my sins, but when Ariel Sharon says

involvement in the World Trade Center attack. Our clients are seeking compensation for the harm they suffered in the Metropolitan Detention Center by prison officials. In addition, the lawsuit will serve as an important forum to debunk the lie that Israel or the Mossad was behind the 9/11 terrorist attacks. It will show that there was no Jewish conspiracy as the Arab world continues to claim and put an end to this racist blood libel."'

24. According to the Bible, the prophet Deborah lived an independently wealthy and dauphinesque life in Ataroth. She was the wife of Lappidoth and an independently minded judge of Israel in the twelfth century BC. After enlisting the help of Barak, she is credited with seeing off the Canaanites. However, after singing of herself too boastfully, she was deprived of the spirit of prophecy for a time. Tamar was a daughter of King David who was raped by her half-brother Amnon, after rejecting his advances. Tamar's brother Absalom bided his time, and when the opportunity arose, took revenge by having Amnon killed.

he will continue his programme despite the people's wishes, he puts himself above them. It's hard to identify with such a government.

Outside Israel, people still believe in Judaism and having a strong Israel, but living here makes you see things differently. Being loyal to your country means that, as a soldier, you have to obey orders even if they go against your conscience, but does it mean you have to respect your government?

Are there cases where conscientious refusal would be defensible?

Some Rabbis say that disobeying an order to evacuate settlers is permitted under Halacha. Religious people would have a conflict because they are obligated first to Jewish law. On the other hand, people who won't harm a Palestinian because it's against their conscience don't have a law system (laughs). So that's not defensible at all.

In Shurat Hadin, we wrote a brief about how Jewish law permits you to assassinate people, including civilians. But you don't go and assassinate civilians. If, in the course of a mission, some civilians get killed, it's permitted (laughs). According to Jewish law, you have the right to kill whoever wants to kill you first.

Since the day of creation, Israel's enemies desired to eat it. Yes, since ancient times, all the people surrounding Israel wanted to destroy it because of its Jewish identity. Obviously, when Israel is surrounded by non-Jewish countries, it will live in a time of a war. That's why security is so important for Israelis; the state would not exist without it. For religious Jews, living elsewhere with autonomy might be the ideal solution. You don't need security for Jewish identity but you definitely need it for Israeli Jewish identity.

What goes through your mind when I say the word 'Palestinians'?

There is no such thing (laughs). They didn't even call themselves Palestinians until the PLO was created. They should join Jordan or Egypt where they belong. They should never be given autonomy. I know, I know, it's not realistic. But I believe that they were nothing to begin with. They were never a people. They don't have their own history, places or language. They're nothing. They're just a bunch of Arabs who were living here before '48, and Oslo was a terrible mistake that brought them back to life. I think the Palestinians are our enemy. They declared war on us and Israel should do anything it can to destroy them.

How did you become a lawyer?

I originally wanted to be a doctor. Later, I decided that becoming a *pro bono* lawyer would help people more. As a student, I argued human rights cases before the Supreme Court. I went on to represent terror victims and slowly Shurat Hadin became a civil rights organisation.

Is it now a law centre, a campaign, or an alternative tourism group?

It's all of them! It used to be a law centre but you can't do law without propaganda. Sometimes you need the media to get the information out. We're a non-profit organisation and we try to take cases that accord with our beliefs. All our income comes from fund-raising. We used to go to the US to do it but then we thought of bringing people to fund-raise here. At first, Ultimate Mission was geared to lawyers who wanted to learn about the security situation. Now, we get judges and doctors too and after the course, they help us with cases around the world.

On their first day, we bomb them with lectures. They hear a Palestinian collaborator's story and receive lectures from the defence minister, IDF chiefs and Shin Bet and Mossad officials on how Israel fights terror. We observe a Hamas terrorist trial and get briefed by the chief justice of the Supreme Court. We go to frontline checkpoints in Gaza and the Lebanese border where they can eyeball Hezbollah and we have a tour of the Defence Fence. It not only shows how bad or strong Israel is – although that's one of our goals – but how in spite of the horror we face, Israel still cares about human rights. We go with Raanan Gissin to the prime minister's chamber and meet his assistant, Dov Weinglass. Benjamin Netanyahu and Shaul Mofaz[25] addressed the group last time and we really appreciated that.

How did you persuade them to come?

We bribed them (laughs). Everywhere we go in the Israeli government, all the ministries and politicians like our work. They know what we do and they want to help us in any way they can. They appreciate our work and this helps us get it done. I don't think the head of Mossad would send his assistant to speak with us if he didn't appreciate what we did.

What do they want to pay you back for?

For doing the things they wish to but cannot (laughs). Everyone would like to wreck Arafat and the Palestinian Authority. Everyone would like to bankrupt Syria and Iran. Everybody wants to take revenge on the European Union but they can't do it as a government. So if we try to do it civilly and legally, they'd like to assist us.

But isn't this 'terror tourism' in bad taste?

You know, the symbol of the Mission is an Israeli gunman (laughs). It's fanatic, yeah. Maybe we should moderate it a bit. Look, we're not a tourism company.

25. Benjamin Netanyahu is the former prime minister of Israel and current finance minister under Ariel Sharon. Shaul Mofaz was appointed Sharon's defence minister in November 2002. Prior to that, he was the chief of staff for the IDF.

We do this to get funding and find people who want to help the organisation. Although we're not affiliated to any group, you see a line towards where it's going. Ultimate Mission is geared to the people who're prepared to take a risk – after all, it's not a safe time to visit – because they're dedicated to Israel and scared for its fate. Many people are concerned about Israel's security, so we could have used a lighter logo, but our goal is to teach people so they will go back and spread the word.

Do you feel any discomfort at hosting Christian Zionists whose ultimate goal is that a third of Jews will be converted and the rest killed?

Right, you know, until the bottom line (laughs), I like them very much. I shouldn't worry about it. It won't happen in my time. We had some Christians on our Missions and they were very nice people. They really believe that Israel should be strong. Their motivation is a little different but as long as it doesn't contradict ours, they're ok.

How were their reactions to the tours different from those of Jews?

They cry (laughs). They are very sensitive. I think they never thought about Israel this way and it touches them. Like 'Small Israel', they learn about tiny and weak Israel and then hear how Israel can also fight. It makes them proud that they're supporting this country. You know, it fits all their nice Bible stories. Jews in the Diaspora take Israel for granted but if they come on the course, they're not unaffected by it. They send me letters saying, 'I've been to Israel 25 times and this is the only time I've seen what it really is.'

Why have you pursued an action to get EU member states classified as sponsors of terrorism in Washington?

The EU supports the Palestinian Authority and, accordingly, Palestinian terrorism. These actions may involve western democratic countries, but so did the Holocaust. You can't ignore or forgive them. The European Union gave the Palestinian Authority $10m a month, when they knew that Arafat was the mastermind of terrorism. They didn't care. They blocked their eyes and ears and continued to support terror. The EU's own report said he stole $9bn. What makes you think he didn't use it for terrorism?

You also campaigned in defence of the soldier accused of killing Tom Hurndall.

He was a scapegoat. Listen, everything might be true. Maybe he was protecting a child. But what was he doing in Gaza in the first place? It's a war zone, not a playground. Wherever these ISM activists go, a bunch of bored kids follow after them. So you know who was born first, the chicken or the egg? If he wasn't there, the child wouldn't have been there. But it's not the thing. He might have been shot by someone else and the cause of death might not have been the bullet.

Do you think the war on terror will ever be won?

No! The US didn't fight against it until they got hit themselves and they still limit the steps Israel can take. Until it cuts your flesh, countries don't get involved. Even then, they don't do it in the massive way. Only countries that constantly get hit hard will fight this war. Primarily, this means Israel alone. How can you beat terrorism? You're talking about insane people whose motivation is to kill. They don't do it because they are promised 72 virgins in heaven. I read their confessions and everyone has his own reason: they killed my cousin or our group's leader, so I took revenge; I was threatened; I wanted to prove that I wasn't a collaborator. They're not afraid to die so you can't beat them. We can't fulfil their demands because they don't have demands.

Aren't they fighting for a homeland?

Yeah, a national state on the land of Israel, maybe that would satisfy them. You can consider that if you want. But you know what, none of their leaders ever says, 'If you give us the West Bank, Gaza, the Golan Heights, Jerusalem, we're going to live peacefully with you'. This is a nation that wants a war. You see 200,000 Israeli leftists demonstrating for peace, you don't see five people in the Muqata doing the same. They don't want peace. The only way to achieve their goals is terror and, even if it subsides, you still have Al-Qaida. The sides are too far away to even try to compromise.

When people talk about a Palestinian state, they don't think about giving them control of their borders, airports, or sea ports. They wouldn't let them buy tanks, artillery or explosives, because it would be national suicide. So the Palestinians are thinking about a completely different state than we are. I'm not even talking about Jerusalem. There will never be a way to compromise on it, or the right of return. So, Israel has to be strong and protect itself until whenever. That's what we did for the last 50 years.

Does Sharon's Gaza plan do this?

It's not a step towards peace. It may be the opposite. It will increase terrorism, just like it did in Lebanon, and that's why the Second Intifada occurred. If you give in to their demands, you pump them and give them reason to fight. Even Sharon didn't say it would reduce terrorism.

Politically, I don't know if we have an impact but we've been able to freeze a lot of money that belonged to the Palestinian Authority. We got judgments against Iran. I represented a belly dancer in a rape case against the Egyptian ambassador. With the Druze soldier against Tom Hurndall, we showed that people still support the IDF, and I know it meant a lot to him. This tool gives you a lot of satisfaction. I'm not holding a gun. I'm not shooting anyone. But I'm able to win some aspect of this war with law.

9
Across the Green Line

After 1967, Israel justified its conquest of the West Bank and Gaza to the world in terms of 'security' – preventing Arab invasions and terrorist attacks. Within Israel, however, it quickly became a matter of faith. In the run-up to the 1967 war, Israeli media and politicians contributed to a widespread expectation of imminent invasion and national catastrophe. Moshe Dayan described how the public came to view 'what was at stake [as] the very survival of Israel'.[1] The religious constituency in Israel, which had once expressed such scepticism towards Zionism, began to explain the lightning victory and conquest of substantial parts of biblical Israel by reference to divine intervention.

The biblical instruction in Deuteronomy (11: 24) that 'our border shall be from the wilderness, from the river Euphrates to the western sea' was suddenly back in vogue. The Messianic ideas popularised in Rabbi Tzvi Yehuda Kook's Merkaz HaRav yeshiva spread like wildfire. Kook advanced his father Rabbi Yitzhak HaCohen Kook's metaphorical reinterpretation of scripture. According to biblical lore, the new Kingdom of Israel would be presaged by the return of the Messiah, a poor man, riding into Jerusalem on a white donkey. Kook postulated that the Messiah had returned in 1948 as the collective spirit of religiously conscious Jewry. The 'donkey' was a singular allegory for the secular atheists who pioneered the Zionist state. It was thus incumbent on all true believers to fulfil their side of Abraham's covenant with God by resettling biblical Israel and dwelling in close proximity to the holy sites.

Religious settlers began fanning out across the occupied territories and putting down roots. In early 1974, Kook's followers founded Gush Emunim (the Bloc of the Faithful) to initiate new settlements and expand already existing ones. Yitzhak Rabin and Shimon Peres, the then-prime minister and defence minister, offered the settlers every assistance.[2] The seizure of strategic high land and,

1. Moshe Dayan, *Story of my Life* (Warner Books, 1977), p. 373.
2. Israel Shahak and Norton Mezvinsky, *Jewish Fundamentalism in Israel* (Pluto, 1999), pp. 55, 84.

crucially, water resources[3] also advanced a more secular national security interest. The settlements united religious and secular Israeli Jews around a self-concept that merged faith and security and held out the prospect of an integrated Israeli Jewish identity.

The resulting consensus stretched far and lasted beyond the mass national awakening of the first Palestinian Intifada. In the summer of 2004, a Jewish activist in Ta'ayush, a far-left Jewish–Arab solidarity movement, told me that even some of her comrades had a sneaking sympathy with the settlers. 'People admire them because they walk it like they talk it,' she said. 'While they're putting their lives on the line for Israel, we're eating sushi in Tel Aviv cafés'. The religious camp constitutes a minority in Israel and probably a minority among the settlers as well. But they are a crucial minority. Deconstructing the settlements threatens to unravel the religious–secular alliance, which in 1967 led even Uri Avnery, the founder of Gush Shalom, to vote for the annexation of East Jerusalem.[4]

Thirty-six years later, when Ariel Sharon first used the 'O' word (occupation) while accepting the US 'road map' to peace, the settler and Likud MK Yehiel Hazan told him, 'I want to know whether I can stay in my home. Will my children continue to bleed?' Hazan is a far rightist who attributes murderous Palestinian anti-Semitism to a genetic defect and describes Arabs as 'worms'.[5] If Sharon had wanted to begin unravelling the settlers' alliance, Hazan's intervention offered him the perfect opportunity. His reply was decisive. 'It will definitely

3. Jessica Mccallin, 'Making the blooms desert', *Red Pepper*, May 2002. 'More than a quarter of [Israel's] water supplies now come from the West Bank Aquifer – and over a third comes from the Jordan Basin. But it has no legal right to the water – and it is not using it sustainably. Private swimming pools and green lawns are not a priority in desert areas. Over-extraction from the Jordan River is the main reason the river flow has dropped nearly 90 percent in the last 50 years. It is now just a small stream, too small to replenish the Dead Sea, which is also fast disappearing. Many hydrologists predict that it won't exist in 50 years.'
4. Warschawski, *On the Border*, p. 21. 'In the fall of 1967, the dissident deputy Uri Avnery voted for the annexation of East Jerusalem. His decision could not have been based on security considerations; the rationale was the historico-religious reasoning that would become an essential component of the new Israeli consensus, the very same that would justify the full scale policy of settlements in the future.'
5. Aljazeera.net, 'Israeli MP: Arabs are worms', 14 December 2004. Yair Ettinger, 'Israeli minister muses on Palestinian "genetic defect"', *Ha'aretz*, 24 February 2004. Aljazeera.net quoted Hazan as saying, 'The Arabs are worms. You find them everywhere like worms, underground as well as above... These worms have not stopped attacking Jews for a century.' In defence of the Israeli Defence Minister, Ze'ev Boim, who made the comment about a genetic Arab defect, *Ha'aretz* quoted Hazan as saying, 'It is well known that Arabs have been slaughtering and murdering Jews for more than a generation. I think that it is in their blood. It is something genetic.'

be possible and there is no restriction here,' he said. 'You can build for your children and grandchildren and, I hope, even for your great-grandchildren.'[6]

However, whether Hazan's offspring live in West Bank domiciles under Israeli sovereignty may be another question. For a little-noticed intricacy in Messianic philosophy holds that while the land is sacred, ownership of it is not. In June 2005, Drori Stuan, a community leader in Kadim, one of the settlements pencilled in for evacuation under Sharon's disengagement plan, even requested political asylum for 75 of the settlement's residents from Mahmoud Abbas: 'If the state of Israel doesn't want us, we don't want it,' he told *Yediot Aharonot*.

> We are people who intend to carry on living in Samaria under Palestinian rule and not under Israeli rule. There are Jews everywhere in the world: in Syria, in Iraq, in Iran, in Pakistan, so we want to be Jews under Palestinian sovereignty. We are not afraid and I believe it will be good for us and we will live safely, like Jews in other parts of the world.[7]

The Palestinian Authority's chief foreign ministry policy analyst, Majdi al-Khalidi, responded favourably to the request. If secular Israel is unable to tackle the vicious circle linking faith with security, a spectre haunting secular Zionism is that some settlers themselves could break it from the inside out.

ESTHER LILLENTHAL

A foothold to hang on to

Because Israeli Jews were not allowed to travel freely in the Gaza Strip, there were only two ways to visit settlements there in 2004: in a settler's car (with Jewish licence plates) or on a military bus. The armoured coach I travelled on had reinforced opaque windows, which blurred the ragged Palestinian families scattered around meagre allotments and rubbish tips in the distance. Few of the soldiers on board seemed to notice them. The Jewish-only roads we travelled at breakneck speeds were pockmarked by tanks around the settlements we entered to pick up and disgorge passengers. 'I won't evacuate settlements and all my friends say they won't do it either,' one soldier from the Golani Brigade told me. 'I believe in war. They want war and we should give it to them. Otherwise Israel will be a tiny country'. Esther Lillenthal, an erstwhile American Jew, spoke more diplomatically. She lived in Neve Dekalim, a settlement in the Gush Khatif bloc. The town resembled an anonymous American

6. Megan K. Stack, 'Occupation must end, Sharon says', *LA Times*, 27 May 2003.
7. Lawrence Smallman, 'Palestinian Jewish settlers?', Aljazeera.net, 5 June 2005.

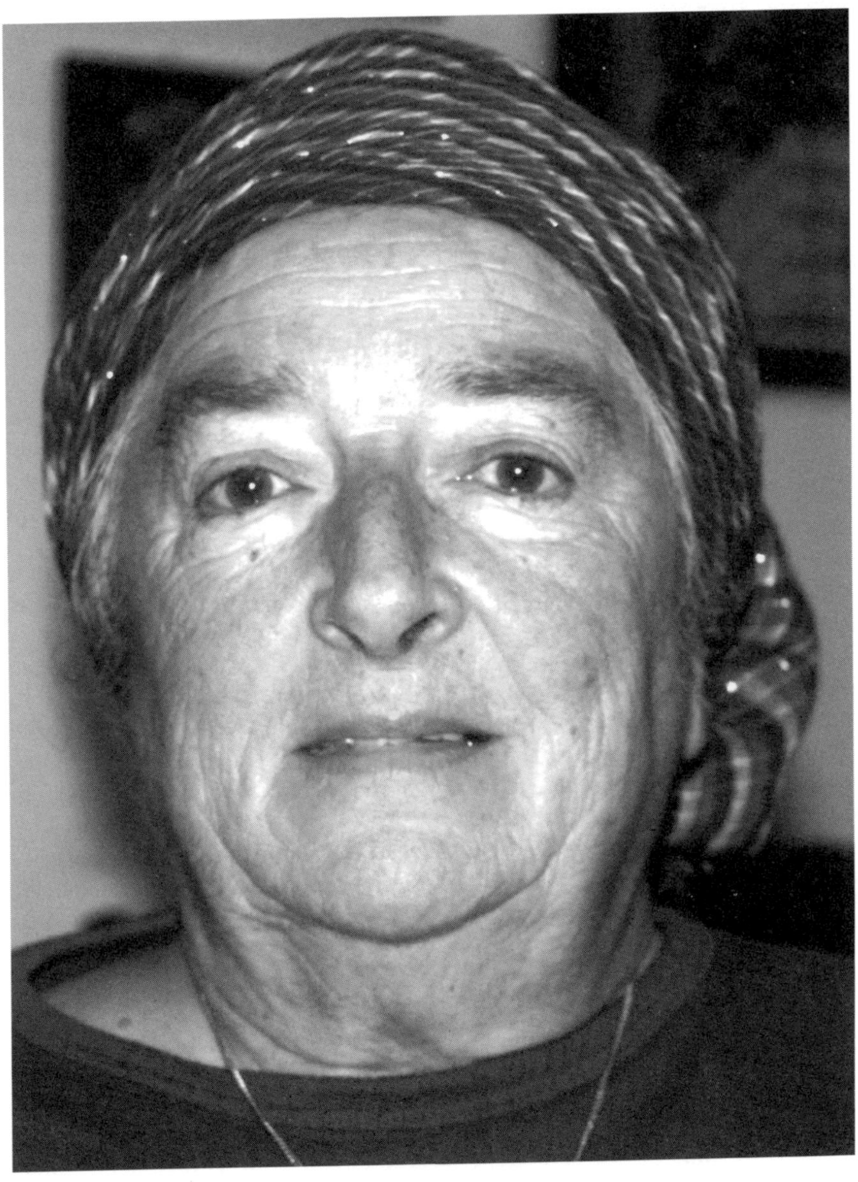

Esther Lillenthal. *Photo by Arthur Neslen*

suburb, except for the soldiers at the entrance, and military helicopters that compassed menacingly overhead.

I was born in Shtetin, Germany. Today that's in Poland. After World War II, the townspeople were given 24 hours to pack their bags and leave, so I am not in favour of the transfer of anyone. I was two years old when my family fled to London in 1939. We stayed there until the end of the war. My father was interned in an aliens' camp on the Isle of Man. He never talked about it. I remember the bombing of London, the pilotless planes and going to school with a gas mask. I remember a lot of things.

After the war, we moved to an Irish–Jewish neighbourhood in Brooklyn and I went to the Yeshiva Jewish High School for Girls. After university, I became a teacher and married an Israeli. We had four children and in 1971, after my sister made *aliyah*, we packed our bags for Israel. That was what I was taught to do. Zionism was my future and I always knew that when I grew up, I would go home. This is where the Jewish people have their roots, history, language, culture, everything. Here you have the opportunity to stand up and defend yourself. You don't have to go like cattle to the slaughter. Every Jew who visits Israel has that feeling of being among your own. Some people suggested that it mightn't be a good place to raise children. I replied that there were wars elsewhere too.

We moved to Neve Dekalim 13 years ago. We were in Jerusalem and I had two sons living in Gush Khatif, one of whom was expecting triplets. I told my husband, 'They don't have enough hands to hold all those babies. We'd better go help'. We've been here ever since. Generally, it's been a beautiful life, paradise. You couldn't ask for anything more. We had good relations with our Arab neighbours. I have a friend in Khan Younis who told me the Arabs were less against the Jews than the Christians because Judaism is closer to Islam. I didn't really understand that. He used to teach us Arabic but things changed. We still phone him but we can't visit any more. I won't tell you his name because I don't want to hurt him, God forbid.

Of course the people in Khan Younis were also evacuated from their homes.

When? They may be refugees but they weren't evacuated. Their own people told them to leave so it would be easier for them to wipe out the fledgling Jewish state.[8] The Arabs who stayed are still living in Haifa, Acco and Ramle. If the

8. This contention began with Yosef Weitz, the director of the Jewish National Fund's Lands Division and chairman of the Government's Transfer Committee. Weitz argued that the flight of refugees in 1948 was 'deliberately organized by the Arab leaders in order to arouse Arab feelings of revenge, to artificially create an Arab refugee problem... and to prepare the ground for the invasion of Palestine by the Arab

Arabs are not ready to live side by side with us here, they should be given the opportunity to leave.

Every other day, mortars fall here now. It's a miracle more people haven't been killed. The day before Yom Kippur, a young woman who worked in our little zoo was killed by a mortar that fell on her house. I'm on the absorption committee so I was there when she was accepted into this town. I don't think we can do anything but stand firm in response. Where are we going to go, Shtetin? I don't even speak Polish. If people pack up and run, Tel Aviv and Haifa will be threatened tomorrow. Arabs have killed Jews since before Israel's existence. There was a Jewish community in Gaza City itself until 1936[9] and some Gazans tried to protect their Jewish neighbours. My gut feeling is that most of them are good people. Given a chance the two peoples could live side by side.

But you see Gaza as part of Israel.

Certainly, have you looked at a map lately?

Even though there aren't any significant holy sites here?

That's not true. You should read the Bible a little more! In Gaza City, there used to be an old Jewish neighbourhood and a mosque with Hebrew writing and a menorah on its wall. There's also a magnificent mosaic floor in Gaza-by-the-sea of King David playing his harp with Hebrew inscriptions. It's the symbol of Neve Dekalim.

The people from Yamit[10] pooled their reparations money and built a new yeshiva here when they were uprooted because their old buildings were

States who could then appear as saviours of their brothers'. Weitz argued that the Palestinians believed that they would 'return not only to their own homes but also to the houses of the Jews and… inherit the possessions'. This version of history has been discredited by Israeli historians and others. In an article called 'The Other Exodus', published in *The Spectator* (12 May 1961), Erskine Childers, the British–Irish son of the president of Ireland, produced evidence of repeated Arab appeals for Palestinians to *stay in their homes* during the 1948 fighting. He concluded that 'official Zionist forces were responsible for the expulsion of thousands upon thousands of Arabs and for deliberate incitement to panic'.

9. Jewish Virtual Library: Jewish settlements which had existed in Gaza for centuries were attacked during the 1936–9 Palestinian uprising. In the aftermath, the British Mandate authorities forced these Jews to leave their homes and prohibited Jews from living in Gaza and Hebron. The Shaw Commission's report subsequently blamed the riots on Palestinian disappointment that their political and national aspirations had not been met and fears about their economic domination by a group with seemingly unlimited finances from abroad.
10. Shlaim, *The Iron Wall*, p. 398. Yamit was a Jewish settlement built in Sinai after Israel's 1967 conquest of the peninsula. Following a peace agreement with Egypt's President Sadat, a withdrawal was negotiated. 'As minister of defence, Sharon was responsible for implementing the withdrawal… Generous financial compensation was offered

destroyed. They left their synagogue standing. The soldiers who came back from there told us the Arabs were using it as a barn for their animals. What's going to happen to our synagogues? It's hard to imagine them being destroyed.

The prospect of evacuation may make me question my behaviour but not my faith. I regret that so many people have been killed and injured, on both sides. My oldest son in the Shamron was attacked by terrorists when he was travelling to Bnei Brak. The driver of the car was killed, and he was shot in his legs. He still walks, with a crutch.

We're only God's tenants. If he wants us out of here, we'll be out, like it or not. But we believe he promised the land to our ancestors. When there was a famine, God spoke to Isaac and said 'don't go to Egypt, stay here'. Where was he when God said that? In the land of Grar. The village below the bridge on the way here is called El Grara. It was right here.

Before Israel was established, the Arabs here thought of themselves as Syrians and Egyptians. The *Palestine Post* was a Jewish paper, the Palestine Orchestra was a Jewish orchestra, the Palestine Bank was a Jewish bank.[11] They didn't need to play the underdog then because they were part of a great nation. If they want to call themselves Palestinians now, they may. But this is my one and only homeland and they have quite a few options.

Don't white European Jews have many different homelands?

Do they? I don't think so. In Belgium there are Belgians, in Germany there are Germans, in Poland there are Poles and in the land of Israel there are Israelites.

Well, in Jordan there are Jordanians, in Iraq there are Iraqis…

But they're all Arabs! And they speak the same language.[12]

---

to these settlers but many of them refused to leave of their own accord… Resistance to the withdrawal lasted several days and was accompanied by heart-breaking scenes on television. But in the end, the IDF succeeded in evacuating all the settlers and demonstrators without bloodshed. Sharon ordered the IDF to destroy the town of Yamit to its foundations instead of surrendering it to the Egyptians as envisaged in the peace treaty.'

11. In the Yishuv, settlers created their own banks, orchestras and newspapers. For example, *The Palestine Post* was an English-language Zionist newspaper founded in 1932 by an American journalist, Gershon Agron. In 1950, its name was changed to the *Jerusalem Post*. The paper supported the campaign for a Jewish homeland in Palestine and opposed British policy restricting Jewish immigration during the Mandate period. It still publishes today.
12. In fact Arabic exists in three forms: the Classical Arabic of the Qur'an; the literary language developed from the classical and referred to as Modern Standard Arabic, which has virtually the same structure wherever used; and the spoken language. Uneducated Arabs may have problems understanding Modern Standard Arabic, and huge variations in dialect, accent and pronunciation between Arab countries are

Do you see the hitnatkut as a dispute between religious and secular Jews?

Maybe, I don't really know how secular Jews feel. They'd give up the lands that we took in '67, which were the impetus for my family to return to our homeland. We didn't start that war, and if God put these lands in our hands we have no right to make light of that. It's a black mark on our education system that some of the seculars don't even see themselves as Jewish. All that stops them from becoming lost to the Jewish people is living here. The minute they leave, they're the first to assimilate. You need some hold on your background and many of them don't have one. Their idea of civil marriages would divide us. The people who follow the Torah would have to keep records of who-married-who, to know that their children were actually marrying Jews. The Jewish people are a family and they marry within the fold. It keeps it a tribe.

Would you prefer an Israel governed by the laws of the Knesset or the halacha?

Halacha means 'walking'. It's a moving thing that changes with the times. In years gone by, the Knesset tried to govern according to the laws of the Torah. It would take some adjusting to do it now but Torah education could solve many problems in our country. Religious Jews have a more secure identity because we continue the traditions of our forefathers so we have a foothold to hang on to. Other people get into trouble because they're really floating around. We're living in a pre-messianic age and according to our sages, it's a time of upheaval. This land is acquired by suffering and we're living through that terrible period now. I hope it won't last long.

What do you think will be lost if disengagement goes ahead?

I'm hoping that it won't, you understand? It would be a very bad precedent. Yamit was earth-shattering for those who lived through it, some of whom now live here and are determined not to go through it again. They're reminding everybody that it was Arik Sharon who brought them here. One man in Elai Sinai told me that Arik Sharon took him to his place and said, 'This is it. Put down your roots. This is the land of Israel and here you will stay.' For Sharon now to tell us to go somewhere else is a dangerous betrayal. When we're gone, the Arabs will be able to fire their mortars into power plants, Ashkelon and Sharon's farm.

It's impossible to imagine them living in the houses of people they've killed. How could you even think about giving the Arabs the house of, say, Tali Hatuel and her daughters in Khatif.[13] The young people are anxious. The uncertainty

---

such that a Syrian would find colloquial Moroccan Arabic, for example, virtually incomprehensible.

13. Tali Hatuel, a pregnant Israeli social worker, was killed along with her four daughters on 2 May 2004 by armed Palestinians. She was shot while driving out of the Gush Khatif settlement bloc entrance on her way to protest at Ariel Sharon's disengagement plan.

is more difficult for them. I'm retired but a lot of them have lost their jobs. Even the telephone company has pulled out. Most people are calmly going about their lives but some want to take more strenuous action. Few will take the money and run. In secular settlements like Nisamit, where people mainly came because they were offered housing benefits, they're just sitting and waiting for the reparations, which is sad.

I voted NRP but I'm very disappointed in Sharon. He ran on a right-wing platform but is governing on the Labour party's. I wonder whether he was moved by his money problems. It's still not clear why he made such a complete about-face and he certainly hasn't explained himself. He was a hero in our wars. He laid his life on the line but he's almost become my enemy. He's carrying out an extreme leftist policy that's unheard of. If the government doesn't fall, a lot of people will come here and physically try to prevent the *hitnatkut*.

So should soldiers disobey orders to evacuate you?

Well, after World War II, German soldiers were called to account and they weren't allowed to say, 'I was following orders'. I would say to our soldiers: keep that in mind. You're accountable for your deeds. If you think that what you're ordered to do is immoral, don't do it. But don't think that a Jewish soldier would shoot one of us. It won't happen.

What sort of people have moved here to join your movement?

Some are activists from Likud and Lieberman's party. There are some Kachniks[14] living here. Bibi Netanyahu's brother-in-law, Ben Artzi, has moved to Atzmona to take a stand. In America, though, people seem to think that it's a trick of Sharon's and he'll pull some rabbit out of the hat to halt it at some stage. We're very grateful for the support of Christian Zionists who've come and encouraged us.

How often do you see your family here?

My children are gone. Two of them live in Gush Khatif. We see less of the other two. This Shabbat, my son from Atzmona is coming here with his nine children (chuckles). We're already great-grandparents. I see a future for the family who've stayed here.

14. Avigdor Lieberman's secular National Union party supports the 'voluntary' transfer of Palestinians from the West Bank and Gaza. The term 'havdalah' or transfer was first coined by Rabbi Meir Kahane of the Kach party, who some call fascist. A poll in October 2004 for Israel's Channel 2 TV found that 58 per cent of Israelis between the ages of 18 and 22 supported the expulsions of Arabs from Israel.

What will you do if you're evacuated?

I haven't the foggiest. I haven't given it any consideration. If and when they come to evict me, I don't even know if I'll open the door. I'm certainly not packing yet.

HANAN PORAT

We have nuclear weapons to prevent another Holocaust

Hanan Porat is one of Israel's most famous religious Zionists. A former leader of the far right National Religious party, he achieved notoriety in 1994 when, on national television, he appeared to echo Baruch Goldstein's last words before massacring 29 Palestinian civilians: 'Happy Purim'. Porat was born in Kfar Etzion, a town in the West Bank first settled by Jews in 1927. Despite receiving financial support from Shmuel Holzmann and the Jewish National Fund, the settlers were finally forced by Palestinian uprisings to evacuate their homes in 1948.[15] The sons and daughters of the pre-1948 settlers re-established Kfar Etzion after Israel's conquest of the West Bank, in 1967. In the years that followed, Porat, along with figures such as Moshe Levinger and Menachem Froman, was a high-profile student at Rabbi Tzvi Yehuda Kook's Merkaz HaRav yeshiva. With them, he went on to found the Gush Emunim [block of the faithful] settlers' movement. Porat was a five-times elected MK, Chairman of the parliament's Constitution, Law and Justice Committee and member of several other panels including the Foreign Affairs and Defence Committee. Prior to this interview, no serving or former Israeli Jewish MK had admitted on the record the scale of Israel's nuclear programme.

My memories of Kfar Etzion, the town where I was born, are not a sequence. They are like still pictures, flashes of things. I remember the view, the mountains, the roads. I remember going with my father to milk cows by lamplight and the children picking flowers in the mountains with such joy. I was almost five years old when Gush Etzion was occupied in 1948. Just before it fell, we walked to some fruit trees on a hill, dressed in white costumes – parents carrying their children on their shoulders – and we picked fruits. The town was already under siege and we were waiting to be evacuated. I was put on the roof of the Beit Knesset[16] with a guard who had lit the surrounding villages with a spotlight. I

15. *Gush Etzion and the Hebron Hills Booklet* from the Keren Kayemeth Le'Israel (Religious section) and Educational Center Kfar Etzion.
16. A synagogue or 'house of gathering'.

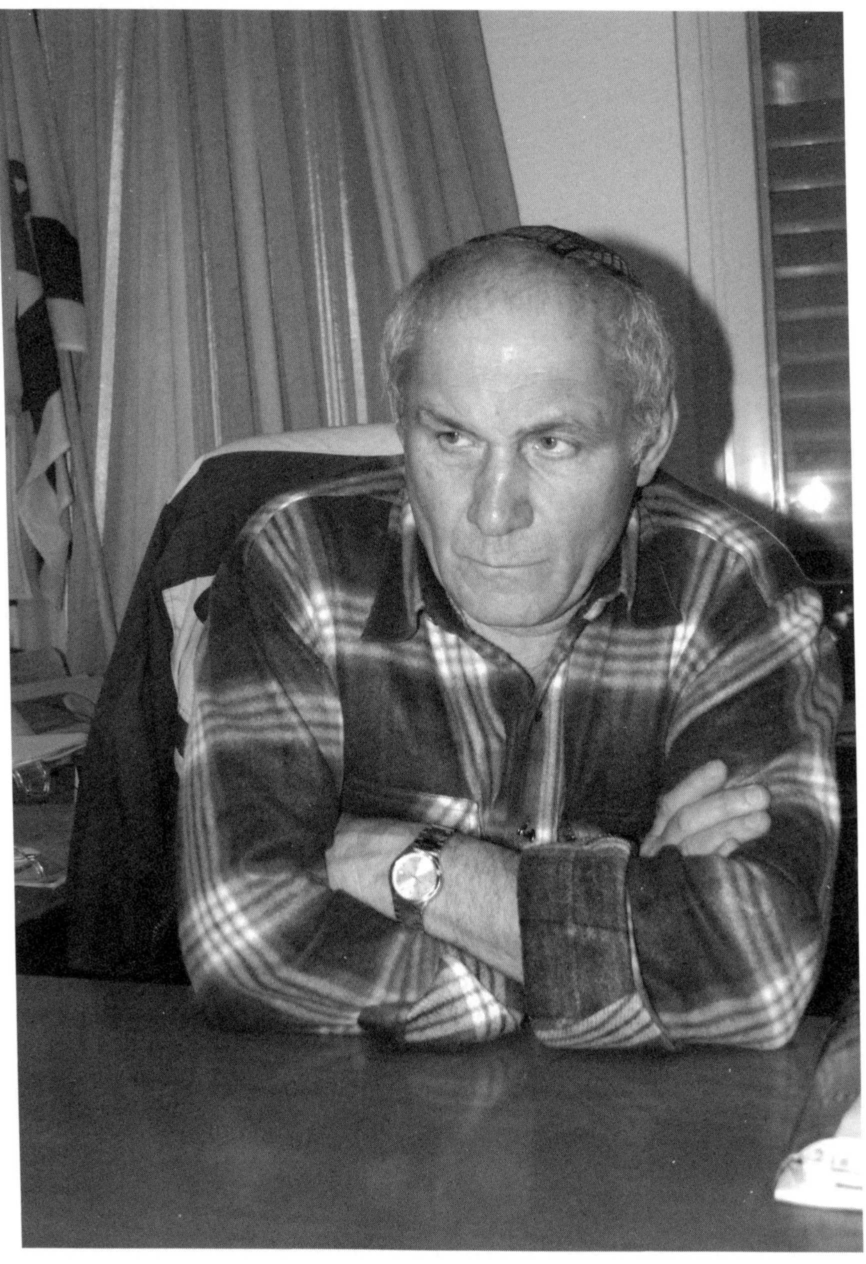

Hanan Porat. *Photo by Arthur Neslen*

was frightened and I told him, 'See how small we are compared to them? They are so many!' He replied, 'But they are in darkness and we have the light.'

Most of our parents were killed in the fighting but, thankfully, the Hagana sent my father to organise the troops who brought food and supplies to Gush Etzion. He had to stay in Jerusalem because the roads back were closed. We went there with our mother when the situation deteriorated. I don't know if I should say 'exile' but we felt that we'd been torn away. They cut our roots brutally. In the last battle, more than 140 people were killed in one day.[17] Most died in battle, the others were shot and bombed in a bunker after they surrendered. Only three men survived.

The power of the tragedy connects Kfar Etzion and the Hebron events of 1929,[18] but there was one big difference. Kfar Etzion fell the day before the state of Israel was declared. We really felt that despite all the pain, they had given their lives for the state and their blood was not in vain. My father came from Poland and most of his family were killed in the Holocaust. That taught me that this is the only place for Jews, and that evil in this world has no limit. You must be strong and never give in to it. Chamberlain, for instance, passively took part in the Holocaust.

Do you see any parallels between Chamberlain and Sharon's Gaza plan?

Undoubtedly, it's not just Sharon, it's the general attitude in the western world that you should understand and compromise with terror. Arab terror is a whole philosophy which wants to control the world. In that context, Sharon's plan is a criminal act because it cuts people off from their land for political – not security – reasons. That's why I objected to the peace-time transfer of Arabs.

But haven't you supported transfer?

I never used the term 'transfer'. But of course if people want to leave for personal reasons, there's no cause to stop them. Many Arabs want to leave Israel but other Arab countries are preventing them going. Transfer is forbidden but so is preventing free movement.

Would you like them to leave?

Yes. In the current situation, when the Arabs are so overwhelmingly hostile to Jews, I would, of course, be happy if there was a migration, especially of those

17. Jewish Virtual Library puts the number of dead at 127.
18. A community of Arabic-speaking Mizrahi Jews had lived peacefully in Hebron for centuries but in the early years of the twentieth century, tensions grew when Ashkenazi – and explicitly Zionist – immigrants began to settle in the town. On 23 August 1929, the town exploded into rioting and 67 Jews were killed, 55 of them Ashkenazi's. The survivors of the massacre were relocated to Jerusalem by the British authorities.

who don't want to be here, or don't want us to be here. I think we can find a way for Arabs to live here happily and peacefully under Israeli sovereignty. If someone raises his hand and acts with violence or terror, though, he should be expelled.

Why is blowing up civilians on a bus to get a national state different from blowing up civilians in the King David Hotel[19] *to get a national state?*

I don't automatically support all the actions taken by Etzel and Lehi before 1948 but at least that action was targeted on the British and civilians were given a warning. Palestinian terrorists directly target civilians. It's partly our responsibility. If we ruled over them more strictly and prevented anti-Semitic Arab media from getting into people's minds and affecting children, things would improve.

Apart from Zionism and religion, what else to you defines Jewishness?

Jewish consciousness is an eternal trait. That's why we define all Jews as belonging to one family, even if they're secular anti-Zionists. We don't have an entrance test for Jews. Every Jew is still my brother. The resurrection of the people of Israel is the way to resurrect the world. The people of Israel who live moral lives under God's light will become a great apostle for the world.

Is that light underwritten by the ability to visit darkness on others, in extremis with nuclear weapons?

God forbid no, it's an automatic contradiction and a distorted picture. Israel is the only small place that Jews have. The Arab world is one unit of millions of square kilometres, even though it's divided into many separate pieces.

So should Israel get rid of its nuclear weapons?

Today, of course it shouldn't because this is part of the balance that prevents the Arabs from destroying us. I have no doubt that Israel is responsible enough not to use these weapons in an attack, but only in a defensive way, if threatened with destruction. We have nuclear weapons to prevent another Holocaust here in Israel. It's clearly the only purpose. When Arab states say that if Israel has

19. On 22 July 1946, 91 people, most of them civilians, were killed when Jewish underground fighters loyal to Menachem Begin's Irgun bombed the King David Hotel in Jerusalem. The southern wing of the building was then being used as the headquarters of the British Secretariat, a military command and criminal investigations centre. Of the dead, 28 were British, 41 were Arabs, 17 were Jewish and five were other ethnicities. The Irgun claimed that they had delivered a warning to the hotel's telephone operator well in advance. However, an internal police report in the 1970s claimed that the warning was just being delivered to the British officer in charge when the bomb went off.

nuclear weapons, they should have them too, it's illegitimate because they don't want them for the same purpose.

What is more important to you, your faith or the land?

My connection to the land stems from my faith. God wants me to build the real world of faith and morality in Israel, personally and as part of a nation because a man is not alone. His faith is a national faith. The Zionist philosophy cannot exist without it.

Can't you have a connection to the land without owning it?

Of course, I don't myself own the land. God gave me my soul, and he gave this land to the people of Israel. It's an organic part of us, like part of my flesh. The ingathering of exiles and establishment of the state of Israel clearly point to a resurrection of the Jewish people. Even if there are severe crises, it's not a glass that's half empty. It's a very big glass which also has these moments of crisis in it. All the problems in Judea, Samaria and the Golan Heights stem from our mistakes, our corruption and the way we spoiled ourselves. The real question is whether freedom of choice can spoil God's choice. I can't give you a guarantee that the *hitnatkut* won't happen. But I'll do everything in my power to prevent it.

Will you support soldiers refusing orders or settlers wearing Orange Magen Davids?

I think it was a big mistake to wear this Magen David,[20] although I understand the psychological sorrow that brought them to it. The evacuation is immoral, unJewish and violates human rights. If Jews were expelled from Scotland, everyone would say it was anti-Semitic. That's why it's right to protest. If I were a soldier, I couldn't carry out these orders but I won't attack a brother Jew, whatever the price.

If a Palestinian state was created with security guarantees on your right to live and worship freely as a citizen in the West Bank, would you stay?

I would stay in Gush Etzion even if it was part of a Palestinian state, hoping that it would become part of Israel in the future. That's what happened in '37,

20. BBC News Online, 'Settlers' Star protest sparks ire', 22 December 2004. 'A group of settlers opposed to Israel's plan to force Jews out of the Gaza Strip have begun wearing orange stars recollecting the Holocaust... The move has touched a raw nerve in Israel, where many support the Gaza pullout and see the settlers' protest as trivialising the Nazi genocide... Said Moshe Freiman of the Gush Katif settlement bloc, "I sense that I am a victim of a new expulsion of Jews and that a Shoah is being visited on my home where I have lived for the last 28 years."'

when the Jewish establishment decided that settlements should stay, even under Palestinian authority. We're not ashamed to be called Messianics.

How did you feel when you saw a Palestinian violinist being forced to play for Jewish soldiers at checkpoints?[21]

This story is an anti-Semitic lie. Our soldiers don't want to hurt Palestinians. They didn't force him to play. He decided himself and they just opened the violin case to check if there was anything there. You can't compare it to the Holocaust. It wasn't like the Jews who went as sheep to their slaughter.

Why did you say 'Happy Purim' after Baruch Goldstein killed 29 people in Hebron?

This is also a lie. I told the people in Hebron that they should cleanse themselves of this horrible act by Baruch Goldstein, so it wouldn't stick to them.[22] I said 'Happy Purim' because that's what you say when you come to someone's house during Purim. Of course, Baruch Goldstein was a terrorist. But you can understand his distress.

21. Jonathan Freedland, 'Let's take off the blinkers and see clearly', *Jewish Chronicle*, 3 December 2004. In a strongly worded op-ed, Freedland wrote that the video of the incident, which was shot and released by the Israeli feminist group Women in Black, 'showed a Palestinian musician, forced by Israeli soldiers to play his violin at a military checkpoint. The Israelis suggested that Wissam Tayem "play something sad." Once he obliged, they jeered and laughed at him. For some reason, and I think we can all guess what that is, the image of the musician at gunpoint shook Israel from its slumber. Playwright Yoram Kaniuk, who had written about a Jewish violinist forced to play for a Nazi camp commandant, demanded that the soldiers involved be charged "not for abusing Arabs but for disgracing the Holocaust." In a rare move, the mass-circulation daily *Yediot Ahronot* moved columnist Meir Shalev to the front page where he echoed Kaniuk: "Once we were the people who played the violin…".'
22. Witnesses to the Hebron massacre reported that after walking into the Tomb of the Patriarchs, Baruch Goldstein said 'Happy Purim' before he began indiscriminately shooting Arab worshippers. On the same day, Hanan Porat appeared in a report on Israeli television. The only words he was reported to have said to camera were 'Happy Purim'.

ADAM BEN ZION

Intelligence is a dirty business

'Adam Ben Zion' is an anonymous-looking man in his mid-40s. Until a few days before this interview, he was one of the Israeli state's most senior intelligence analysts. He insists that there was 'no drama' in his decision to take early retirement and seek a second career. 'People from our place usually leave early,' he said. 'You cannot work in Nablus or Gaza for 25 years.'

I grew up in a protected upper middle-class neighbourhood, elite high school, university, good units in the army etc. Most of the time, I lived in Big Israel. I was nine when Jerusalem was liberated and 17 when I first went abroad. My father was a Holocaust survivor and this was his final stop. We didn't move. We'd had enough of that in exile. Until his death, he never left Israel.

I first became aware that Israel was surrounded by enemies in 1967. We watched the news and discussed politics so I understood the situation well. In my first year at a nationalist-religious high school, I decided to learn Arabic. At 14, I fell in love with the language and I went on to study it at University. We and the Arabs hate each other but we basically speak sister languages.

Looking back, I think my parents wanted to give me a normal childhood. My father occasionally told me frightening stories about his escape from Poland and the Ukrainian collaborators who betrayed him to the Nazis. For me, it proved that we needed our own state, army and political independence to defend ourselves.

If all Jews had lived here in 1941, couldn't the Holocaust have been successful?

Yes. I'm no determinist. Jewish independence is not enough. I believe that we should normalise as a nation like other nations rather than be a light unto the nations.[23] Despite my schooling, my family wasn't religious. We went to synagogue on Shabbat mornings and football matches in the afternoons. Today, the religious police expel children from schools for doing that. There was a

23. The debate about whether Israel's mission was secular and assimilationist or religious and Messianic. The phrase 'a light unto the nations' comes from the original covenant between God and Abraham in Isaiah 42:5–8, 'I, HaShem have called thee in righteousness, and have taken hold of thy hand, and kept thee, and set thee for a covenant of the people, for a light of the nations'. By contrast, the early Zionists, influenced by the more earthly nationalisms of their age, aimed at something less ambitious. The phrase 'a nation like other nations' was used by Herzl, Buber and

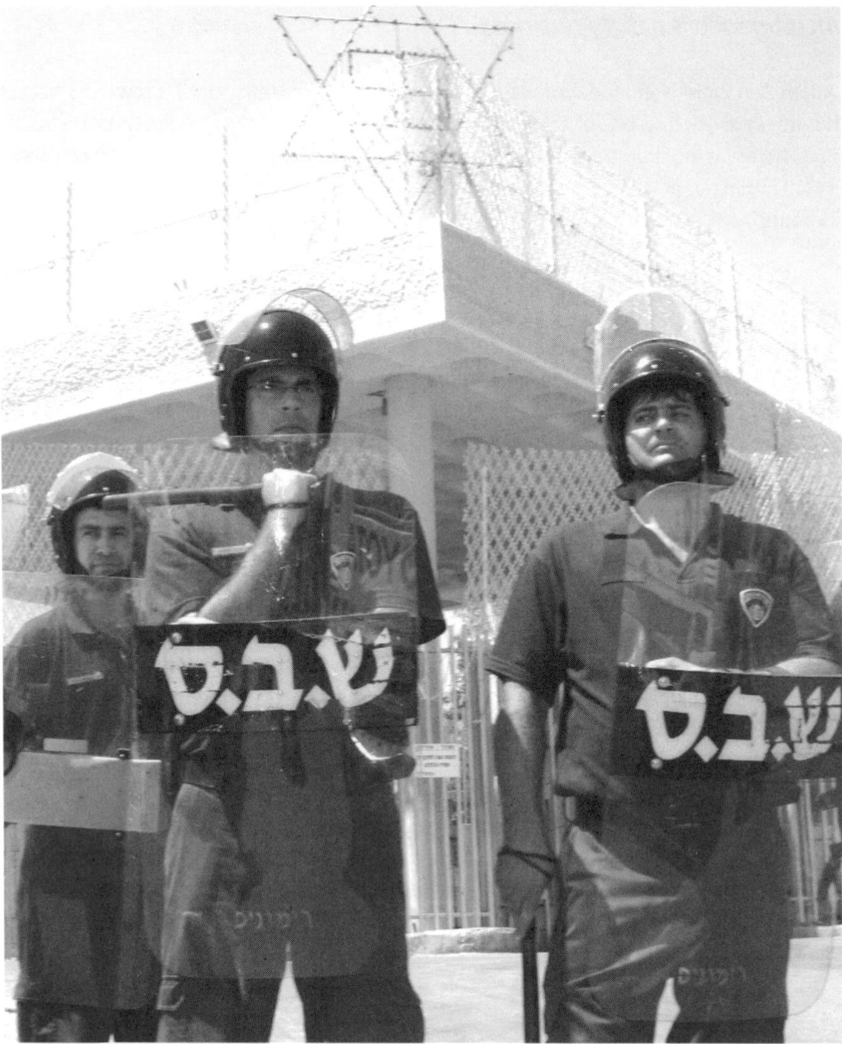

Security forces protect the Ha'Sharon prison during protests in support of Palestinian hunger strikers in August 2004. 'Adam Ben Zion' wished to remain anonymous. *Photo by Arthur Neslen*

terrible religious radicalisation after 1967 and my classmates often became more religious than their own parents. To me, being Jewish meant taking pride in our contribution to world history and culture. We were among the first to profess monotheism and that is linked to our social values, language, prophets and scholars.

In the army, I was a jobnik. See my glasses? I was no fighter. I'm a chess player. That's why I went abroad at 17, to play in a big tournament in France. The winner, David Goodman, quit chess later.[24] I worked in Israeli military intelligence as an analyst during the Lebanon War. I learned that many Palestinians knew our history well and considered themselves, paradoxically, the Jews of the Arab world. To some extent, I agree but I can't wipe out the impression of the last four years. It shocked me that the Fatah and Barghouti people so quickly became our foes.

My career in intelligence really began during the First Intifada. It was an unpredicted 'orphan failure' which no-one took responsibility for. I was one of the analysts recruited to foresee the next one. A process of greater public oversight was beginning, with the 'hidden kingdom' becoming more scrutinised by the press and Knesset. These were positive aspects.

We produced policy-related ideas, papers and recommendations but only analysing the Palestinians. We reported and were obedient to the prime minister and the highest echelons. Their decisions were not so influenced by what particular analysts were saying, even the chiefs. I was dealing strategically with terrorists in the West Bank and Gaza, and Israeli Arabs. In governing circles at the start of the First Intifada, the Palestinian issue had been considered a nuisance. It grew to be perceived as a war. There was no official declaration, but when Rabin stupidly expelled 400 Hamas terrorists,[25] he considered them an existential threat. After Oslo, Arab terrorism aimed at derailing the peace process came

---

Ben Gurion. In contemporary Israel, the debate has polarised issues in the separate Jewish particularism versus universalism debate. However, every time secular Israel has attempted to answer the question decisively, it has provoked a crisis necessitating a postponement of the debate.

24. David Goodman was an international chess master who subsequently became a reporter for the Associated Press.
25. Shlaim, *The Iron Wall*, pp. 509–10. '[Yitzhak] Rabin's decision to deport 416 Hamas activists to Lebanon, following the kidnap and murder of an Israeli border policeman… was without precedent and in flagrant violation of international law. It out-stripped the toughest measures of the Likud and out-Shamired [Yitzhak] Shamir. None of the alleged Islamic activists had been charged, tried or allowed to appeal before being driven blind-folded into exile in Lebanon. This act was intended to discredit Hamas but it had the opposite effect… Worse than a crime it was a mistake.' The Hamas men, mostly university graduates, were subsequently readmitted into Israel in 1993.

to influence the Israeli government's most basic decisions. Maybe one of our successes is that we lowered it again to the level of a 'dangerous nuisance'.

Is it true that in the 1980s, Israel supported Hamas as a counterweight to Fatah?

Yes, this happened. We cannot deny it but Hamas then adhered to the traditional ways of the Muslim Brotherhood,[26] educating people and not taking part in militant activity. They became active in terrorist operations gradually. There was basic short-sightedness on the Israeli part but it's difficult to condemn. They tried to weaken the PLO, which was then the most powerful group. It was not necessary that this should happen. History could have gone in other channels. We saw that we couldn't go on with Dayan's policy of 'open bridges'[27] forever. It exploded in our faces and Palestinian society was radicalised in a process that we failed to interpret accurately.

We didn't totally ignore what the world was telling us. As a private citizen, I think Sharon has sincerely sought to improve the situation but I'm not a friend of his or Netanyahu or Barak's. Intelligence analysts tend towards the political centre. If you're discovered to be from the super-extremes, a supporter of Azmi Bishara or Meir Kahane, I don't think you'd be recruited to intelligence services, only to the army (laughs).

Would such people's phone and email communications be monitored?

It's possible. But Israel is not recruiting informers in synagogues or political parties without a clear and imminent terrorist threat. This isn't a securitat state. If we'd had an informant in Ygal Amir's synagogue maybe things would be different today. I hope more resources will be focused on the extreme right now because they've proved to be more dangerous. But, good for me, I didn't work against Jews, I only analysed Arabs. Maybe I would have refused.

What political mistakes do you feel were made in the years after Oslo?

The most basic flaw of the Oslo process was that so many important issues were left open so there was always a cloud over it. There was no agreement on

26. Ibid., p. 459. Hamas was actually founded by Sheikh Ahmed Yassin as a wing of the Muslim Brotherhood. It was obliged to pledge that its fight for Palestinian independence would be conducted lawfully and without recourse to arms. However, the group was radicalised by the Intifada.
27. Two months after the 1967 war, Moshe Dayan formulated the 'open bridges' policy between the West Bank and Jordan, reopening the Damia and Allenby bridges and so improving relations with Amman. It allowed the transit of Palestinian goods and workers between the occupied territories and the Arab world and encouraged Palestinian emigration. Palestinians between the ages of 20 and 40 who left could not come back before nine months had elapsed but would lose their rights of residence if they did not return within three years. The policy ground to a halt during the 1990s under the weight of border checks and blockades of Palestinian enclaves.

refugees, Jerusalem or the final borders. The idea was that gradually confidence would be built and the Palestinians would feel the fruits of peace. I basically supported it but it wasn't part of my job. The crucial period to check for mistakes in is between 1994 and 2000. I'm sure the Second Intifada wasn't inevitable. Many say it was pre-planned but I believe it evolved until it reached a state that couldn't be stopped by the politicians. Arafat didn't want peace but he didn't think things would deteriorate as far as they did. When he realised that, he was too weak or passive or ill-equipped as a leader to end it.

What do you base that assessment on?

Let's say an accumulation of information and impressions. I am convinced that on the 28 of September 2000,[28] Arafat did not have a well-organised plan for the uprising. However, he tried to profit from events as much as possible. As a politician, Arafat was not a changer or generator of realities; he reacted to them on a tactical basis without seeing the larger picture. Our mindset for six years had been that incidents, however serious, would not degenerate into all-out war. There was a level of cooperation between Israeli and Palestinian security forces. The speed with which they turned to force shocked Israeli society and us too, to some extent. Israel may have used too much force in the beginning but did we have an alternative? The targeted killing only began in November and then on a very small scale.[29] I must say I blame the Palestinians for the deterioration. I know how to analyse their excuses.

If an Israeli bomb killed a Hamas leader in his home and two children who lived next door also died, would the operation have been a success?

No, if we were sure that young children would be killed, I don't think we'd have done it. It happened, I know it happened but even today it's under jurisdiction. There was a petition to the High Court to disqualify Dan Halutz,[30] you know?

28. The date that Ariel Sharon visited the Al Aqsa Mosque and the Second Intifada began.
29. Anthony Dworkin, 'The Killing of Sheikh Yassin: Murder or lawful act of war?', *Guardian*, 30 March 2004. The Fatah activist Hussein Abayat was the first victim of an Israeli assassination or targeted killing when he was killed in a helicopter attack near Bethlehem.
30. As commander of the Israeli air forces, Dan Halutz ordered the dropping of a one-tonne bomb on the Daraj neighbourhood of Gaza, where the Hamas activist Salah Shehadeh was sleeping on 22 July 2002. The bomb also killed 14 civilians, many of them children, and injured more than 150 people. Halutz later told his pilots he slept well at night and outraged *Ha'aretz* readers with a remark that all he felt when dropping a bomb was 'a slight tremor in the wing of the airplane. It passes after a second'. Shortly after this interview, Halutz was promoted to the position of chief of staff of the IDF.

But I really wasn't involved in it so I can't comment. This is very sensitive. The outcry over say, Jenin compared to Fallujah shows the double standards and injustice in this world. I'm reluctant to cry anti-Semitism against any criticism of Israel, but Israel is a scapegoat. We understand the plight of the Palestinians is not easy but with the recent Tel Aviv bombing,[31] this guy woke up in Nablus and despite all the so-called so-terrible checkpoints – which I agree make the lives of Palestinians quite miserable – at 11am there was a suicide attack.

So checkpoints won't solve an essentially political problem?

Yes, but it reduces the scope of terrorist activity to a tolerable size. We didn't begin this way. There were mediation efforts by Powell and Zinni to try to reach the cause. It was a mistake to go to Camp David. It would have been better to manage the conflict and try to solve the crucial aspects later, to create a critical mass of Palestinians who would respond peacefully even to serious disputes. If the Second Intifada had followed the civil disobedience pattern of the first, Israelis would have accepted – or even supported – it. This was the Palestinians' biggest failure.

I'm aware that we also used violence against the British and the Arabs, and every national movement has its upsets. But still I don't think the Palestinians are ready for a state. Israel will not provide concessions in exchange for words again. New concessions will only follow a clear position against terror that emerges from an internal Palestinian struggle. Hamas is going to be a political party but there must be a monopoly on the use of force, like in Israel. Hopefully this won't encourage a civil war on the other side but if necessary, there is a comparison with *Altalena*.[32] But Sheikh Yassin was no Begin and Yasser Arafat was no Ben Gurion, and neither is Abu Mazen.

31. On 1 November 2004, three people died in the Carmel market bombing by a 16-year-old Palestinian from the Nablus area. Three suspected members of the Al Aqsa Martyrs Brigade were subsequently killed by Israeli undercover agents that night in Nablus.
32. Morris, *Righteous Victims*, pp. 236–7. 'On June 19–20 [1948], there occurred what Ben Gurion and his ministers regarded – or said they regarded – as a rebellion. An IZL ship, the *Altalena*, carrying about 900 immigrants and members of the organisation, as well as arms, arrived off Israel's shores from France. The IZL demanded that the weapons be distributed to "its" battalions in the IDF and the independent IZL troops in Jerusalem; the government refused. Ben Gurion maintained that the country could only have one army, the IDF. IZL troops took control of a beach area near Kfar Vitkin, north of Netanya and began to offload the vessel. Government troops surrounded the area and a number of firefights ensued. On June 21, the IZL troops surrendered but the *Altalena* sailed south to Tel Aviv, where on Ben Gurion's orders, the IDF artillery opened fire on it. At the same time Palmach troops took over the IZL's headquarters in downtown Tel Aviv and disarmed the dissidents. The *Altalena*, hit and on fire, soon sank; most of the arms were lost. Eighteen men died in the clashes, most of them IZL members.'

Did you ever deal with information obtained through immoral methods?

I'm sure there were cases where people were not interrogated properly, but this has been dealt with. In '99, the Supreme Court made a judgment about it.[33] Things don't always go smoothly for arrested Palestinians but no-one in the recent Intifada died during an interrogation. We are better than the Americans, I'm sure about that. I'm not happy that we have 10,000 Palestinians in Israeli jails today. It's terrible. It consumes so many resources. But the people who perpetrate the many excesses are usually soldiers or border guards. The professional interrogator understands that the less force you use, the better your chances of gaining information. The aim is to get intelligence, not revenge. The soldiers taking pictures with the corpses of dead Palestinians were terrible. But some Palestinian informers are tortured by their own people. It's a problematic society but you can understand it. It happened in Israel in the '40s too.

Arabs in Jaffa say that many of the informers you recruited were criminals and drug addicts who could be easily controlled or blackmailed. Afterwards, they say you dumped them in their town without back-up and increased crime and social problems.

This is a big problem, yes. Well, you must understand that intelligence is a dirty business. It's not a charitable organisation and if you want to recruit people, you don't usually go to the best, highest or most educated echelons of society. I don't take part in their recruitment in the initial phase but my basic approach is that it's something that happens all over the world. The British now recruit spies even against the Americans and French. It's the international game. Here it's a necessity. Sorry to be cruel, but it's the price that must be paid. Israel's official policy is to try to rehabilitate them but it's not easy. Sometimes it doesn't work and they indulge in criminal activity. We try to minimise it but it is a social problem. Still we're only talking about a few hundred people in Israel. It's logical that they would live among Arab populations because that's their natural milieu. Maybe we don't provide them with enough support. Israeli Arabs know that these people betrayed their Palestinian brothers in the territories and they don't want them to dwell among them. But ok, they send their children to schools so at least the next generation will integrate. It doesn't leave me

33. Alexander Cockburn, 'Israel's Torture Ban', *The Nation*, 27 September 1999. While the Supreme Court reacted to international condemnation of Israel's use of torture on 6 September 1999 by banning such acts as 'shaking, sleep deprivation, "frog crouching", chair perching, bag over the head', Cockburn noted that 'it also said there might be circumstances in which the interests of the state require torture: "If it will nonetheless be decided that it is appropriate for Israel, in light of its security difficulties, to sanction physical means in interrogations this is an issue that must be decided by the legislative branch..." So the court carefully left the door open for the Knesset to rush through a "ticking bomb" law.'

feeling emotionally upset. We didn't kill them and if every other Palestinian was an Israeli spy we wouldn't have faced such a strong Intifada. We treat the nationalists with respect.

To what extent have Israeli Arabs been seen as a fifth column within Israel?

I believe the situation between Israeli Jews and Arabs is one of this country's biggest success stories. Some Arabs have helped the Palestinians infiltrate homes and there was even one Israeli Arab suicide bomber. But as we're talking about a minority of almost 20 per cent with close family links to Palestinians in the territories, it's a huge success. Perhaps in the end they will become a fifth column. There is a new, more assertive generation, more ready to voice their nationalist demands than their parents who lived under military administration until '66. The establishment must make more effort to integrate them. Sakhnin winning the Israeli football cup was a positive development.

But every week Israeli Jews shout 'Death to the Arabs' at them...

They also shout 'Death to the Jews' so this is very Israeli. It's the utmost of integration.

It sounds more like racial war than racial integration.

It symbolises the essence of the problem and the solution. Both teams play in the national league, both stand for the anthem – although the Arab players don't say the words because it only speaks about Jews. There is talk of writing a symbolic new verse. Of course, there is a danger of Islamic radicalisation. We will have to deal with this Hamas-like movement among them. But the proof of the success is that they are viewed with suspicion by the Palestinians. They are largely considered as traitors who prefer immediate material interest to the national interest. The October 2001 riots were terrible but there was never a danger of them joining the Intifada. Even the radical leaders still wanted to be Israeli citizens. Please God, it stays that way. They don't want to give up their advantages.

As an intelligence officer presumably you looked to divide and rule the Arab constituency because if they're fighting each other then they're not fighting you.

Well, it's difficult, what would you like? The establishment is treating Israeli Arabs as citizens, ok? We in the security establishment prefer that they are integrated and given as many rights and opportunities as possible because it reduces the danger of terrorism. It's not 'divide and rule' because we don't deny them their affiliation with the Palestinian cause or the right to protest when Israel is fighting their people. We just say, 'Don't be involved in subversive activity and don't break the law. We don't want you to chant Bialik's songs. We appreciate your culture and identity but the law is a common denominator.' There were demonstrations of grief after Arafat's death. It's not pleasing for the Israeli establishment but it's normal.

How worried is Israeli intelligence by extremist settlers?

Really, they are worried. I thank God that I don't have to deal with this. There is popular hatred of Arabs because more than a thousand Israelis have been killed. The official Israel is trying to minimise it to some extent. Not everyone is capable of distinguishing between good and bad Arabs, and the tendency to use excessive force is one sad aspect of Israeli independence.

Undoubtedly, the settlers are a problem Israel has created for itself. Even the Labour party considered them to be the new pioneers. It was Rabin, Peres and Ygal Allon who encouraged them. But should Jews be denied the right to live in the historic land of Israel? I don't think that the West Bank should be 'Judenrein'.[34] And I do think that given the circumstances we've remained quite humane so far, to some extent, I hope.

THE WIEDER FAMILY

Waiting for a miracle

Not all settlers want to stay in the occupied territories. Many working-class Israelis, like the Wieder family, were seduced by government sweeteners a decade ago and trapped by a collapse in the settlement housing market. In the Wieder family's house, almost all the upstairs rooms were furniture-less, bare and white, with an unlived-in feel. The exception was their son Ron's room, which had a wall painting of a man doubled over with arms outstretched in supplication and key-ring size images of what looked like a screaming skull dotted about. Ron appeared to be suffering from a trauma-related stress disorder.

Eliezer: I work in a chemical factory and I was born in Clujnapoca, Transylvania in 1948. We were children when our parents brought us here.

Sally: He lost his mother, three sisters, and 60 other members of his family in the Holocaust. I didn't lose anybody close but my sister was born in a ghetto. I was born in Bukovina, Romania and I was ten years old when we made *aliyah*. I'm a technician now.

34. The Nazi policy of 'cleansing' areas of Jews by deportation or murder.

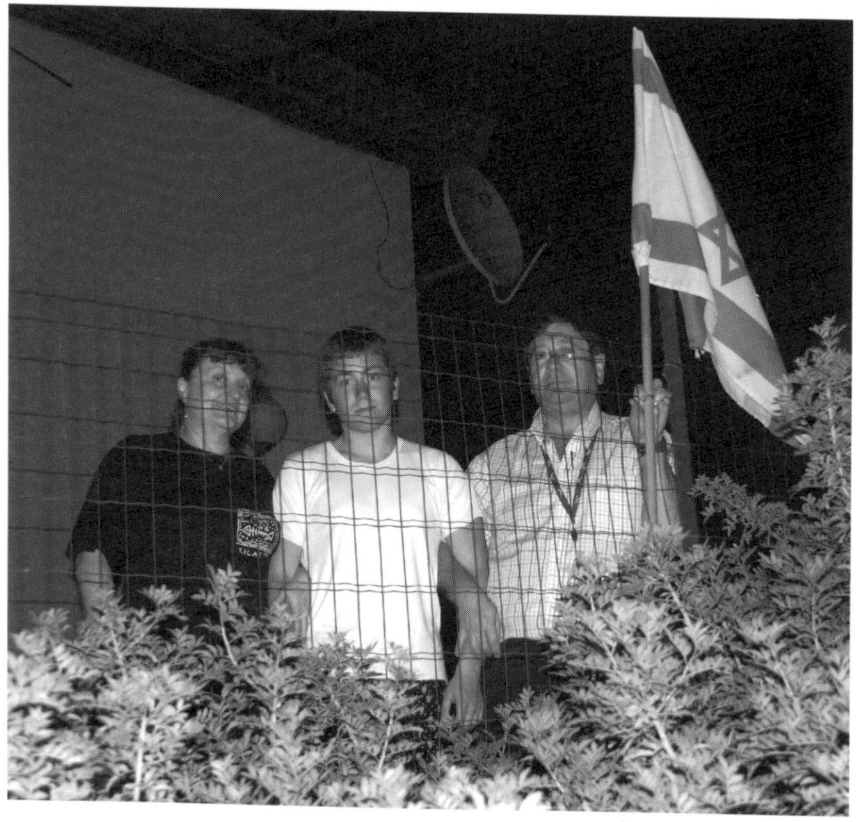

The Wieder family outside their house in Tene Omarim. *Photo by Arthur Neslen*

Eliezer: I didn't feel very Jewish in Romania because my parents had been afraid to give me a Jewish name after losing so much family. I was given a Christian name and identity.

Sally: His name was Ivan! They didn't even give him a *bris mila*. We lived in a small community which felt like a ghetto. I always felt afraid because policemen came every few days and checked under our beds to see if we had any money or gold. We didn't even have what to eat.

Eliezer: I don't like to speak about the Holocaust. I don't like to hear about it and I don't like to ask about it. I don't even know the names of my sisters who were killed in Auschwitz. I don't want to know. I came to Israel in 1962 and we settled in Be'ersheva with immigrants from Morocco, Tunisia and Bolivia. Sally lived in a block on the other side of the street. That's how we met. We moved here in 1990. Ygal Allon, the head of Palmach, said this place would never be given back to the Arabs.[35]

Sally: We thought life would be better here. We were offered a big house with a nice view. My eldest son and I are both asthmatics and it had clean air with no factories or trucks.

Eliezer: The government gave us a lot of help. They gave us cheap loans to buy the house and they lowered our income tax to 7 per cent – but only for three or four years.

Sally: We put $130,000 into this house, and we're still paying the mortgage.

Eliezer: You couldn't even sell it for $10,000 now. Nobody's looking at property here; there are more than 20 empty houses that can't be sold. They built this place shoddily with the worst materials on the market. The wind comes in through the window and the rain comes in through the patio door.

Why do you think the government built this settlement?

Eliezer: They thought it would be ours for good but I've studied history and you can't conquer and occupy another people forever. There has to be two countries for two nations. This is Palestine. When we came, the situation was different. We could shop in Dahariya, the nearest Arab village. You can see its lights from here. Now, you could visit but you couldn't be sure you'd get out.

Do they visit here?

Eliezer: A few of them. They are not so afraid.

Sally: Yes, they are coming!

35. Allon believed that the West Bank should be given to Jordan but that there should be a 'protective belt' of Jewish settlements along the Jordan Valley.

Ron: … if they have a pass.

What was it like growing up here as a teenager?

Ron: It was great. Until a few years ago I wasn't afraid or sad. I didn't think about the Palestinians or our distance from Be'ersheva. It's very hard for me not to see my friends there now. It takes an effort because sometimes I just want to sleep and rest.

Sally: My daughter and my elder son's wife don't even come any more and I'm afraid for their safety when they do. We feel like ducks in shooting season when we're driving them home.

Eliezer: Even the people who came here for ideological reasons want to leave. Maybe 10 per cent of the settlement wants to stay.

Sally: They are waiting for a miracle, like the Jews in the Holocaust.

Some people see the settlements as embodying of the pioneering spirit of Zionism

Ron: Not us.

Eliezer: I tell you, Zionism is not about keeping more and more land. It's about keeping the lives of people. These crazies who won't even join the army want to keep all the settlements with my children's blood! That 10 per cent of the people are put on television because they scream and make noise. The silent people aren't invited.

Sally: Sh! There's an alarm call (announcement over loudspeaker outside). It's ok, they're just killing mosquitoes. They make the same announcement when there's shooting.

Eliezer: Sometimes you can even hear the shooting in your house. It drives us crazy. When they attacked us, they were lying in wait outside the settlement. We just disturbed them. It was on June 17th, 2003. They were two metres from the left side of the road and as we passed…

Ron: You couldn't see the gunman. It was 10pm and I was driving in the pitch black. It was only four days after I got my licence. My parents were in the passenger seat…

Eliezer: … he was 17 years and four months old. I didn't hear the shooting. Ron suddenly put his head on my knees and said, 'They're shooting at us!' The car began to roll backwards because they shot the engine, wheels and handbrake. We thought Ron was dead, because we called him and he didn't answer us. Then he opened the right-hand door of the car and jumped, shouting 'Get out of the car!' We hid in the car and waited. Luckily, they didn't come to see if they'd killed us.

Sally: They ran away because they thought someone would come to help us.

Eliezer: They heard the shooting at the security gate but nobody came to see.

Sally: They were scared.

Ron: I kept thinking 'I don't want to get hit by a bullet. What can I do? I can't see anything'. The bullets were whizzing past my face. You could just hear them like 'weow'. I thought, 'This is it, I'm going to die'. I didn't have a weapon. I couldn't protect myself. I couldn't protect my parents. They couldn't protect themselves. They couldn't protect me either. You can't see bullets. Afterwards, I started to cry and then scream, yell and curse. I began punching and kicking the wall until my hands and feet hurt. It was difficult for me to sleep after that. I had nightmares and I was angry with everyone.

Sally: He's had a problem with his memory ever since. He's a genius with an IQ of 145 but since the attack, he hasn't been able to go to school. He always has to shut the house lights off. He said that if we didn't leave this town he'd kill himself.

What nightmares did you have?

Ron: I kept running this script through my head with different variations. Like how would it have played out if it had been a different time of day, if I was sitting here, if they were lying there? This sort of thing...

Eliezer: ... he got very frightened. If he heard any small noise, he'd close the doors and windows.

Ron: I wasn't afraid.

Eliezer: You were.

Sally: To emerge without a scratch from the bullets, I believe that God saved us because we've done so many good things.

Eliezer: Now I live in fear for my life and my son's. We want to move but I haven't the money to rent another house. We're paying almost 3,000 shekels a month here.

How did this community react to the incident?

Sally: For a few months they didn't go out at nights.

Eliezer: Most of them are still afraid. Some carry weapons but a gun can't help you. If I'm driving and they shoot 44 bullets at me, what can I do with a gun?

Sally: The crazies carry guns.

Does the Wall make you feel safer?

Eliezer: Not at all because we're on the Palestinian side. I wouldn't support it if we were on the other side either, but it would better than it is now. They want to build us another ghetto with an electrical fence.

Sally: Our parents were in enough ghettoes.

Ron: There is no connection! Would I like to be here if my grandparents hadn't lived in a ghetto? I don't want to live behind an electric fence because I don't like ghettoes!

Eliezer: The point is we didn't come to Israel to live in ghettoes. We want to be free and if this isn't our country, they should evacuate us.

Sally: The terrorists can't get to Be'ersheva so they come here to kill us. When they've built the Wall, it will be much easier for them. I can't sleep here with the bullets, fear and nightmares. I think they're attacking me, and I start to scream, 'It's not my house!' People on the other side of the Wall say that we have to be strong and stand against the bullets. Why aren't they coming here to get killed?

Eliezer: A religious workmate told me, 'You mustn't give them back the land.' But he's too afraid to go to settlements himself. The religious pray for the land, not the people who live on it.

Do you ever guard settlements, Ron?

Ron: No, I'm a jobnik.[36] I was due to join the air force as a pilot but after the attack, they lowered my profile. Now I sit doing nothing for 90 per cent of the day. All my life I wanted to fight even after the attack, but not any more, after the way they treated me.

What would you say to soldiers who refuse to implement the hitnatkut?

Ron: Nothing, I'd like to hear what they have to say.

Sally: We don't like any refuseniks because if the country needs soldiers, they should go where they're sent.

Eliezer: I was in three wars and I did what I was told. The army isn't a democracy and those who refuse orders take from the country without giving back.

What if the army told you to repopulate Judea and Samaria?

Eliezer: No, then we'd be being sacrificed for the faith of the religious. I'm a part of the occupation but I don't like it. I would rather Israel was like it was

36. 'Jobnik' is slang for non-combat soldiers who are given odd jobs around the military base by their commanding officer.

before 1967, smaller and at peace with our neighbours. We have a beautiful country, I'm very proud of it.

Ron: I'm not. I don't like the people here. I hope that it will get better for the people who stay, but I want to go to Canada to study and raise a family. Solving the problems among ourselves is more important than solving our problems with the Palestinians.

Eliezer: The religious hate the secular, the right hate the left, the Sephardim hate the Russians...

Sally: ... we don't need outside enemies. We have enough inside.

RABBI MENACHEM FROMAN

To love my Palestinian neighbours

Hailed by some as a prophet and others a traitor, Rabbi Menachem Froman is a Kabbalist, settler, peace activist and joyful iconoclast. For decades and from the most unpredictable of latitudes, he has opposed both war on Palestinians and the removal of settlers from the West Bank and Gaza. A high-profile Merkaz HaRav student, Rav Froman was instrumental in setting up the Gush Emunim settlers movement. However, he broke with the organisation in 1994 and went to work as a religious advisor to the Knesset. Religious figures denounced him for his son's decisions not to wear the *kippa*, and his own decision (as a rabbi) to keep a dog. More trenchantly, Froman appalled many of his erstwhile friends when he began holding meetings with the spiritual leader of Hamas, Sheikh Ahmed Yassin, and Yasser Arafat, with whom he forged a close friendship. He was the last Israeli to see the PLO leader alive. At the time of our interviews, Rav Froman was receiving police protection because of threats to his life from right-wing extremists, yet he would not carry a gun. On one night-time visit to his settlement in Tekoa, during the festival of Chanukah, the deafening wail of muezzins from surrounding Palestinian villages echoed around the darkened settlement streets like an indigenous people's battle cry. On another, teenage settlers at the settlement bus stop cowered as the sound of gunfire echoed around the surrounding mountains. Both times, Rav Froman was in good spirits, effortlessly confounding all secular and religious expectations, playfully embodying more contradictions in Israeli Jewry than perhaps even he is aware of.

I'm the rabbi of Tekoa and a teacher in another yeshiva near Hebron. I have ten children, thank G–d, which is perhaps a lot for an Englishman...

Menachem Froman. *Photo by Arthur Neslen*

It would be a lot even in Tel Aviv.

You mean Tel Aviv is not part of England, or America? (laughs) I was born in the Galilee, in Kfar Hasidim, a unique village founded by the Hasidim. I went on to study at the Yeshiva Merkaz HaRav where all the leading members of Gush Emunim[37] studied. Part of the Yeshiva's concept was to serve G-d by being a pioneer in the army's front line, and in '67 I fought in 'Motte' Gur's famous parachute regiment which conquered Jerusalem. While I was studying, I married in 1972 and lived in the Old City's ruined Jewish Quarter among Arabs who were staying in the destroyed houses.

When the war finished, we felt we had finally arrived in the heart of the land, the biblical and Talmudic holy places like Hebron and Shiloh that we had dreamed about for years. We were drunk on the feeling. Tekoa, for instance, was the city of Amos the prophet, of King Rehav Ha'am, Josephat and Bar Kochba.[38] Here (points) you see Herodion, the cave of King Herod where Bar Kochba, the last independent 'president' of Israel made his final camp. His famous letters were found here. One by one, we left the yeshiva to settle and become rabbis. I first became the rabbi of a kibbutz called Migdal Oz, and then I came to Tekoa.

How did the Palestinians there treat you?

I had excellent relations with them, especially my neighbours who lived there illegally. Their houses belonged to Jews who had fled in the War of Independence and the authorities tried to persuade them to leave by turning off their water. So they came to me for water (laughs).

37. Shahak and Mezvinsky, *Jewish Fundamentalism*, p. 55: 'Rabbi Tzvi Yehuda Kook... possessed a strongly charismatic personality and exerted great influence upon his students. He elaborated orally the political and social consequences of his father's teachings. The rabbis who graduated from his yeshiva in Jerusalem Merkaz Harav or "Centre of the Rabbi" and remained devoted followers of his teaching established a political sect with a well-defined political plan. In early 1974... Rabbi Kook's followers with their leader's blessing and spiritual guidance founded Gush Emunim (Bloc of the Faithful) ..., Gush Emunim succeeded in changing the Israeli settlement policy. The Jewish settlements which continue to spread throughout the West Bank and to occupy a large chunk of the Gaza Strip provide testimony of and documentation for Gush Emunim's influence within Israeli society and upon Israeli governmental policies.'
38. Between 132 and 135 CE, Shimon Bar Kochba ('Son of a Star') led a Jewish rebellion against the occupying Roman empire that would come to be known as the Bar Kochba Revolt. Bar Kochba was famed as a dictator and military leader and, according to documents discovered in the Judean desert between 1952 and 1961, an observant Jew. He died in the final battle of the war at Bethar in Judea. Thousands of Jewish refugees had fled to Bethar during the war. All were killed when Bethar fell. Jews were heavily persecuted in the years that followed. Many were sold into slavery. The Roman emperor Hadrian changed the country's name from Judea to Syria Palestina.

Rabbi Tzvi Yehuda Kook was our teacher and inspiration. He was a very warm personality with a lot of love for his students. When his wife died, he invited me to live in his apartment and take care of him. It was an honour. Rav Kook continued the work of his father, Yitzhak HaCohen Kook, whose religious philosophy legitimised secular Jewry.[39] Traditionally, if you were religious, secular Jews existed outside your nation because the nation is a slave of G–d. But Rav Kook thought that in their way, non-religious Jews were also serving G–d as part of the religious enterprise. You couldn't say this was a 'Messianic' atmosphere, in the Christian sense of feeling constant tension every day that the Moshiach was coming.

Part of Rav Kook's philosophy was to understand the term 'Moshiach' in a cultural or (whispers) secular way. The Messianic Age was a process of developing the spirit of the Jewish nation and advancing it to another stage of understanding and reality.

To a stage where it is a duty for Jews to settle the West Bank?

Yes, it's a *mitzva* to settle here and meet the energies of the land. You get power and inspiration from this place. I am a teacher of the holy Zohar, and teaching it in Tekoa is totally different from teaching it in Tel Aviv. My yeshiva is the formal continuation of Rav Shimon Bar Yochai's.[40]

For 15 years, we've also run a unique school here that breaks down the barriers between religious and non-religious Jews. Usually in Israel, the communities are separated. Our system is quite the opposite. We teach the Bible and critiques of the Bible. Half of our students are religious, half are non-religious. They're roots and branches of the same tree. Rav Kook always said that real belief was based on the possibility of freedom.

What do you think Tzvi Kook would say about the current political situation?

I think it's unfair to try to answer. The spirit of man is free and people change their views. It wouldn't be fair to ask what Moses would say either.

You see Tzvi Kook as Moses?

No, but he gave us this direction to the holy sites. For him, faith was not just abstract. It was about the touch of the land.

39. Rabbi Avraham Yitzhak HaCohen Kook, who migrated to the Yishuv in the early 1900s, was the first religious figure to innovate traditional interpretations by way of Zionist metaphor.
40. Shimon Bar Yochai was the 'author' of the mystical Kabalistic text, *The Zohar*, which he received in spoken form from his teacher, Rabbi Akiva. Bar Yochai was also a pacifist who bitterly opposed the Bar Kochba revolt.

In Leviticus, G–d said, 'The land is mine, and you are but tenants and travellers.'

But this is exactly the essence of my interpretation of Rav Kook (laughs). This is not the territory of the land of Israel. This is not Palestine. This is the land of G–d and we are His guests.

As a supporter of a Palestinian state, how can you settle when the land is occupied?

This land is not occupied (laughs). The Palestinians, Europeans and Americans might say that but I think it's a conceptual mistake to compare me, in Tekoa, to a Frenchman in Algeria. I am the son of many generations who defined themselves as Palestinians, as men of the land of Israel. The invitation to my late parents' wedding said, 'The ceremony will take place in the Temple Mount (shouts) unless the Moshiach doesn't come, in which case it will be in Pavunitz, Poland'. These lands are not 'occupied territories' but our homeland. We don't see it only as a result of historical processes. We see the connection between Jews and the land as divine.

A Palestinian living under curfew, whose olive trees, water and land have been appropriated by soldiers and settlers might question your definition of occupation.

The Palestinians are under Israel's control for the same reason that the tigers in London Zoo are not free. If most Israelis didn't have a justified suspicion that they would use their freedom to destroy the state of Israel, there would be no soldiers here. The Palestinians would have their state and their freedom. I say that as a personal friend of Yasser Arafat. I am the last Israeli who talked with him.

What did he say to you?

'My brother, come to visit me.' He usually called me his brother. I phoned him and said 'Ya Rais,[41] I have a new plan for you, involving concrete and critical steps that will enable you to see the establishing of a Palestinian state in your lifetime.' We both knew that he was an old man. We had met many times. Despite the difficulties, he always invited me. The problem was that, often, my government would decisively and repeatedly try to stop me from visiting him. Formally, they said it was because they cared about my safety but perhaps there were other reasons too.

Because it wasn't always possible to meet, we corresponded by letters and had long telephone conversations. So I called him and said, 'Ya Rais, this time we can't speak on the phone or correspond. We have to meet. I will make the effort.' How I would have managed to get there is another question. Arafat, as usual, said, 'Of course, my brother, come to me tomorrow!' I told him that one of my

41. 'Leader' or 'chief'.

sons had married a few days before on the Temple Mount.[42] He wanted to give me a gift for the wedding, as he traditionally did, but this time we never met.

The next day, a Friday, I couldn't go.[43] Gideon Ezra, the Israeli minister of internal security affairs, said that he wanted to see me. Usually, I would tell the Rais that I could go to him every day – and I'd tell the minister that it would take me a week. This time, however, it was part of the plan to establish a Palestinian state and get out of the vicious circle of terror and Israeli reaction. I missed one day because of the meeting with Gideon Ezra. Then when I phoned, they told me that the president was sleeping (laughs) and I understood that something was wrong. After a few hours my friends put me in the picture and I realised that his health was going downhill.

My plan had a number of stages. One was that a group of Palestinian representatives would gather in the Seven Gates Hotel in Jerusalem where the PLO was founded. It is symbolic and, more importantly, it has the Temple Mount in the background. There, Abu Amar, Abu Ala and Abu Mazen[44] would declare – and I still have the words of the declaration that I wanted to suggest to the Rais – the founding of a Palestinian state in Jerusalem. The plan was that it would happen three weeks after the US elections. I worked for connections with both presidential candidates. Bush would recognise the state which would, despite the problems, have had borders more or less on the Green Line.

Do you think America would have accepted that?

(Confident) Yes! I think it would have happened. The two governments would discuss the problem of the thousands of Jews in the Palestinian state afterwards. This was a very detailed and complicated plan with the support of the most important rabbis in Israel. They supported the general direction and with G–d's help they will support a future plan.

My activities towards the Palestinians were really a part of my identity as a Messianic Jew. I'm responsible for promoting the Jewish spirit, making it more gentle and less egoistic and nationalistic. That's what I understood by Rav Kook's messianic prophesy and Hillel's definition of Judaism as loving your neighbour

42. 'Follow up to the Temple Mount Wedding', *Arutz Sheva*, 10 September 2004. 'Menachem Froman's son and daughter-in-law Netayah and Techiya Froman were secretly married on the Temple Mount or Al Aqsa Mosque, the holiest site for both Judaism and Islam in Jerusalem in September 2004.'
43. Suzanne Goldenberg, 'No way to die', *Guardian*, 16 December 2004, Avi Ischaroff and Amos Harel, 'The final days of Yasser Arafat', *Ha'aretz*, 8 September 2005. Physicians first diagnosed Arafat with a disease of the digestive tract on Tuesday 12 October, three days before Froman was to have met him. By Sunday 17 October Arafat was unable to stay upright at a meeting of his own security council for more than 10 minutes before staggering out.
44. The *nom de guerres* of Yasser Arafat, Ahmed Qureia and Mahmoud Abbas, respectively.

as yourself. My neighbours are Palestinians so the essence of my religion is to love my Palestinian neighbours as I love myself. If I have a state, they have to have a state. If Jerusalem is my capital, Jerusalem has to be their capital. If I have freedom and prosperity, they must have the same. All my activities with the Palestinians are a part of my Jewish self-definition.

You've said before that you'd like to live in a shtetl on the West Bank in a Palestinian state. Would Palestinians be allowed to live in the shtetl?

I think they would be allowed. I don't see it as my dream because a community is a cultural unit and I don't see settlements only as places where people live. We are also building our culture and Palestinians are building theirs. They are not part of the Jewish tradition so I think it's not the way. I am a primitive Jew. I'm a primitive rabbi and the Palestinians are also primitive. You perhaps are less primitive. 'Primitive' is not defined by a lack of sophistication. A primitive man is also deeply connected to heaven and the land. Not every fool is a primitive.

How have other settlers reacted to your views?

Some oppose me, some support me. I'm not sure that all of them respect me. Some of them think I am a traitor. But Rabbi Kook was also persecuted. At his Jerusalem synagogue, people threw raw sewage over him. I have not been honoured to be so persecuted. Every person who tries to develop his cultural tradition must expect opposition because men are connected to their traditional ways of thinking. There is the possibility that Menachem Froman will be murdered. Some good Jews have threatened to kill me, my wife and my children in a fire big enough to 'burn all my tribe' (laughs). The police arranged cameras all around my home after one good Jew wrote on my house, 'Froman is a traitor and traitors must die', in nice handwriting.

Why do you call them good Jews?

Why not? They don't want to rob me. They haven't any personal interest against me. They're idealistic Jews who think they're defending their tradition. I can understand them because I'm a Messianic Jew who wants to change and sublimate my tradition so they're right to oppose me. I don't recommend killing me. More than that, I don't compliment those who plan to kill my wife and children, but they understand well that I want to change the current Jewish spirit, to affect *tikkun* by taking the spirit to a higher level, so they are justified in opposing me.

10
Away from Zion

After the calamitous expulsion of Spanish Jewry in 1492, followers of the mystic Kabbala increasingly turned to an apocalyptic messianism that explained exile in terms of an imperative for Diaspora Jewry to affect *tikkun olum* (or healing the world).[1] Since 1948, the concept seems to have found expression in Zionism as a need for the Jewish people themselves to become whole again. But the Kabbala itself differentiates between a first Messiah, the militant 'Son of Joseph' who would prepare the conditions for the Messiah's return, and the more spiritual 'Son of David' who would subsequently redeem the world through spectacular miracle-making.[2] Jewish mysticism can potentially advance universalist notions, as well as particularist ones.

For an ever-increasing number of Israeli Jews, the ingathering of exiles has brought cultural anomie and *yerida*. Some young Israelis have 'descended' to the patron saint of secular Zionism, North America, where assimilation is the norm. Others have opted for more spiritual, exotic and affordable destinations like India and Thailand, often bemoaning a narrow and restrictive religious orthodoxy as they go. Nearly 60 years after Israel's establishment, the trend is for the grandchildren of Zionist pioneers to emerge from the tube of *aliyah* in new and foreign landscapes where their identities are as provisional as any in the globalised age. A silent 'outgathering' of the exiles is in process that may have profound implications for Zionism and Jewish identity. The diaspora clock, which Zionism tried to turn back to year zero, is ticking again.

1. As a means of advancing the Messiah's return, see Cantor, *Jewish Women*, pp. 40–1.
2. Shahak, *Jewish Fundamentalism*, p. 66.

YARON PE'ER

Something we lost along the way

During the last decade's travel boom, the Middle East has been the one travel destination Israelis have largely shunned, whether out of choice or necessity. The only exception has sporadically been the Sinai, a post-occupation drug-fuelled playground for demob-happy soldiers and refuseniks alike. On New Year's Day 2005, two months after the bombs that killed 11 Israelis on the Sinai peninsula,[3] I travelled to Ras-as-Satan, the site of one of the blasts. Despite a collapse in hedonistic tourism, young musicians and artists from across the region still congregated on its pebbly beaches. One of them, a follower of Menachem Froman, introduced me to Yaron Pe'er, an accomplished musician with a quasi-mystical persona. Yaron was esteemed by Egyptians, Sudanis and Israelis alike. Together, they shared joints and songs around starry beach camp fires at sunset in a latter-day minstrel commune they viewed as a model for the region's future.

From my point of view, it's like this: we are the third Israeli generation and maybe the first who've had the chance to see beyond our need to survive and build the country. I had a beautiful childhood. Although my background was mixed, I saw myself as a Sephardic Jew because I was more attracted to the eastern side. At that time, the Mizrahim were a bit discriminated against.

I believe there is something in Judaism. God is not Jewish. The people are Jewish, God does not belong to the people. The reverse is true. Every face comes from the same source, which means one unity. Whichever aspect of God you worship, it gives an amazing richness to the community. But you lose that richness if you talk about the Jewish God because it's also the Muslim God and the Christian God. Through the one you can see the many. When these exist at the same time and people let go of their structures, something might happen.

These days, some of us travel far from Israel to search for the old culture. Underneath the surface something is happening. A new culture of unity is developing. The Arabic and Jewish mentalities are often negative. Like, there's a

3. Thirty-three people, more than ten of them Israelis, died in the two bomb blasts at Ras-as-Satan and the Taba Hilton in the Sinai peninsula on 7 October 2004. Of those, only two were killed in Ras-as-Satan, one Israeli woman and a Bedouin. The attacks were initially blamed on Al-Qaida although police later said they were carried out by a Palestinian resident of Egypt.

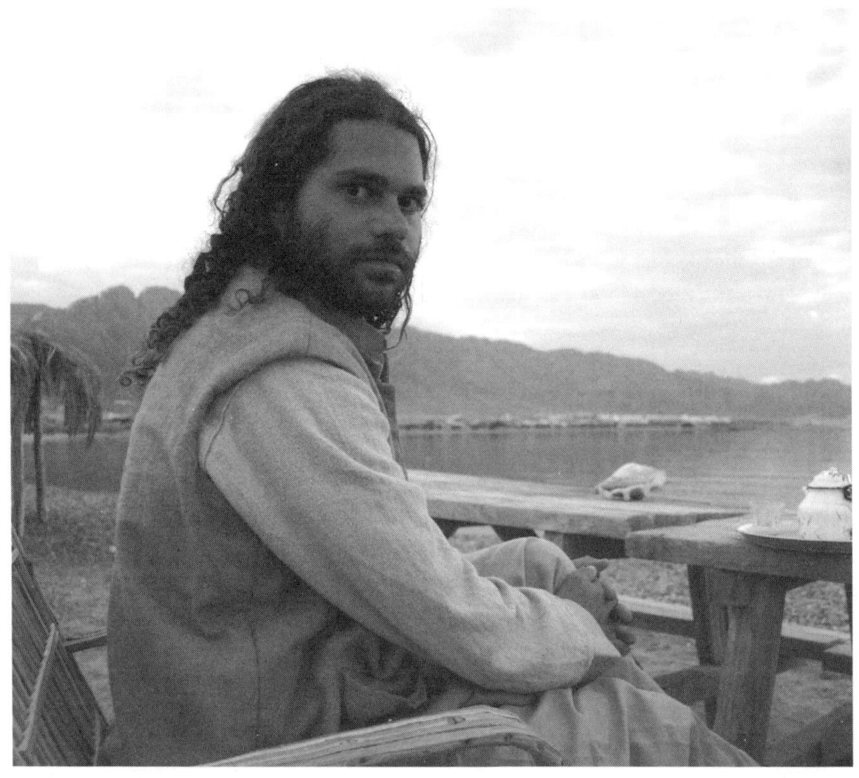

Yaron Pe'er on the beach in Ras-as-Satan, Egypt. *Photo by Arthur Neslen*

cake and everyone says, 'If I can't have the piece I like, I'll ruin it for everybody.' Masada is in a way the positive side of the same coin.[4]

I'm 29 years and a day old. I had an amazing weekend. I'm so lucky that I found this place and these people to be with. I don't know if you realise what's going on here but there are people from Israel, Cairo, Mexico, Spain, all meeting like brothers and sisters. It's like a miracle, the point where our differences become an advantage. I feel this place is protected. Two months ago, the people who wanted to bomb it couldn't get in. It was very close. In the Qur'an, the Sinai is called Ard el-Muminim or 'Land of the Believers'. People here are more centred and free. They lose their identity a little bit. It's good because if you're sure of something, you might miss new things that are emerging. When you give up something you were born with, you become more human.

My father's family come from Greece. My mother died when I was 17. Their generation was occupied with duty. Mine is more free to wander. I began travelling pretty late, at 22. I'd visited my family in Saloniki before, but it took my father years to understand why I was travelling so far.

How far have you been?

Sometimes the whole world can be the distance from your chest to your nose. I studied Indian classical music for the last six years in Varanasi in India. My teacher, Santosh Kumar Misha, is of the fourteenth generation of sarangi players.

4. The fortress of Masada is one of the most enduring of Zionist myths. Today it is a national park, complete with cable car, ferrying tourists and Israeli soldiers who ritually swear an oath at the top of the mountain. However Josephus's unreliable account of its demise in *The Jewish Wars* offers the only historical record of events there. As the story goes, towards the end of 74 CE, 960 Jewish fighters sought shelter from the advancing Roman tenth legion atop the mountain fortress, where they were subsequently besieged for seven weeks. Night and day, the Romans worked inexorably building a platform of ladders, bridges and planks to assault the camp. When they reached the apex, they found that the inhabitants of the camp had elected to commit mass suicide, preferring to die as free people than live as slaves. All bar one woman, who related the story. Questions about the story's veracity were first raised when the Israeli archaeologist Yigal Yadin discovered the Masada camp site. There was no evidence of the lots the Jews were supposed to have drawn to select their killers, and the remains of only 25 people were found scattered around a cave at the cliff's south side. Yet it remains a powerful symbol of national martyrdom. So powerful that the unsuccessful US presidential candidate John Kerry visited the site and in an article, 'A powerful journey, an essential dream', recorded his belief in Josephus's account despite the lack of any historical evidence. 'I will never forget a moment on top of Masada... We shouted across the chasm – across the desert – "Am Yisroel Chai" and across the silence we listened as the voices came back – faintly we heard the echo of the souls who perished – Am Yisroel Chai. The state of Israel lives.'

I also studied Arabic music under Yair Delal.[5] He said that if in the 1970s we'd brought Middle Eastern culture to Israel instead of American culture, we'd be more connected to the land. Before Israel, you could take a train from Alexandria to Damascus. Today you can't even dream about such a thing.

I'll never play like an Arab but I have a talent for mixing things. Have you seen the musicians here today? There's a santur player from Lebanon, a guitarist and drummer from Cairo and we're all equal. We drop our used skins and learn from each other. This is the movement. Religion is structure and many times it stands between us. We do want to define God, but this is the one movement you can't catch unless you are also moving. You can go with it but you can't understand it at the same time.

I feel connected to the land I stand on by music. The culture has been here for thousands of years. Every generation of Jews has been rejected, repelled, erased. I believe that we were too proud and disconnected from our neighbours and that caused jealousy. I think our fathers' biggest mistake was not appreciating that. You can reach the top but you must remember who you are. There's a chance that this generation will act differently. You can see it here.

But Israel was supposed to end the wandering of the Diaspora, why is it resurfacing?

You have two kinds of wanderers, the Israelis who have faced the ugly reality of the army and need a place to break loose. The fact that they stayed in one piece means a lot. You see this in India, they are the most selfish and arrogant people but the Indians accept it. These Israelis talk to them like masters to slaves. It's very ugly. The other Israelis believe in something higher and deeper. The Jewish people were dispersed for 2,000 years and we think that there's something we lost along the way. Maybe we can find it. On one side, people's identities are based around the Holocaust. The other side accepts that Jews were victims in the Holocaust but asks what we can do with that knowledge. When you conquer people and hold power over them, you have a choice. You can do what was done to you. You can do worse – if there is worse – or you can act differently. You decide.

What do you think might have been lost along the way of Israel's founding?

In my field, the Jewish story-telling tradition by which knowledge was passed from grandfather to grandchild. If you smash a pot of clay and the pieces end up in India, Australia, Baghdad and Denmark, you have to wander to find the

5. Yair Delal is a popular Mizrahi-Israeli musician of Iraqi origin who had pursued artistic collaborations with Arab musicians from other Middle Eastern countries, and the occupied territories. He has spoken out against the occupation and supported Israeli refuseniks.

lost pieces. The Jews that stayed in Turkey, Greece, India and Morocco hung their dreams about a sacred land and realised that they were happy where they were. When they came to Israel, the teachers would ask the parents not to speak Arabic to their kids. They asked them to forget where they came from, the same with the Palestinians. They were exposed to modernisation in Israel – which is positive – but also discrimination. You say you know a Jew from Baghdad who wants to return? Please tell him to come here. He would enjoy this place.

I'm learning about the things we have in common. I speak a little Arabic and maybe in a few years the ideas of this place and time will become better integrated. The Bedouins here speak Hebrew and relate better to the open-minded generation of young Israelis than to the Egyptian authorities. We're like family members. There is a connection developing.

When I am with Israelis here now, I feel like a local and in front of the locals I feel Israeli. When I'm in India, I try to build bridges between the two. One of the problems is that Israelis separate themselves into a scene, the same as happened in past generations. We give them good reasons to expel us. You (addresses me) may be Jewish but you're not Israeli. You're lucky. You don't have common ground. One moment you belong, the next you don't. Even one piece of the clay pot contains knowledge of the whole.

Do you think Israel could be seen as a modern day Golem?

Is he the one from the Lord of the Rings?

It was a Kabbalist legend about a rabbi who moulded a piece of clay into a being that would defend the Jews of Prague but it turned into a monster that destroyed everything, including the Jews it was supposed to protect.

I don't know the story. It sounds interesting.

When do you feel you are home?

When I am here, now, accepted and not judged by the way I look. In Israel, I sometimes have to be creative to find a key to the situation but yes, there too. I feel good when I go back but the situation there is miserable. My family are like slaves that worship material things. To see a ray of sun here is beautiful but to see it in the grey city is more special. When you don't find the people, you should become one. When you don't feel humanity, you should be a human. I hope eventually to be in a place where everything is becoming one, and the different parts start to connect, know each other and use that wisdom.

Israelis who haven't lived outside of the country have no idea about life. In a way I feel more secure outside Israel. I think a big disaster is coming which will take Israel to the bottom of the bottom, a place where the father will finally understand that the one child he lost was also lost on the other side, and the one child that is left is very precious. It's human nature to worship the shell and forget what's inside it. We all have two eyes, one nose, two nostrils, one mouth, two ears. Nobody is the same, you know. But we are all created *b'tselem elohim*, in the image of God.

Glossary

Adon	Mr
aliyah	lit. 'a glorious ascent'; immigration by a Jew to Israel
Ashkenazim	East European Jews
balagan	confusion, mess
barmitzva	ritual coming-of-age religious service when a boy turns 13 years old. A batmitzva is held for 14-year-old girls
Betar	revisionist Zionist movement drawing inspiration from the Bar Kochba rebellion of 135 CE. The movement sponsors the soccer team. Betar Jerusalem FC
Betuach Le'umi	'security of the people', lit. social security
bitachon	faith or security
bris mila	circumcision
Bund	Jewish socialist trade union and political movement in Russia and Eastern Europe, from the late nineteenth century to WWII
cheder	lit. 'room' in Hebrew; a Jewish religious school
chuppa	a wedding canopy
chutzpah	cheek
din rodef	Jewish fundamentalism's equivalent to a *fatwa*. In 1995, West Bank and Gaza rabbis decreed a *din rodef* against Yitzhak Rabin shortly before his assassination
doikayt	'hereness'
Eretz Yisroel	the land of Israel
Fallashmura	Ethiopian Jews
fellach	Arab peasant
Gada	West Bank
goyim/goys	non-Jews
Gush Emunim	the 'Bloc of the Faithful'; a Messianic movement founded in 1973, claiming that Jews had a divine right to settle in the West Bank, Gaza and the Golan Heights
Hagana	Name of the Israeli army during the War of Independence and before
Halakha	Jewish religious law
halutzim	Zionist pioneers/settlers
Ha'rabait/ Temple Dome/Al Aqsa	the holiest site in Judaism and third holiest in Islam, built around the stone on which Abraham was thought to have offered his son Isaac as a sacrifice to God
Haredim	ultra-orthodox religious Jews
Hashem	God

Hashomer Ha'tzair	youth wing of the Meretz party; influential 'Socialist Zionist' youth movement inspired by Baden-Powell's Scouts, founded 1914
Hashura	military arm of the Iraqi Zionist underground in the 1950s, formed after Rashid Ali's pogrom of 1941
Hasidim	ultra-orthodox movement formed by Rabbi Israel Baal Shem Tov in eighteenth-century Ukraine
Haskala	Jewish enlightenment between the 1770s and 1880s
Herut/Likud	rightist party founded by Menachem Begin around the ideas of Vladimir Jabotinsky
Hesder	military service programme for religious students
hitnatkut	disengagement
imma	mother
Irgun/IZL/'Etzel'	far-right Jewish militia in pre-1948 Israel led by Menachem Begin
Kaddish	a mourners' prayer
kashrut	Jewish dietary laws
kavanot	mystical statement regarding intentions of worship
Kiddush	a Sabbath prayer
Kur Hitukh	lit. 'a melting reactor' or pot
Lehi	far-right militia, aka the Stern Gang, which split from Etzel in 1940
Loshn koydesh	'the holy tongue', Yiddish
madricha	teacher and guide
magid	itinerant preacher
Mapai	the Israeli Labour party
Mapam/Meretz/Yahad	Israeli left-wing party
maskil	a kibbutz secretary
Masorti	religious movement in Israel associated with conservative Judaism worldwide
matsav	war/situation
menorah	religious candelabra
Midrash	a combination of legal, exegetical or homiletical teachings on the Tanach (three parts of the Holy Bible)
mikva	ritual bath for religious ceremonies
minion	the ten men needed in a synagogue for a Sabbath service
Mishna	written and codified form of Jewish oral law
mitzva/mitzvoth	good deed
Mizrahim	Middle Eastern Jews
mobarot	transit camps in which refugees were processed
mohel	circumciser
moshavim	rural agricultural settlements that allowed farmers to own private property
Moshiach	the Messiah
Muqata	the late Yasser Arafat's presidential compound in Ramallah
Neteurei Karta	ultra-orthodox anti-Zionist religious sect
Olim hadashim	new immigrants
Palmach	Israeli army units during the War of 1948
pigua	terrorist attack

Sabra	prickly pear; a Jew born in Israel
Schechina	lit. 'God's presence'; a feminine concept representing God's dwelling and immanence in the created world; the personified spirit of the People of Israel
Sefer Tehillim	Book of Psalms
Sefer Torah	the Hebrew Bible, or Five Books of Moses
Sephardim	Mediterranean Jews
shahid	'martyr' in Arabic
Shabbak	Israeli domestic security service whose initials are Shin Bet
Shabbat	Sabbath
shaduch	match
Shas	ultra-orthodox Mizrahi religious party
Shinnui	secular centrist party
shiva	seven-day mourning period for a departed loved one in Judaism
shmud	to quit being a Jew
Shoah	Holocaust
shtanz	stereotype
shtetl	East European Jewish village in the pre-WWII period
Tikkun Olum	lit. 'healing the world'
Tsenna	a period of rationing and shortages in the 1950s
Ulpan	subsidised English-language school for new immigrants
Yerida	'descent' or emigration from Israel
yeshiva	religious school
yeshiva boche	religious student
Yishuv	pre-1948 Jewish settlements in Mandate Palestine
Zohar	holy book of the Kabbalists

Index

Compiled by Sue Carlton